AVALANCHE & GORILLA JIM

APPALACHIAN TRAIL ADVENTURES
and OTHER TALES

ALBERT DRAGON

NEW YORK

AVALANCHE & GORILLA JIM
APPALACHIAN TRAIL ADVENTURES
and OTHER TALES

by ALBERT DRAGON

ISBN 978-1-61448-170-6 (paperback)
ISBN 978-1-61448-171-3 (eBook)
Library of Congress Control Number: 2011943242

Published by:
MORGAN JAMES PUBLISHING
The Entrepreneurial Publisher
5 Penn Plaza, 23rd Floor
New York City, New York 10001
(212) 655-5470 Office
(516) 908-4496 Fax
www.MorganJamesPublishing.com

Cover Design by:
Rachel Lopez
www.r2cdesign.com

Interior Design by:
Bonnie Bushman
bbushman@bresnan.net

To Barbara, for everything.

and

*To Jim, for reasons you'll see
when you read this book.*

Contents

PART ONE

3   Chapter One

9   Chapter Two

PART TWO

19   Chapter Three

33   Chapter Four

43   Chapter Five

51   Chapter Six

55   Chapter Seven

59   Chapter Eight

69   Chapter Nine

75   Chapter Ten

89   Chapter Eleven

101   Chapter Twelve

113   Chapter Thirteen

127   Chapter Fourteen

137   Chapter Fifteen

149   Chapter Sixteen

PART THREE

155   Chapter Seventeen

167   Chapter Eighteen

175   Chapter Nineteen

PART FOUR

193   Chapter Twenty

211   Chapter Twenty-one

221   Chapter Twenty-two

223   Chapter Twenty-three

231   Chapter Twenty-four

PART FIVE

249   Chapter Twenty-five

261   Chapter Twenty-six

271   Chapter Twenty-seven

279   Chapter Twenty-eight

289   Epilogue

291   Acknowledgements

293   Bibliography

295   Endnotes

PART ONE

Chapter One

Loud ungodly screams shattered the forest night, reverberating in the darkened woods. It sent chills to every part of my body. I was separated from whatever beast lurked out there by only the thin material of my small tent, and that thought doomed any hope of sleep.

How I came to be alone in a dark forest far from civilization is part of the saga of an adventure that led to my long hike on the Appalachian Trail, and how it changed my life for the better.

Where did it all start? In the heart of a city boy a long time ago. Raised in Philadelphia, I was of average height and weight, dirty blond hair that stuck up in the back, and glasses. I despised my nearsightedness because it prevented me from being involved in contact sports, which I would have loved.

Going backpacking was a lifelong dream that I thought was going to go unfulfilled. When I was younger I was fascinated by the thought of backpacking in the woods, going somewhere new and different. Maybe it was because I wanted to be set free in the outdoors. I wanted to be boundless as the wind, blowing through fields, over mountains, along the roads of this great country. I wanted to be on my own, to be able to survive in the forest, to roam, to be independent!

The Tacony Park was the closest I got to the wild outdoors. It was near my home in the Feltonville section of Philadelphia. A big wonderful playground of trees, tall grass, the park was a fun place where my friends and I lolled away our summers, climbing trees, playing in ditches, and in the fall, jumping out of trees into piled up straw they cut in the meadow area. It was a carefree life.

Train tracks separated the park from the woods beyond the tracks. It wasn't really wilderness, but to us the densely wooded area was a mysterious backcountry we walked through with caution, kids not sure of what to expect in the forest beyond the bounds of a civilized world. The train tracks crossed the Tacony Creek on a trestle bridge. Next to the tracks was a slender wooden planked pathway with a pipe railing. Sometimes we walked on the bridge—boys looking at the wide creek below, dropping ballast stones from the railroad bed and counting how long it took before they hit the water. "That one took two seconds. Let's see if this big stone falls faster." Often we met under the bridge between the concrete abutments that supported the trestle and listened to locomotives noisily clattering overhead, spraying us with lube oil that smelled of a hot engine.

Crossing over those tracks, to a space hidden from the streets, into the world of trees, deep bushes and a hidden abandoned stone quarry was magical. There were no rules; we would just run wildly and enjoy the exploration, imagine wild animals, and hike without care. The idea of being in the wild excited me. I read everything I could about backpacking and even thought of a summer forest service job. I knew my parents would explode at the mere suggestion, so I never told them. I was alone with these daydreams. There was no one I knew who backpacked. Let's face it...the people I knew didn't even know what backpacking was! They thought a backpack was something you put on an achy back. My dream of long overland hiking was just that, an empty dream.

When I was in the second year of high school, I had a friend named Shel whose father took us hunting in the Pocono Mountains of Pennsylvania. We stayed in a rustic cabin in the woods. It was early December, and so frigid that a wooden box outside the window served as a refrigerator. I had read a book on deer hunting and knew everything from how to stay downwind from the prey to how to gut out the animal. (Don't start to cut until you're sure the animal is dead. Take a branch and brush the deer's eyes—if it doesn't move, its dead!) We didn't get a deer, but I got a great kick out of being in the mountain forest. We went hunting in the early years of college. I never shot a deer. Had one in my sights once, but I didn't shoot it. By the time I counted the points on the deer's antlers to make sure it was a legal buck, it was gone. It was just as well; for me it was the trek in the woods that was important.

Being in woodlands was so great, I volunteered to stalk the prey for my friends Shel and Lou. I would go around the mountain and come up to where my buddies waited with their rifles. The idea was that the deer would move away from me and towards them. Most people don't like to be the stalker because you lose the chance of shooting your own deer, it takes effort to walk through the woods, and someone could mistake you for a deer. (I never worried about being accidentally shot; my pals were sharp shooters. Besides, I didn't owe them any money.)

One cold November day my pals took their places in the woods. I walked down the mountain, turned around and headed up to where I thought they were waiting. It started snowing. Being late afternoon and overcast, everything turned light gray, and I lost my bearings. I tried to backtrack, thinking I could retrace my footsteps in the snow. Then, gently falling snow covered my footsteps, and I ended up wandering aimlessly. The trail itself disappeared beneath heavier falling snow. I was cold and didn't know which way to go. My worst fears were coming true. I was lost in the woods...in a snowstorm. Lost. Freezing. Panic set in, wreaking havoc in my bowel. I suddenly wished there was a bathroom nearby.

My heart was thumping. I wanted to throw down my Winchester rifle and run. I looked to the right. I looked to the left. Everything looked the same, drab shades of gray, tall bare trees, darkening spaces between, a lost, lonely, forgotten bleak world. I was falling into forlorn empty space. Something inside reminded me the international distress signal is three shots. Should I shoot three times into the air? I saw an object move ahead in the gloom. What the heck is it? Nearer, I made out red and black plaid...a hunter crossing ahead of me. I ran to him and asked if he knew where the trail is. Gruffly he said, "Over there," and started to walk away.

I stared through flurrying snow to *over there*, but didn't see any trail. Just a blanket of dirty white snow in the approaching dusk. I stopped him and demanded with fierce, desperate determination, "Put me on the trail!" It wasn't just melting snowflakes beading on my reddened forehead; it was the moisture of desperation and fear. He looked at my hand clutching the

Winchester's trigger guard, maybe thinking my index finger was perilously close to the trigger itself. Never taking his eyes off my hand, he walked me to the trail.

The following year I was better prepared. It came to my attention that if you get lost it is best to stay calm by chewing a piece of gum. Amply supplied with sticks of Wrigley's chewing gum, I ventured forth. Lou dropped off first to take his stand. Shel and I walked down the mountain and then Shel dropped off to take his stand. Enjoying the walk in the woods better than anything, I trekked on and at some point—to give some legitimacy to my alleged hunting—eventually stopped and waited for deer to arrive. The day wore on—no signs of deer.

Walking back, it occurred to me that the scenery was not familiar. I really didn't know where I was. As luck would have it, I stumbled into Shel who was also wandering aimlessly in the woods. I said, "Do you know where the trail is?"

"No."

So I searched in my pocket. "Have a piece of gum!"

Shel's anguished face softened into a smile as he reached for the stick of Wrigley's. We walked for a while chewing and trying to figure out where we were. After a short time, Lou arrived, laughing almost hysterically at the sight of us. "What's so funny?" Shel asked. Lou said he had seen us from his perch on the hill, and we were roaming around aimlessly—less than thirty feet from the trail.

We had a good laugh, but I will never, ever forget the gut-wrenching horror of being lost the year before.

Those were my only experiences with the backcountry. After college I went to law school. After law school I started to practice law in Philadelphia, got married, bought a house, and became very busy. My wife, Barbara, is pretty and petite, yet hardy. She accommodated my woodsman spirit and was willing to be more physically active than her generation was raised to be—mainly because it was something I enjoyed. She agreed to join the Outdoor Club of South Jersey with me. We went on day hikes in the New Jersey Pine Barrens and took some trips to Vermont and Maine for short weeks of day hiking.

The day hikes were fine, but what I really longed for was long-distance backpacking. However, there was no way Barbara was going to sleep on the ground in deep frigid forests, and do without a daily shower.

For too many years I became captive to an office of law books, phone calls, depositions, investigations, trials, settlements, and emails. I got up early every day and exercised, went to a gym several times a week to work off stress.

Any ideas of being free and hiking long distances in far-off mountain forests disappeared, fading into a far away past. Buried were any conscious thoughts of ever backpacking.

Chapter Two

The Appalachian Trail attracts many different people. Here is another person who—through the struggles of war—would eventually find his way to Appalachian heights and adventures.

Khe Sanh, Vietnam, 1968

Khe Sanh is on a barren plateau sometimes veiled by mist. The bloodiest battle of the Vietnam War took place there.

From January 30 to January 31, 1968, a devastating salvo of artillery shells, mortars, and rockets crashed into the American air base at Khe Sanh in an isolated spot near North Vietnam. Eighteen Marines were killed, forty were wounded. For several months the enemy relentlessly bombarded the Khe Sanh air base, home to five thousand U.S. Marines. On one day alone, thirteen hundred artillery rounds rocked the American base and its outposts. On some days the shelling continued at the rate of a hundred explosions every hour.

Carl James Saxton was twenty-one years old of medium height and slender build. Jim, as he was called, arrived in Vietnam as part of the U.S. 1st Cavalry Division. On April 1, 1968, Jim's division started Operation Pegasus to relieve the besieged marines. After five days of fierce battle the army linked up with the marines, and the enemy siege was officially lifted. The U.S. 1st Cavalry suffered 92 killed and 629 wounded.

The North Vietnamese Army [NVA] overran a U.S. Green Beret camp on the Laotian border. Three days of intense fighting followed. The U.S. military retook their special forces camp, lost it to the NVA, and finally the

U.S. forces recaptured the camp. The enemy continued bringing supplies over the mountains and harassing fire over the border from Laos on the West. A decision was made to stop them—take them out by sending U.S. troops on a clandestine mission into Laos.

Following Jim's fighting in Operation Pegasus, the 1st Cavalry moved to the boarder between Vietnam and Laos near Khe Sanh. Jim was a grenadier. He used a 40mm grenade launcher that looked like a sawed off shotgun with a very wide bore. Jim was in the war close-up, firing high-explosive grenades at targets only 50 to 250 meters away. "As a grenadier, I have a rifleman with me to protect me as I use the grenade launcher," Jim Saxton said. "We got to the top of the mountain—that's where the bunkers were—and we fired into the bunkers." He held the short stubby weapon to his shoulder, supported the barrel with one hand, and pulled the trigger with his other hand. The weapon jolted back as the explosive missile flew toward its target at 250 feet a second. The bunker exploded into flames, smoke, and debris. "The squad leader at the bottom of the hill was supposed to send support up for us." Jim added, "He didn't."

Enemy bullets were whizzing around. There was the sharp yata-ta-ta-ta of machine gun fire. The rifleman next to Jim screamed out, "Ow, fuck, I'm hit!" The rifleman dropped his weapon and fell to the ground with a thud as his leg collapsed beneath him. He grabbed his leg. It was squirting blood between his fingers. Jim quickly looked around to assess the situation of bullets and explosions around them.

"Gimme your first aid pouch," the rifleman murmured.

Jim was feverishly thinking, *I'm a rookie...new to battle...what the hell am I supposed to do!* Jim knelt, dodging several pinging bullets, set down his grenade launcher. The rifleman was in agony. Jim knew he had to say something to keep him from passing out. "Use your own first-aid pouch. I'm supposed to use mine and you're supposed to use yours."

"You gonna let me bleed to death?"

Jim was half listening. He couldn't see any hostiles, but zinging bullets were coming from somewhere. *Got to say something*, he thought. "You're not gonna bleed to death...'cause...'cause you got a canteen cup and I got a canteen cup...and...you can drink your own blood," Jim said making a grim joke to keep the man conscious. Jim thought, *That was dumb and crazy, but it's keepin' him from going into shock.* Jim had already been busy opening the man's first-aid pack, quickly applied the thick bandage and tied it around the area of spurting blood. "Got to get you out of here, brother." Jim—slim at 160 pounds—lifted the man over his shoulders in a fireman's carry.

With his human cargo, Jim ran down the hill through a storm of bullets. Yata-ta-ta-ta—"Damn," he said to his buddy. "They got two machine guns cross firing at us." The region had been thoroughly bombed. It was open and desolate. There were craters everywhere. Jim tried dashing in a different direction. His feet slid in loosely exploded dirt. Shots whistled close by. There was a clanging at Jim's hip, and he felt wetness at his side and sudden lightness in the load carried on his belt. A bullet had smashed through his canteen and another severed his hip belt, dropping his ammunition pouches. Jim kept running down the hill, around deep gaps in the ground, in and out of crater holes to avoid wicked machine gun fire and explosions around him. Later, Jim confessed, "It's a wonder I didn't get shot. It's a miracle!"

His comrade was not so fortunate. Jim felt a jarring of the body across his shoulders as the already wounded warrior recoiled from another bullet wound. It burned into his right arm and sent a spray of blood across Jim's shirt. The soldier weakly uttered, "Oh, shit," went limp, and then was silent.

They reached the bottom. From Jim's blood-stained shoulders, a medic and another man lifted the limp soldier. He was medevaced out by helicopter.

For this stunning act of bravery, Jim was awarded the Army Commendation Medal: a bronze hexagon with an American bald eagle grasping three crossed arrows and bearing on its breast a shield suspended from a green ribbon. The document accompanying the Army Commendation Medal states, in part:

> For heroism in the connection with military operations against hostile forces in the Republic of Vietnam. Specialist Four Saxton distinguished himself by heroism in action… When his assault mission unit became heavily engaged with a larger enemy force and sustained a casualty, Specialist Four Saxton exposed himself to the hostile fire as he crossed an open area to his wounded comrade, administered first aid, and evacuating him to safety.

Eventually, the ribbon bore three oak clusters, denoting Jim's award of this medal for bravery in battles again and again during his military career.

A Shau Valley, Vietnam April 1968

The A Shau Valley was the scene of fierce fighting in Vietnam. It was long and narrow, really several valleys and mountains. The sides of the valley were thickly forested. A Shau Valley was critical to the enemy. They used it as a main pipeline for supplies and troops. Because of its importance to the North Vietnamese Army and the Vietcong (VC), it was the target of numerous military actions by allied forces, particularly the U.S. 101st Airborne Division. The NVA and VC vigorously defended A Shau. It was an area of much fighting throughout the Vietnam War and had a terrifying reputation for soldiers of both sides. A soldier who fought in A Shau had an honored position among combat veterans.

Jim and his men followed the motto of the 11th Armored Cavalry Regiment: Find the Bastards – Then Pile On! The men moved quietly through low foliage, sleeves rolled up, flak jackets unzipped due to the heat. Some were seasoned veterans. A few had already received several Purple Hearts.

Jim thought back to when he arrived in Vietnam, amid bedlam. As the young raw troops got off the plane, artillery and mortar blasts surrounded them. "You FNGs are gonna have to learn fast," the MP said to them with a sneer.

A quavering voice in the rear asked, "What's an FNG?"

The MP, a knowing smile on his face, responded, "Fuckin' New Guy, you jerkoff!"

In war, one way of promotion is when the guy above you gets wounded or killed. You take his place temporarily. If you do well, you get promoted. Such advancement is called blood stripes. Jim received blood stripes and was promoted to sergeant, commanding a squad of nine soldiers.

After months of battle, Jim became a hardened squad leader who was looking at the new guys around him. When one of the new guys had gotten killed in front of him, it wasn't just another FNG who "bought the six-by-three farm," it was a young man—a person Jim felt responsible for. Somewhere back home, a mother, girlfriend, family would cry, and deep inside—beyond explosions and past his steel surface, where no one could see—Jim wept... and longed to be in peaceful mountains.

Danger came in many flavors: booming artillery shells, clacking machine-gun fire, fearsome and quiet booby-traps. These death traps were typically hand grenades attached to trip wires, or baskets of clay with slender, sharp sticks jutting out that would swing down from a tree and kill a soldier instantly. Then there were the legendary punji pits. They were camouflaged grave-size holes in the ground with scalpel-sharp stakes sticking up from the bottom. Unknowing soldiers stepped on what they thought was solid ground and fell several feet onto the stakes. Although punjis could kill immediately, often the victims would die from infections caused by feces that was smeared on the sticks.

The constant awareness of death was around each bend. There was no rest. Jim loved the outdoors, but hated always being wary of danger. He longed for a place where he could walk in peace—without fear.

Jim's squad had been on a reconnaissance mission. Nine men quietly communicating with each other only through hand signals and eye contact. Their mission: find the enemy and take them out. There were two rookies in the squad, FNGs only in this country for a few weeks. They took a much-needed break from creeping through the dense forest on high alert. A private sprawled on the ground, his head against a tree, bandoliers of bullets draped across his chest like deadly necklaces. Between the belts of bullets dangled a chain with religious icons. Two men sat on debris, the grimness temporarily slid off their faces as they smoked cigarettes. In a few minutes Jim had the squad on the move again.

The soldiers went uphill in triple canopy area—treetops so dense you couldn't see the sky. The enemy was cunning. They could hide anywhere, even in indentations on the forest floor covered with branches and leaves. They lived in elaborate tunnel systems, some 130 miles long—one clandestine tunnel was found to exist beneath an American army camp. The enemy would send one of their men running near the American soldiers to draw them into an ambush. Seasoned troops know to resist the temptation to chase, assess the situation, and carefully take action. But the FNGs would give chase.

That's what happened to Jim's squad. A single pinging sniper bullet killed his point man. The second and third men in line were total rookies. The second man yelled, "I seen him, I seen where the fire came from. Let's go!"

The third man's adrenaline was up, and he also started screaming, "Let's get the mothafuckers." They took off running.

Jim yelled for them to stop. The sniper fire increased. One of their own had been killed; everyone's adrenaline was pumping. Chaos. Running and shouting, "lousy bastards...fuckin' NVA...assholes."

Jim was yelling, "Come back!"

Too late. The men rushed right into an ambush. The enemy fire accelerated. There was a distinct whistling zzzzzzz sound of a mortar propelling through the air and then the deafening boom as it exploded two hundred feet away. Shrapnel and splintered tree wood flew in all directions. Jim held his breath against the powdery residue that filled the Vietnam air. When he breathed, dirt stuck in his nose and on his teeth. "Take cover!" he yelled with a southern accent. "Take cover!" With his little finger Jim wiped dust from the corner of his eye and blinked several times to get it out.

One of the FNGs dropped to one knee to pick up his rifle that had been shocked out of his grasp by the explosion. Another soldier dashed toward the safety of a crater and yelled, "How 'bout you, Sarge?"

"I'm okay."

The next mortar boom was ear blasting; it was so close there was no time for the whistling zzzzzzzz sound. The ground shook. A hot blast hit the back of Jim's head and side of his face. Dirt and shrapnel exploded toward him. The filth-filled air rushed at him. In the flourish of dust, huge arms surrounded Jim, lifting, pushing him like he was a puppet on a string. He had a vague feeling of floating as he was blown off his feet, the stink of burned explosives in his nostrils. It felt like someone had struck the left side of his head with a hot iron poker. He felt warm trickles down his face. The immense pain developing in the left side of his head was overshadowed by the more immediate need to focus on the son of a bitch 150 meters away, pointing his rifle at Jim and shooting, shooting. Jim got up on one knee, raised his M16 and squeezed the trigger until the crack of sniper fire ceased.

Three squad guys were killed, several were wounded. Jim continued to fire on the enemy. His squad could not pull back. There was only one way to go—right through the hostiles. The close combat—running and shooting—continued as they moved toward the enemy, forcing them back.

In the last stages of chaos, the rest of the company arrived. The wounded were picked up and moved back. One of these reserve forces looked at the Sarge, "Holy shit!" He turned, waving his M16, and yelled, "Medic, dammit, medic!" It looked like half of Jim's face was blown off, but it was mostly blood. Pieces of shrapnel were embedded inside—and the concussion had taken its toll.

"Who's hurt?" Jim asks.

"It's you, Sarge."

"Take care of the others first."

Jim was medevaced to a hospital at Cam Ranh Bay where doctors performed surgery. Afterward, Jim's eyesight started to fail him. One day, all he could see was carbon blackness—he was blind. People had to lead him around, help feed him, take him to the toilet. He didn't know if he would see again. His mind kept replaying the memories of stealthy Vietcong sneaking up on him, of heads getting blown off. He was angry and afraid of the dark.

There were moments when he could calm the fear and hatred. He would visualize a pastoral path through the trees and up mountains, and it brought him serenity. The outdoors was peaceful and inviting—when it isn't raining down terror. He knew he would walk in quiet, peaceful, green woods someday; he would shake off the veil of anxiety that was war, that traded sleep for nightmares; he would enjoy a path without explosions and punji sticks. Someday.

The doctors operated on his eyes. After thirteen days in the dark, Jim could see the world around him again. In a small compartment of his mind there remained a vivid picture of that peaceful trail—a place he needs to go, to be at peace.

For service to his country, Jim received the Bronze Star Medal, awarded for heroism to those in close personal combat with the enemy. It hangs from a crimson ribbon and comes with the V device for valor. For wounds sustained in battle, he was awarded the Purple Heart, a royal blue ribbon from which is suspended a heart shaped medal with the profile of George Washington against a purple background.

All he needs now is that peaceful path through the mountains.

PART TWO

Chapter Three

In a forest in the heart of northwest Georgia, at the top of a mountain marks the beginning of an exciting, electrifying, life-changing journey... or the worst damned trip you'll ever take. To me, at times, it was both!

March 12, 2002

I'm on a US Airways jet plane flying to Atlanta, Georgia, near where the Appalachian Trail begins. How did I get here—and what is the Appalachian Trail?

Bill Bryson set loose a horde of people walking the Appalachian Trail when he published his book *A Walk in the Woods*. At a party, Barbara heard about this new book—then on the best-seller list—and gave me a copy for my birthday. She had no idea what this would do to me.

My life changed when I read Bryson's book. He wrote about hiking the "A.T." (that's what most hikers call it) with his friend Katz. Through Bryson's good-humored narrative I got a glimpse of what it was like to backpack the 2,175-mile-long ribbon of dirt and rock from Georgia to Maine. What fun! The more I read, the more it rekindled my old dream. I could do that...But, how? What equipment did I need? Where along the way do you get food? How do you know where to go? How do you get to the trailhead in Georgia? Could I really do this?

My age? Let's just say that when I started practicing law there were no computers in our office. Several times a week I work out at the gym and hike in the woods with Jack (our Rhodesian Ridgeback). I can still ride a bike a hundred miles from our summer home in Brigantine to Cape May and back—and then go out to dinner with Barbara.

I contacted the Appalachian Trail Conference and got a list of books on the A.T., checked their website for info, and other websites of those who were conversant with the trail. I asked questions at outfitters stores.

What is the A.T.?

Think of it as a narrow path extending from Springer Mountain in Georgia to Katahdin, a mountain in Maine. Climbing up and down mountainous heights, through dense forests, across cow meadows, and crossing streams on stepping stones and small bridges. A slender trail where thousands of like-minded people hike with one thought in their brains: to get from a mountaintop in Georgia to a mountaintop in Maine.

I look out the plane window to mountains of North Carolina and wonder how long it will take to hike to this point. There is a thrill of joy and excitement about fulfilling a lifelong dream. Still, everything below looks desolate. Relentless forests with steep rocky elevations sticking up between them—ridge after mountain ridge as far as anyone could see, even from five miles up. No signs of civilization.

Somewhere below, a thread of trail goes through the forests and over the mountains, heading north-northeast to Maine.

Dark clouds are coming in, making the mountains eerie—warning of unknown dangers hidden within vast stretches of vegetation clinging to the mountainsides.

With a shaking chill my thoughts go back to Pennsylvania when I was younger—the time I was lost in snow. It scares me. Yet, there's one lesson life teaches: It's okay to be scared, but it's not okay to let fear prevent you from doing what you want to do.

I stare out at the bleakness and wonder *what am I in for*.

After landing in Atlanta, I take the MARTA train to meet the man who had agreed to drive me to Springer Mountain, the southern starting point of the Appalachian Trail. When I get off there is a bear of a man waiting for me.

His mustache is the color of gunmetal, and he wears a plaid shirt and white baseball hat. "I'm Hacksaw," he says, referring to his trail name.

I don't have a trail name, so I reply, "I'm Al."

"This here's Mr. Boo," he says, pointing to a sturdy looking guy carrying a green backpack, hiking poles, and a broad smile on his full face. "He's doing the trail too."

Before I could shake Mr. Boo's hand, he starts telling me how he hiked the A.T. end to end a few years ago and is out trekking for a few weeks this time. We throw our gear into Hacksaw's Chevy pickup truck, which had a cab over the cargo area, and pile inside. Both Hacksaw and Boo are enthusiastic about hiking and between the two of them they answer my questions about the A.T. before I ask them. We go to a supermarket to get last minute food items. When we are through shopping, Hacksaw looks at our grocery bags and bulging backpacks. "Looks like we better go to my place and get you squared away."

Hacksaw's house is a homey single with trees around it. I dump the contents of my backpack and the grocery items onto the kitchen table. The airlines don't allow a stove on the plane; consequently, I shipped mine to Hacksaw's house. It hadn't arrived, so Hacksaw lends me his Whisper Light white gasoline stove. Standing, chin in hand, Hacksaw studies the pile. Mr. Boo walks around examining it briefly; they both confer on the best way to cram all the stuff in, and gently told me where to stick it—in the backpack that is. Amazingly, everything fit. Boo loads his pack. Then, we take a bouncy ride on back roads up Springer Mountain.

Most people hike up Springer Mountain from the south, climbing eight tough miles north to the crest, the spot where the Appalachian Trail starts. That's the approach trail—not part of the A.T. Instead of spending a day struggling up a mountain we take Forest Service Road 42 to a place where we can hike a mile south to the starting point. It is raining and cool, making me doubly glad I had decided on this shorter route. The pickup bounces to a stop at the side of a small parking area. "This is it," Hacksaw declares.

I look around. "This is what?"

"Trail's *over there.*"

I'd heard those ominous words before. I squint through windblown light fog but can't see anything "over there." Thoughts of not finding a snow covered forest trail in my distant past make me more than uneasy. Mr. Boo doesn't seem concerned. He grabs his pack from the rear of the vehicle and starts putting it on. I take my cue from him and try to do the same, fumbling with the buckles and straps. As Boo starts on his way, I am still fumbling with my straps and hiking poles. Hacksaw, smiling at me, leans a hand against the cab of his wet truck and says "Take care, boys."

"Yeah," says Boo, and he starts at a brisk pace into the blowing mist.

I step lively to catch up with the now receding new hiking buddy. We hike uphill, stepping onto wet stones and mud puddles. My legs rebel against my over-crammed and overweight fifty-plus-pound pack.

The views from Springer Mountain are supposed to be excellent, but by the time I huff my way up to the boulder marking the official start of the A.T., mist and fog make it hard to see anything a hundred feet away. The boulder has a bronze plaque on it proclaiming:

APPALACHIAN
NATIONAL SCENIC TRAIL
SPRINGER MOUNTAIN
ELEVATION 3782
Southern Terminus
CHATTAHOOCHI
National Forest

This is it! I reached the holy land. I want to cheer and cry. I'm having a religious experience. But I have to have it fast, it's starting to drizzle, and the fog is thickening. I quickly take the register from the Ziploc bag and sign my name to record my presence on the trail.

Mr. Boo heads for the shelter about the distance of several city blocks away, but I'm lucky to see seventy-five feet in the moving thickening mist. A sign indicates where the shelter is, points down a small maze of paths. My backpack has a slight wobble to it, and I realize I hadn't taken the time to fasten one of the adjusting straps.

The Springer Mountain Shelter is like a three-sided wooden shed, open in the front with a shingled roof. It is built to hold ten people, but twice that many eager hikers are already jammed into it. In front of the shelter is a jumble of large backpacks with things like cups and camp shoes hanging off them. "It's too crowded," Mr. Boo complains. "I'm going to the next shelter." And he leaves.

It is getting dark and is muddy and cold. The next shelter is about two and a quarter miles north on the A.T. I am not about to hike several miles in mucky, foggy, darkness.

I step up into the shelter. It is crowded, and I can barley see anything the light is so dim. "Check the second level," says a voice from a shadowy figure on the floor who is pointing toward a ladder leading to a sleeping deck above. "Ouch," cries a female whose leg I almost step on in the darkness.

"Sorry," I say as I gingerly make my way to the ladder. The bulky pack on my back makes it awkward going up the steps. With my head just above the second level, I look around at a dark environment. No way of telling what is vacant, if anything. I don't like the thought of not seeing well in the dark, and tripping down the ladder steps at night to go pee. Breaking a leg doesn't seem like a good way to start my journey.

I leave the shelter and find a path leading to a field where some tents are already set up. By then it's difficult to see more than fifty feet in front of me. Putting up the tent, the contents of my backpack are strewn all over the ground. I search in the darkness for pegs to nail down the tent so it won't collapse on me. There is no place nearby to set up the stove to cook a meal. I am glad to be out of the misty rain, and I settle for a cold dinner in my tent.

I crawl out of the tent and bump into Tom, his coat collar up and wool hat pulled down over his ears to keep out the miserable cold dampness. Tom had left his wife and daughter in the slightly warmer confines of their tent. "Gotta hang the food bag," he says. "Keep the food from attracting bears." In his hands are two bulging blue water-resistant bags.

"Do you know where to hang them?"

He nods, and points with one arm gripping a blue bag.

"Hold on, I'll get mine." I reach into my tent, fish around, and pull out my equally bulging green food bag. He leads me to flagpole-high trees that have pulley and cable systems for hanging the bags. He shows me how to use the contraption to raise our food way out of reach of bears or other hungry marauders. The fog is very dense, and we hesitate, looking for the right direction back to the tents.

It's real damp, and being up in the mountains, it is getting colder. I shiver as I crawl inside my messy tent. Gear and clothes are scattered through the tight space the size of a refrigerator carton. Where's my warm fleece? I'm in a dark tent, sorting through my stuff unable to find anything. I have the creepy feeling that I don't know what the hell I'm doing. Everything seems to be a bundle of confusion. What am I doing?

What have I done?

I don't sleep much. I am too excited, and two rocks bulging beneath my thin sleeping pad dig into whatever side I lay on. The winds blow and shake my tent, and it rains all night, sometimes heavily. It is comforting to know the tent is dry.

Something would happen tomorrow that would put a whole different light on my lifetime trip.

March 13, 2002

Wake early, retrieve my food bag, and nibble at a blueberry Pop Tart. I begin to pack up, pulling up the tent stakes; they are coated with a thick dark mud that got under my fingernails and became so deeply engrained in my fingerprints that wiping them on wet leaves doesn't clean them. I wondered if my fingers would ever be clean again.

The fog lingers but isn't as thick. It just melts into a silver-gray haziness that reminds me of photos of California smog. The temperature is in the upper forties, and it is drizzling off and on.

I lift my pack—it hadn't gotten any lighter—and begin looking for the trail. As I move in the general direction of where it should be, I see something unusual. Walking toward the A.T. is a hiker, red bandana around his forehead, salt and pepper beard, army issue camouflage brimmed boonie hat. In his left hand is a hickory staff as tall as he is, about five foot nine inches. Attached to the staff is a large, green stuffed gorilla!

I think to myself: Am I going to be stuck hiking over two thousand miles with crazies, toy animals attached to their hiking sticks? Is the Appalachian Trail populated with these kooks? As I near him, he presses the gorilla's chest. The stuffed creature bellows a loud gorilla scream. It's all too comical. I laugh as loud as the big ape's roar, and so does the nut with the large stick. "I'm Gorilla Jim," he says with a southern drawl, offering his right hand.

I want to say, *You're a monkey's uncle*, or worse, but I just extend my hand and say, "I'm Al." He shakes my hand with a firm grip, and his friendly blue eyes and wide grin tell me he's not as wacky as he otherwise seemed. In his mid fifties, Gorilla Jim and I are over a generation ahead of 80 percent of those who are stirring awake at the Springer Mountain Shelter. "Thru-hiking?" I ask.

"All the way to Katahdin in Maine."

"Me to." For the first time it hit me. I'm on my way to Maine. The years of dreaming, the preparation, accumulating equipment, sweaty exercising... *this is it*. My anxiety about finding my way in shitty weather and doubts about whether I can actually do it all brush away with the happiness of being on my way.

He looks me over. I'm wearing a red zip-up shell (jacket) over my wind shirt (an insulating layer), pants with zip-off legs, khaki wide-brimmed hat, green backpack with a blue sack strapped to the top, and heavy boots. In my hands are two hiking poles that fold up like long thin telescopes. Attached to the straps across my chest and stomach is a black pouch holding my map, trail info, snacks, and a holster for my water bottle. And he sees that I am not sure where the starting point is to my two-thousand-plus mile journey.

I search around. "Which way's the trail?"

He accommodates my ignorance and nods his head to the right. We start to walk down the mountain.

I can't say much about the trees along the sides other than they are bare... scant of any foliage, look old, thin and alone. I can tell you less about the view because of colorless low visibility conditions again this morning.

"What's with the gorilla?" I ask.

Gorilla Jim pats the green stuffed animal. It roars, making us both crack up. "My wife gave it to me. I thought it would look neat on my hiking stick."

I smirk, "It's different, all right."

"That's how I got my trail name, Gorilla Jim. My real name is Carl James Saxton. Usually, other people give you a trail name. I gave myself this name. I like giving people trail names. You got one?"

My parents did not even give me a middle name. "Na, not yet."

"We'll find one for you before long."

My last name is Dragon. I didn't need another animal name. To be social I respond, "We'll see…Where you from?"

The trail from Springer Mountain is mostly downward, and as we walk in light rain, it has the smell of woodsy wetness. Jim tells me he is from Murphy, North Carolina, close to the A.T., an area we would reach in a week or so. He recently moved to Owasso, Oklahoma, because his wife got a job at a hospital there. As we pass Forest Service Road 42 where Hacksaw dropped me off the day before, our yakking is interrupted while we cross a stream. Gorilla Jim tells me that he had been a career army man, twenty-two years in the service, served a long tour of duty in Vietnam where he was in a lot of combat and became a drill sergeant. He isn't clear on it, but somehow he was wounded. He loves the military and being outdoors but hasn't done much hiking since moving to Oklahoma.

We are trekking through primitive areas of the Chattahoochee National Forest, along the broad ridge of Rich Mountain. We walk on a narrow bridge over a stream with water so clear we can make out each rock at the bottom. Hiking side-by-side as much as the trail would allow, Gorilla Jim turns and asks, "What about you?"

Rain dripping from tree branches splashes off the brim of my hat. I tell him I was a lawyer and resented being confined to the indoors. I talk about my love of hiking and how I am fulfilling my dream of backpacking the Appalachian Trail.

"Done much backpacking?" Gorilla asks.

"No."

Jim looks around into the drizzle and foggy haze that seems to conceal a hidden mystery. "Well, Al, how do you know how to live in the woods?"

"I went to every outfitter in the Philadelphia area. Asked them all kinds of questions about equipment, what to expect, food and water, tents… everything." I carefully step over a mud-slicked rock and continue, "Read books, got two videotapes on backpacking, and got info off the Internet and from the Appalachian Trail Conference. Gradually, I bought the equipment I needed. I'd put the stuff on the work bench in our basement and go over it at night after work, trying to think of what I'd need and how I'd use it."

Then, Jim asks me, "But, did you get any *real* hiking experience?"

"No. I don't know what it's like to live in the forest, to use this equipment in real life situations."

Jim is interested. "What did you do?"

The trail widens and we walk side-by-side. I continue, "I wanted to go out for a few days on my own in the Pine Barrens of New Jersey, near where I live, to experience backpacking and test the equipment. The Batona Trail is a fifty-mile-long trail back through pine forests with several places to camp out. Every weekend I planned to go, it snowed or was bitter cold, so the trip had to be postponed. The weeks went by, and I knew if I was going to do the A.T. I had to get some experience and learn to use my new equipment. One February weekend I told my wife I was going no matter what. She said, 'The woods are full of snow.' I said, 'I don't care, I have to go.' She gave me the "you're as stubborn as your father" look, but she knew I was headed into snowy backcountry for three days."

Jim stopped hiking and looked at me. "You were going into snowy woods without any backpacking experience? This I gotta hear."

"I was familiar with the Batona, having day-hiked every part of it—in good weather—so I figured how bad could it be. Barbara dropped me off at the northern end of the trail at a place called Ong's Hat. Back in colonial times there was a tavern there. Mr. Ong got drunk one night and his pissed-off wife threw his hat up into a tree…Anyway, it was below freezing, I was wearing my shell, an insulation layer, gloves, and I was still freezing my ass off. Barbara took one look at the snow covering the trail and tried to conceal her concern. No, she looked horrified. I said, 'Look, Barb, if conditions are bad, I'll hike to the state forest station and call you to come get me.' I kissed her on the cheek and started to slog through the snow. She sat in the car and cried.

"The woods were beautiful, all white, quiet. Not a soul. Not a human footprint in the soft white covering. Only occasional paw print of a raccoon, rabbit, or maybe an Eastern Coyote marked the snow. The trail was invisible. I tried to recall its turns and contours. Sometimes I could follow the pink blazes marking the trees, but the previous day's blowing snow had obscured many of them, and I didn't know if I was still on the right path."

Jim shakes his head as he listens.

I continue. "I came across a road, flagged down a pickup truck, and asked the driver how to get to the ranger station. I hiked for about half an hour before I got to the station. I explained to the woman behind the counter what I was doing. She sort of gasped and said, 'You better talk to the supervisor.' She returned with a guy in a brown uniform with a logo patch on his sleeve. When I told him what I was doing, he asked, 'What kind of tent do ya have?' I answered, 'A three season tent.' He said, 'You know what season's not covered?' I said, 'Of course, winter.' He said, 'That's what we're having now.' 'Look,' I said, 'I've got a fifteen-degree sleeping bag and its only going down to sixteen degrees tonight.' He looked at me kind of peculiar, 'That's in Philadelphia. Out here it's going down to eleven degrees *and lower*. You better come back in April.' He stared at me strangely for a while then went back to his desk. I called Barbara and she picked me up in an hour."

Gorilla Jim is looking at me with a "you got more guts than brains" expression. "Did you go back to those pine woods?"

"Yes. I couldn't wait. When the weather was better I spent a few days hiking the Batona and testing out my stuff."

"Alone?"

"Yeah, by myself."

"Were you scared to spend nights in the forest alone?"

"I was scared shitless."

Jim pictures me hiking along a trail through pine woods of New Jersey, no one else in the forest. "What happened?"

"I spent a pleasant sunny but cool day hiking. I set up my tent while there was still plenty of light and made a nice dinner. Before it got dark I gathered wood and made a fire to ward off the feeling of emptiness. I watched the darkness set in and the fire die down. Nothing to do, so I went into the tent and got into my sleeping bag; it was quiet like earth was before people were created. Feeling drowsy I dozed off.

"I was rattled out of sleepiness by a screaming, penetrating uproar that filled me with a terror of the most frightening horror movie. The monstrous sound echoed back and forth through the blackness and turned my blood cold. It was as though the voice of Death, deafening, was bellowing the incomprehensible cadence: 'Who cooks, for youoo! Who cooks, for youoo!' At first, I was afraid to move. Like a sudden cold steel hand locked around my throat, fear gripped me. It blared again, yelling in the darkness with the force of a shattering bullhorn, riding back and forth on the forest gusts. It was enough to turn your blood to ice. This was no ordinary beast. It was the Jersey Devil for sure. I hoped it wouldn't notice my little tent in the vast pine darkness. It ignored me, but shouted again and again.

"When it finally went away, I sat shaken in my tent, sleeping bag up over my ears. I didn't know what made that sound, but just after it left I heard something equally frightening—a pack of vicious dogs."

"Dogs barked. So…?"

"I once read a book about a guy who was pursued by a pack of ferocious wild dogs in those same woods. With fangs bared, they chased him up a tree. They would have ripped him apart. They finally went away."

"What happened to you?"

"The beasts must have been trying to kill a deer. I heard their growls and barking and then yelping. I stayed awake almost the whole night. At some point the racket died down and disappeared. I got a few hours of troubled sleep."

"Sounds awful."

"My days of test-hiking ended at the Wharton State Forest office. While waiting for Barbara to pick me up, I described to one of the rangers the horrible noise I heard that first night. The nerve shaking uproar that had this tempo: *hoo-hoo, hoo-hoooo — hoo-hoo, hoo-hooooo!* The ranger recognized it immediately and said 'Sounds were not of this world, right? That would be a barred owl. Ghastly isn't it? Sounds like a madman loose outside your tent. But it's just a huge owl's mating call.'"

Gorilla Jim and I trek the trail. A few college age hikers pass us, guys still clean shaven. The equipment they couldn't ram into their backpacks is hanging on the outside, attached with carabiners or straps. "Crummy weather, dude," says one with long hair. Lashed to the rear of his pack is a guitar wrapped in a garbage bag to protect it from the weather. He spots the gorilla atop Jim's hiking pole, "Hey dude, what's the monkey doing there?"

Jim presses the gorilla's chest, it bellows and we all laugh.

Mostly we have been descending the mountain. We walk along Stover Creek among majestic hundred-year-old evergreen trees, known as Cathedral Hemlocks. Their trunks tower a hundred feet in height. Their crowns are so dense that little light reaches the forest floor. We feel insignificant in their presence and awestruck as though passing through a place of worship.

We cross creeks and walk on log bridges and abandoned logging roads. I keep part of my consciousness on the two-by-six-inch vertical white paint marks on the trees—blazes that mark the A.T. This is how we find our way through the forests and mountains of this weaving dirt and stone line from Georgia to Maine. Sometimes we both stop and peer into the misty rain, trying to see the next white blaze ahead, rainwater releasing rich aroma of moist earth.

We take a break, standing under a tree, as the rain eases up. I eat a handful of trail mix. Jim eats a candy bar and tells me he was married five times. His fifth wife was a keeper. The Gorilla man has many brothers. He had been a top sergeant in the army, which meant he was in charge of other sergeants and was responsible for the well-being of many men and women. Between bites of the Hershey bar, Jim fills in some details. There were women in his outfit who played seductive games with the sergeants. "They were supposed to wear their T-shirts tucked into the top of their shorts," Jim says. "Instead, they pulled their shirts out, covering the shorts so it looked like they weren't wearing anything under their T-shirts. They'd walk by and call out in soft alluring tones, 'Good morning platoon sergeant…good morning sergeant.' In my case because I was in charge of the all the platoon sergeants—I was the senior field—they would say, in a 'come screw me' voice, 'Good morning, Senior Field.' I'd bark, 'Get into proper uniform.' They'd get their blouses back into their shorts pronto.

"The other thing you had to look out for was when the women did sit-ups," Jim explains. "They needed a partner to hold down their ankles. A female would work with a female, and a male would work with a male. Once, one of the women had no female to work with her. I held her ankles. Each time she drew herself up, her big round boobs almost hit me in the face as I was counting the sit-ups. Suddenly, I realized, What the hell am I doing? Every time she was coming up, I was looking inside her T-shirt. One…two… three…, and she was getting a kick out of it. I got a sharp tap on my shoulder from my colonel. 'What are you doing, Sergeant? Isn't there supposed to be a female here instead of you?' I gulped and said, 'There isn't anyone available.' He looked at me like *You're full of bullshit,* and said, 'She doesn't do sit-ups until a female is available!'"

The trail here has been trampled by thousands of feet over the years, and it is not difficult to follow. It is difficult to walk *on.* Ordinarily, when you step down onto solid dry ground, your foot stays in that place until you pick it up to move. When stepping into slippery mud, however, your feet can slide forward if you don't have your body centered. If you're leaning back, your feet continue to slide and you fall on your backside.

Constant rain plus many trekking feet equals mud, loads of slippery grease of the mountains. As we come down one steep mountain, I slide, heels digging into the liquid dirt, starting a small landslide of rocks and coffee-brown water. "Hey," Jim yells to me above the clatter of rainfall. "You're causing an avalanche…That's what we're going to call you: *Avalanche!*" He smiles with the pride of a father naming his first son and repeats it aloud to himself, "Yeah, *Avalanche.*"

I don't care for that trail name and hope with time a better nickname will come along. Instead, from then on as hikers passed us or we stopped for a break at the trailside or came to a shelter Jim introduces me as: "My hiking partner, Avalanche." Hikers only knew me by that name. I begin to respond when someone says: "Avalanche, how far is it to the next shelter?" or "What are you making for dinner, Avalanche?" or "Avalanche, you ever see rain like this before?" I start to like the new name; it is part of being admitted to a new culture of hardy outdoor folks. Hey, Avalanche, aren't you the tough backwoods dude who walks all day in rain and ankle deep mud, sleeps on the ground, and eats crappy camp food?

Weeks later when one of the skinny college-aged guys with wild dark hair and unkempt beard calls out, "Hey, whazzup, Landslide?"

I reply, "It's *Avalanche,* dude."

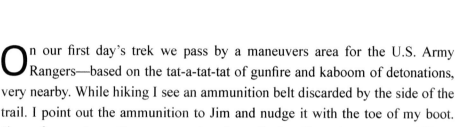

Chapter Four

On our first day's trek we pass by a maneuvers area for the U.S. Army Rangers—based on the tat-a-tat-tat of gunfire and kaboom of detonations, very nearby. While hiking I see an ammunition belt discarded by the side of the trail. I point out the ammunition to Jim and nudge it with the toe of my boot. Jim, a former Army Ranger, examines it professionally and announces, "These are blanks for maneuvers. When I was in the Rangers we weren't allowed to use the trails, had to find our own way through deep woods. You'd never have found anything like this. We'd never be near a trail. Wouldn't let the enemy know where we were by dropping something like this."

At Three Forks, three creeks converge. We cross a footbridge, and awhile later we are on the footpath going up to Hawk Mountain, having hiked seven and a half miles today. The Hawk Mountain Shelter is a three-sided wooden hut. Similar to the Springer Mountain Shelter, the Hawk Mountain Shelter has a peaked roof and an upstairs sleeping loft. There are pegs inside to hang gear and backpacks. Novice hikers, backs aching from the semi-strenuous hike up to this shelter, are rapidly smartening up to the need to lighten their backpacks. In the shelter they discard unnecessary equipment and form small piles of abandoned canned goods.

The Hawk Mountain Shelter is supposed to sleep twelve people. Almost twice that number of backpacks are dropped from weary spines onto the bench of a picnic table in front of the shelter. College students and younger people camp in tents near the shelter. The middle-aged trekkers gravitate to the lodging of the wooden hut itself. We gradually sort through our gear and move into the shelter. The rain lets up.

Dick is in his fifties. He can't wait to take off his boots and replace them with leather sandals. He watches his wife and sister-in-law get out their stove, food, and pots. They are the long-distance hikers who need to develop the rhythm of getting their meals together. Dick is only out for a short while, after which he will go do what he really enjoys: playing golf.

Arthur is in his forties, overweight, and has a bagel haircut (a crew cut with a vacancy at the top where he had been losing his hair). He has on rain pants with mud splashed up the legs and a thick blue vest over lighter blue turtleneck shirt. He looks around for a place to put down his pack and loosen his boots over crying feet.

Almost all of us share two things in common: starting on an exciting adventure that would take us through unending miles of mountains and forests and being exhausted. There are a few section hikers who are on vacation for a week or so, hiking a section of the Appalachian Trail.

We congregate around the shelter, talking among ourselves about equipment, how to cook, avoid foot blisters, difficulty of the trail. Some hikers sit on the front edge of the shelter pouring water into cook pots, dumping in Lipton's noodles, Raman, rice, or whatever else could be assembled into an easy dinner. New friendships form. It is a "first week of school" feeling.

The Hawk Mountain Shelter's rustic outdoor toilet (*privy*) has only three sides—like a tiny closet with the door removed. The front is completely open so the occupant can look at the natural scenery as he or she goes about his or her daily ritual.

Each shelter has a register in which hikers enter their names so people know where to find them. Most folks write short notes in the shelter register about what's happening. There are entries about the privy, trail names, and the weather:

"Great to be able to poop and look at the mountains!"

"... enjoy the three walled privy."

Michael "Yet to be named" Liretto.

"Day one and already have my trail name. Started out as Riverhiker and earned a new name. Going to Springer to start—wrong direction—so—*'Backtracker'* is me."

"fog finally lifted after arriving, and it began to rain and rain and rain."

"It's raining like a Mofu in the a.m."

"The fog finally lifted and it's beginning to dry out and so are we!"
One guy's note took up half the page and then ended with this:
"P.S. I MISS MY WIFE!"
Some people wrote about the shooting and explosions of the Army Rangers:
I hear machine guns!!

Jake exploded latest night. Oh wait, it was the Rangers around Our Tent!! What Are They Shooting at???

Not Me.

I Hope.

Jim and I sign the register under this note:

The Rangers are coming for YOU!

Everyone is so tired from a day of trudging through mud that we are in our sleeping bags by 7:45. I hear the rangers machine-gun fire and explosions in the distance. That was nothing compared to the sound of people's explosive snoring. I sleep on the lower level near a husband and wife. The husband sounds like a concrete-breaking jackhammer amplified through rock concert loudspeakers.

March 14, 2002

The sun welcomes us, spreading its golden glow across the horizon. Jim comes out of the shelter, stretches his arms, looks at the pink rose light that melts the night away, and says, "It's a beautiful thing."

The weather is clear. I take off my shell, and we walk in seventy-degree warmth. Horse Gap greets us with its countless tall sunlit trees casting shadows on a forest floor that is carpeted with last fall's cinnamon-colored leaves. What a pleasure to be bathed in sunlight instead of soaked by cold rain—it *is* a beautiful thing.

Coming up from Horse Gap, climbing and climbing, I realize that in Georgia there are going to be steep lung-busting ascents. Struggling up Sassafras Mountain—the terrain is so vertical the trail actually stares me in the face. Jim and I stop every few hundred yards to catch our breath. The Gorilla man crouches over to help suck air into his lungs.

At one switchback I look above me to a guy in his early thirties and weakly yelp, "How's it going?"

He gulps some air, pauses, and croaks down to us, "I've had better days."

At another switchback, a woman in her twenties is sitting on a boulder, arms up around her knees, head down, beat. Curled up at her feet, snoozing is a large black-and-white dog, a little backpack on its back. She looks up, sighs, and says to me, "This is really something!

I'm glad for any reason to stop. Spotting her large dark blue backpack I ask, "How much weight are you carrying?

"About fifty pounds." She groans.

"Have you hiked before?"

"Yeah, I'm really carrying too much, probably too much food."

"I hear you. I'd like to get rid of some weight I'm carrying." The straps of my backpack dig into my shoulders and chest. My pack weighs around fifty pounds. It is like hauling a six-year-old boy on my back up and down mountains all day long!

Sometimes the trail is just a slight indentation in the ground or faint line through mulched leaves. At other times we are walking on slender ledges going around the mountain with sheer drop-offs on one side of the trail. Through Justus Mountain and Phyllis Spur, the trail is like a roller coaster with steep ups and downs. We cross an old logging road and several streams. Some streams we traverse on narrow wooden bridges, others we cross on stepping stones, the water forming rivulets around the rocks. Going up to Gooch Gap, the trail finally levels out and gracefully curls around a mountainside with views down into gorges and pine-scented, jade-colored hollows. For a while we pass between deep green rhododendron thickets so dense you can't see through either side.

Looking down hundreds of feet below, there are glimpses of a stream and we hear the sound of moving water.

We pass Gooch Gap Shelter, go nine miles, and camp with a group of people we met earlier. Everyone's exhausted from the steepness of today's uphill climbs. They fade into their sleeping bags. This is a peaceful spot and I expect to get a good night's sleep.

Jim is too tired to set up his tent and instead decides to sleep out under the stars. During the night I hear a tumult outside my tent. There is a sudden rain, and Jim is thrashing around, rushing to put up his tent in the dark. The quickening downpour won the race and all of his things got soaked before he could erect the tent.

March 15, 2002

This morning I watch as Jim packs his gear, which was not only wet but weighed more from the rainwater soaked into it. Arthur tries to heave a backpack jammed beyond capacity onto his back, but two large stuff sacks, along with camp shoes and other paraphernalia swinging from the back of his pack, get in the way, and he twists and wriggles his arms into the shoulder straps.

Today's hike takes us through beautiful scenery. High up on dove gray and tan stone outcroppings, we stand gazing at the panorama. Range after range of mountains, the closer ones are craggy, sharp and distinct, rich shades of dark blue; the second mountain chain, miles away, are lighter blue. Each more distant range is lighter and softer, less distinct, until the farthest hazy peaks blend with sky. Big Cedar Mountain has an overlook with a view of Blood Mountain, the highest mountain on the A.T. in Georgia. This is what it's all about! Being rewarded several times a day for carrying a heavy load to the crest and looking down on nature's best handiwork. It is like being inside of a painting.

We are wilderness-trekking through the Chattahoochee National Forest filled with hardwood trees: oak, hickory, and poplar. Being early spring, many of the trees are still bare. When it isn't raining, we look down the gorges through denuded forests. I slow my pace to look across to mountains on the other side of the valley, sometimes catching a view down through and over mountainside trees six stories high.

It's not the primitive forests or the ridges at this three or four-thousand-foot altitude that impact us the most. It is overcoming the tough, weight-bearing climbs on steep ascents and descents—enduring the strength of will—that make this stretch of terrain memorable.

The trails up Ramrock Mountain and Big Cedar Mountain—almost vertical—test our endurance. Hiking up these mountains is like hiking up an endless sliding board. The trails are wet and the earth is soft. With each step we slip and slide and have to jam our poles into yielding mud to keep from falling, which causes unnatural twisting and jarring of our shoulders.

We stagger up steep inclines that pain our thighs. We pause every few dozen steps to suck enough air into our lungs that aren't ready for this kind of work out. Jim stops, puts his arms under his backpack, and shoves it upward to relieve his back and shoulders. He leans forward, hands on thighs, and puffing for air asks, "They tryin' to kill us?"

I lean on my poles, panting, trying to form words, "They could've made the trail... gradually zigzag up the mountains... but, no." I pause to grab more air into my lungs, "... they make the damn trail go straight up... and over... They *are*... trying to kill us."

Jim laughs as well as a breathless man could. "I'm paying $4,000 to be tortured like this!" Then, both of us laugh at the absurdity of paying to be in agony.

My ultimate goal is to get to Maine, to hike the twenty-one-hundred-plus miles of Appalachian Trail, but right now I just want to get to the top of this friggin' mountain, to raise my leg and go one more step, one step closer to the top. Inside us the energy drains away. There is tremendous resistance to lifting 220 pounds (my body plus gear) any higher. I'm helped upward by years of exercise and months of training. I'm held back by decades of living and knowing that this hike should have been done by a much younger Avalanche. Also, there's too much stuff in my backpack! I'm an electric toy whose battery is drained and the toy is fumbling without energy to take it any farther. We could not make it a mile and a half more to the Woods Hole Shelter.

Jim and I have hiked eight and a half miles this day through what were the most grueling mountains, at least up to that point. We camp by ourselves amid tall trees at Jarrard Gap. (A gap, sometimes called a pass, is the low point between mountains.) I can't get the stove Hacksaw lent me to work. I pump the white gas, try lighting it with a cigarette lighter, but it will not light. Gorilla Jim's stove gave him trouble the first night but is working fine now, so I use it to heat my dinner. I miss my Dragon Fly stove and wonder if Hacksaw will bring it to me when he shows up at Neels Gap, or if I would be resigned to eating cold food or borrowing stoves.

Experienced hikers carry only a spoon to eat with—no fork, no knife. Without the spoon you are out of luck. Jim could not find his spoon. He took the plastic coated paper container that had held his dried Lipton Noodles and folded it into a scoop. "I made a spoon, ranger style!" the Gorilla man proclaimed. He tasted his camp food concoction, savored it with closed eyes and said, "It's a beautiful thing." He said the same about the scenery. Whenever something went well, Jim said it was *a beautiful thing*.

The sun sets early at this time of the year. There are bears in this area, so, in the dark I hang our food bags on a cord that I strung up between two trees.

March 16, 2002

We wake up at 5:00 a.m. so we could travel to Walasi Yi where we would get a warm bed and a hot meal and stock up on much needed supplies. We had been looking forward to Walasi Yi for the past few days. After cold Pop Tarts, Instant Breakfast, and banana chips, we break camp and get on our way. It is still dark and the fog is wafting across the beam of my headlight.

The climb from Jarrard Gap is weird and wonderfully beautiful—we are hiking up into the clouds.

Since we started so early, we catch up with the others we had met and who had made it to the Woods Hole Shelter. They are all stirring and eager to get to Walasi Yi Center. Gorilla and I take a break, chat with fellow hikers, and refill our water bottles from the stream. Unlike the cowboy movies, you cannot safely drink water out of a stream. There is the danger of getting giardia, crypto (short for Cryptosporidium) and other intestinal-ravaging germs and parasites. Yes, we're talking about world-class diarrhea out in the forest. (Failure to keep your hands clean—and hand sharing food with others, such as other people dipping into your trail mix—can cause the same intestinal disorders.) These bugs can be eliminated by treating water with chemicals or forcing the liquid through a pumping gadget that filters out the bad stuff. We use a pump canister. It is the size of a soda can with a plastic hose that goes into the stream or spring. A pump forces the water through filters and out another tube into our water bottles.

If you look at a profile of the mountains and valleys of the Appalachian Trail, it looks like the teeth of a handsaw, except the teeth of a saw are all uniform. The profile of the southern part of the A.T. includes one peak that towers above the rest.

Blood Mountain is the highest peak on the trail in Georgia. In the late 1600s, the Cherokee and Creek Indian tribes fought a bloody battle over the resources in the area. So many warriors were killed or wounded that the mountain slopes are said to have run red with blood, giving Blood Mountain its name, and also naming nearby Slaughter Gap. A more contemporary reason for its name: you feel like you're sweating blood climbing it.

As we hike up the mountain, dead trees fallen over in the woods look like collapsed warriors left on the battlefield. Ironically, a few tufts of grass at the side of the trail indicate spring is not far off. In another month the trailside trillium, mountain laurel, and rhododendron will burst into red, yellow, pink, violet—a living rainbow—but not today.

A torrential rainstorm hits us. We hike up in a blasting, cold torrent, crescendos of snoring wind. Rain jacket hoods pulled tight over our heads, we climb against the raging weather.

There are hundreds of large rocks placed as steps, part of the steep trail going upward, and we trudge up the slabs, made treacherous by blowing rain. You step up, leaving the rock you're on, and onto the slippery surface above. There is no place to stop, no place to take refuge from the storm. Jim slips on a smooth rock and catches his balance just before he fell. I can only make out a couple words as he yells to me through the storm: "…be careful…" The noisy rain pounding on my head drowns out everything else.

A hiker ahead of us, his thin polyethylene poncho wildly blowing sideways in the wind, slides on a large flat rock, spins around with the wind, almost drops completely to his left knee, stops in time to right himself, and cautiously moves on. The blaring wind is so loud we couldn't hear him ten yards away, cursing.

It's as though the sky is competing with itself to exceed each prior day's rainfall. Today's deluge is the winner.

If you think I'm painting an overly dismal picture of the weather—don't. On the A.T. in March and April it rains. It rains a lot, and it's cold much of the time. The Appalachian Trail Conservancy (ATC) oversees the Appalachian Trail and says those hiking "in March will often be disappointed to find cold rain, sleet, and snow." In their publication, *Step by Step, An Introduction to Walking the Appalachian Trail*, the ATC asks this rhetorical question: "Will you endure days of rain, when every item you own becomes soggy, including your tent and sleeping bag?" YES!

Near the top of Blood Mountain, the wind-swept trees are bent and crooked. We stop at the summit for just a moment but instead of enjoying a wondrous display of the valleys, mountains, and vegetation of the Blood Mountain Wilderness Area, we are whacked in the face by driving rain. The rustic stone cabin at the peak has been vandalized by locals who could access it by a highway a mile away. There is no drinkable water at this high elevation, just grooves of murky water running across the boulders.

We begin our steep descent to Neels Gap and the Walasi Yi Center—a two-mile slip-sliding slog through thick mud that makes its way into our boots. We don't care. It doesn't matter that we are twisting our ankles and legs on the slippery rocks and jarring our shoulders trying to catch ourselves from falling. The glee of knowing we will soon be out of the driving rain energizes us. We stumble through the slippery muck, fantasizing about the comfort of a hostel, a steaming shower, and a hot pizza.

The rain knew we would soon be indoors, and it mockingly gives up as we come down into Neels Gap.

The Appalachian Trail is a challenge physically and mentally. Your feet blister and hurt. Your toenails are squeezed, sometimes one is crushed until it blackens and falls off.

The ATC gives Difficulty Ratings for trail sections: 1 is flat and 5 is strenuous ups and downs with only occasional flat sections.

The trail in Georgia is given a difficulty rating of *6!*

Many people can't take the rigor. We saw people quit after the first day. Of those who start from Springer Mountain, 20 percent give up by the time they reach Walasi Yi. However, the supreme reward of accomplishing the mountainous conquests makes it all worthwhile. Often the most difficult challenges make the most prized memories.

Every tortured, whined about, wet cold climb is a treasure to each hiker... way after the hike is finished.

When the sweating, freezing and bitching are over, you've come many miles atop steep mountains, slippery trails, over fallen trees and rocks. What an accomplishment—what a subtle rush.

Chapter Five

The Cherokee Indians considered Blood Mountain to be holy and to be guarded by the great frog Walasi. Walasi Yi means "Place of the Great Frog." To us Walasi Yi means a night in a warm bed. Wide stone steps lead to the Walasi Yi Center, a rambling stone building constructed by the Civilian Conservation Corps in 1937 when the A.T. was also completed. It is the only place where the trail leads up to and goes through a building.

Hacksaw said he would deliver my stove to me here. I have my doubts he'd be here. But true to his word, when we trekked up to Walasi Yi, the friendly bear of a man is there, stove in hand. I return his stove, and Hacksaw goes on his way.

Walasi Yi Center's main feature is an outfitter store loaded with outdoor gear. There are racks of colorful clothes and the ever-popular khaki shirts and pants. Several counters display equipment like stoves, pots, knives, maps, sunglasses, and compasses. Boxes are filled with energy bars and various freeze-dried camp food wrapped in individual portions. They have all sorts of downy sleeping bags, and wonderful displays of teal green and red tents. A middle-aged man, a wool cap on his head and an elastic bandage on his knee, examines a large display of boots and socks. A pug nosed nineteen-year-old girl, her powder blue down jacket over one arm, holds up a taupe-colored long-sleeved pullover for the approval or another bright-eyed girl.

Jim loves stores and is birthday-happy looking at the piles of gleaming hiking gear. "Look at these things!" He holds up a new backpack and his eyes shine. Jim buys the backpack, a pair of boots (his Walmart specials were shot), a bladder to hold water, a rain cover for the backpack and nylon bags to hold loose items.

I am glad to get my ill-fitting backpack off and loosen the laces on clamp-tight boots. After Jim gets his things, we collar Nate, a slender, experienced thru-hiker on the staff, and ask him for suggestions to lighten our load. He goes through our stuff and decides what could (1) be sent home, or (2) be sent to our next destination at Hiawassee, or (3) be put in a "bump box" to send ahead to some other place up the trail. My pack towel is about three feet long. Nate cuts it in half, and I send half of it home along with other things I really don't need. This expert-hiker-salesperson repacks Gorilla's backpack, taking out many unneeded items, which Jim sends home.

When I had walked in, Nate noticed my pack was not fitting right. He works on the straps and buckles, improving the fit and making it more comfortable—but, as long as I have owned it, this pack never did feel right.

"How are your boots?" Nate asks.

"Awful. I've got very wide feet. Size 9½ triple E. They always feel tight."

"Where does it hurt, Avalanche?"

I lean down and put my index finger on the side of my left boot, near the base of the little toe. "It hurts here."

"Take 'em off." This is one order I gladly follow. Nate took them to another part of the store where he used a broomstick-shaped metal rod to work the inside of the boot until it stretched sideways near where my painful small toe had been fighting with the inside of the boot. A crowd of young hikers are rummaging through a pile of packages. It is the mail drop where boxes of supplies sent from friends or family are held until they can be picked up. Fresh faced twenty-year-olds search piles of tan cardboard boxes, looking for the valued package from home. I take my turn and, after searching for a few minutes, retrieve the one addressed to me. Barbara had sent me more than enough meals to feed me to Hiawassee.

While browsing through the store I meet Chef Paul. He is a friendly man who wears well the early part of midlife. Chef Paul looks at our gas stoves and explains that many thru-hikers are now using the simpler and much lighter alcohol stoves. I tell him how I have been without a stove for a while and have just gotten my stove back. Chef Paul convinces me that the extra weight isn't worth the trouble. I want my pack to be as light as possible. Jim and I each buy an alcohol stove and send our gas stoves home. I buy alcohol and a small plastic container to hold it, along with a few other items.

While checking out Nate asks me, "Anything else I can get you?"

"Yeah, twenty-one-year-old legs and lungs."

Nate laughs.

Tenderfoot thru-hikers overpack. When they reach the Walasi Yi Center, thirty-one rugged miles from Springer Mountain, these back-weary trekkers are ready to slim down. We are typical novices. When we arrived, we were overloaded. When we leave, we are streamlined with less and lighter equipment—just the essentials. Outside the outfitter store hangs a scale. A hook at the bottom of the scale holds your backpack which is weighed when arriving at Walasi Yi and when leaving the center. When I arrived, my pack, *almost empty of food*, weighed forty-seven pounds. When I leave, my pack, *full of food*, weighs only *forty-five pounds*. What a relief to have a more comfortable and lighter backpack. It's a beautiful thing!

We were going to stay in bunks at the hostel, but I am fighting a cold or something and have a terrible cough so at the registration counter I ask for a room by myself. We are sent to the "Cabin," a nifty house with bunks in the bedrooms. My bed is secluded on an enclosed porch. Many of us share the cabin. The surprise: Chef Paul arrives with food for everyone staying at the cabin. He puts steaks on an outdoor grill, makes a salad, and serves it with beer...even has dessert. He calls it "trail magic." When I ask how to repay him for this unexpected feast, Chef Paul says, "Sometime do trail magic for other hikers."

While Chef Paul grills the steaks, long grilling fork in hand, a few of us chat. I am standing near Chef Paul when he looks up from turning the sizzling beef and asks, "Avalanche, if I dropped your steak on the ground, what would you do?"

"I'd wipe it off, put it on the grill to kill the germs, and then eat it."

"You're a section hiker!"

"Whadaya mean?"

"A thru-hiker would eat it right off the ground."

I begin to consider why a thru-hiker wouldn't worry about the germs when Chef Paul stares at me and challenges: "Avalanche, What's the difference between a day hiker, a section hiker, and a thru-hiker?" Before I even comprehend the question, Paul answers it himself: "A day hiker sees three M&Ms on the trail and walks by. A section hiker sees three M&Ms on the trail, picks them up, and puts them in his trash bag. A thru-hiker sees three M&Ms on the trail, picks them up, eats them, and then gets down on all fours to look for the rest of the M&Ms." Everyone laughs.

After dinner, Gigi washes the dishes and I dry. We talk like cousins who hadn't seen each other for ages and are catching up. With the dishes back in their kitchen cabinet, we sit in the living room—Dick and Gigi cozy on the sofa and I in an easy chair—and chat about the trail and our hopes of completing it. Jim is out on the wooden deck with Chef Paul and Teetotaler who are smoking cigars and listening to a guitar being played by one of the guys staying at the cabin.

That evening Jim sleeps in a bedroom that has two sets of bunk beds. On one side Jim sleeps in the upper bunk and Dick below him. On the opposite wall are Gigi and Susan in their bunk beds. There is a ceiling fan between the upper bunks. During the night, Gorilla gets out of his upper bunk, hits the spinning fan, knocking it sideways, and he falls onto the floor, waking everyone in the room.

I sleep on the porch and cough all night.

March 17, 2002

Gorilla Jim and I say our goodbyes and leave Neels Gap. It is another day of trekking up and down the steep mountainous trail and through a forest of tall hardwood trees. The sky is overcast, a charcoal hue that usually means rain. We come across two guys sitting on a log, eating bagels with peanut butter. They are seasoned hikers—packed light with gear well worn. Jim asks, "Whatta you guys do when it starts to lightning and thunder?"

The taller hiker answers, "Pray."

Playing along I ask, "Is there a special prayer?"

He grins. "No."

"Is there anything you can do?"

His grin widens. "You can try laying on the bagels."

We laugh and continue along the trail. Even without the sun beating down, it turns hot, a muggy saturating heat, feeling as though we are hiking through a steamy wet sponge. After a strenuous sweaty straight up mountainous climb, we come down into a gap, shirts dark with perspiration. There, in a parking area is a young couple. General has a full beard and denim baseball cap, and Monkey Cola is slender with dark hair. Their car trunk is wide open. Inside is a Styrofoam cooler filled with Mountain Dew, beer, and cold water—free for thru-hikers. What trail magic!

Clustered around the rear of the vehicle are half a dozen sweaty hikers in shorts and T-shirts or sleeveless tops. One guy is so sweaty it looks like he had sat in water. All the girls, including Monkey Cola, have their hair pulled back. The cans and bottles drip with condensation. Jim gets a soda, and before opening the cold can, he rubs it across his forehead. I opt for a bottle of cool water.

It restores your faith to know people would give up their Sunday to provide a frosty revitalizing drink to hot and weary hikers. Despite the refreshing break, the strenuous climbing in the hot and humid weather beats the hell out of us. We can not make it to the Low Gap Shelter, so we pull off the trail. Gorilla Jim finds a good spot, and we set up our tents just in time. Rains hit as we finish setting up. We don't care and snooze in our tents. An hour or so later the rain breaks enough for us to cook dinner. We use the new, lighter alcohol stoves we bought at Walasi Yi. They work okay, but we still have to get the hang of how to use them.

Fog rolls in after dinner so thick you can't see a bear napping seventy-five feet in front of you. We had hiked in a misty eeriness part of the day—visibility down to fifty feet at times, which means we couldn't see two bears making love until we're almost close enough to tell which of them is Smokey and see what wine they're drinking.

It gets dark early, so we turn in at 7:30 p.m.

Rain at night followed by high wind.

March 18, 2002

It has rained every day. We expect to be wet, but the mud is as slippery as oil, and we never get used to that.

This morning we hike an hour or so before coming to the Low Gap Shelter. We arrive as two women in their early twenties are getting ready to leave. Periwinkle is so named because she wore light blue hiking shorts. Salamander got her trail name because of her interest in the little amphibians, which, interestingly, have only four toes on their front legs and five toes on each hind leg. We drop our packs at the shelter, chat briefly, and then Gorilla Jim and I go to the stream to filter water. When we return to the shelter to pick up our packs, we see a purple stuff sack hanging from a nail over the same area where Periwinkle and Salamander had been packing up—but they are gone.

"They left their food bag," we say simultaneously.

Jim adds, "I'll carry it until we catch up with them." He makes room in his backpack to jam in the purple sack.

We hike for a few miles and come across several people camped near the trail. "We found a food bag hanging on a nail at Low Gap Shelter," Jim says to a woman eating breakfast. "We're tryin' to catch up with two young ladies who left it there."

The woman says, "I read the Low Gap Shelter register when we stopped there earlier. Someone wrote that they were leaving the purple sack for a hiker to pick up."

Just great! Instead of doing a good deed, we had taken someone's food. We are not about to hike back to Low Gap. Gorilla and I continue hiking north, looking for a hiker going south. There aren't many southbound hikers, but we saw a few of them since leaving Springer Mountain. The A.T. is usually hiked from south to north. However, it can be hiked from north to south. In 2002, 1,875 people started the trek going north. Much fewer, 286 individuals, started the hike going south, but only sixty-two people completed the southbound hike in Georgia.

Surprisingly, I spot someone coming south. Bill Bennett is thru-hiking from Maine to Georgia. He had started in September 2001 and is almost at his destination. He agrees to return the food sack to Low Gap Shelter.

It turned sunny this afternoon. We hike about eleven miles to Blue Mountain Shelter—almost fifty miles from where we began at Springer Mountain! Many people there complain about the mice at Low Gap Shelter. Mice are a real problem at most shelters. We are tenting here at Blue Mountain so the shelter mice should not be a problem for us.

Whatever bug or cold I had cleared up. No fever in several days. I still cough a lot in the mornings.

March 19, 2002

This is almost unbelievable. Today, as we trek through northern Georgia, we stop for Gorilla to fix his boots. Periwinkle and Salamander hike up and ask Gorilla if he had left a food sack at Blue Mountain Shelter. Jim checked his backpack and didn't have his food bag. *In an amazing twist of fate, they* had found it and gave it back to Jim.

We pitch our tents in the woods and are asleep by 7:30 p.m. Around 10:00 p.m. I'm awakened by sounds of a large animal crunching leaves and snapping brushwood outside my tent. I hope it will leave, but it comes closer and closer to my tent. I yell to scare it off. That doesn't work, so I let out an earsplitting stream of curse words that would have scared away inmates from a maximum-security prison. The beast grunts and grumbles but continues moving nearer.

My yelling wakes up Jim who is still half asleep. In a confused voice he asks from his tent, "What's goin' on, Al?"

"Trying to scare off an animal out there." I let loose another string of curses. "...get the hell out of here you big bastard. Get the f*#! away from my tent." Jim quickly becomes alert and snickers at my efforts to get rid of the beast. I fish around a mesh pocket inside my tent, pull out my whistle. "Jim, I'm gonna blow the whistle to scare him off."

As the tranquility of the forest is shattered by my loud shrieking whistle, Gorilla Jim is hysterical with laughter. "Hey, Avalanche. You gonna try a trumpet next?"

"You think it's so damn funny?" I hear the beast grunting and pawing its way in Jim's direction. "The big bastard is now moving toward your tent! Have fun." I turn on my side, go to sleep, and have the best night's rest since arriving in the Appalachians.

March 20, 2002

Today, we hike in a cool raging rainfall—nothing new.

We reach Dicks Creek Gap and the highway to Hiawassee. Gorilla stands at the edge of the road with his thumb up. A pickup truck stops, its windshield wipers swooping back and forth. The driver tells me to get in the cab. Jim jumps in the back just as two men and a woman emerge from the woods behind us. They all get into the truck bed and ride in the rain. Butch, our driver, is a chunky guy with ruddy complexion where his face wasn't covered by a dark beard. I tell him about the animal outside my tent last night and ask him what he thinks it could have been. He ponders the description for a while and then responds in his southern Appalachian drawl, "Couldah been a wild hog. Couldah been a bahr [bear]." Gorilla and I had discussed it while hiking, and we suspected it was either a wild boar or a large raccoon or opossum, but I suppose it couldah been a bahr.

Butch drives us to the Blueberry Patch hostel, which is filled up. Butch waits while I pick up the bump box I had shipped from the Walasi Yi Center and then he drives us to the Holiday Inn Express in Hiawassee. He won't accept any payment for the ride, so we thank him profusely and say our good-byes.

We can't wait to get out of our wet things. Jim pours water out of his boots. We put our clothes in the washer and take our first shower since Walasi Yi. It feels good to get cleaned up and dried out.

There is an all-you-can-eat buffet restaurant called Daniel's near the hotel. We join John, Recycled, and some of the other guys we had met in the past few days. At the next table Bill, Dick, Gigi, and Susan are eating with another couple. On the trail, Gigi, Susan, and Dick always have such a variety of food that Gorilla Jim dubbed them the Holiday Inn. They call us the Odd Couple. I am Felix.

A few days earlier, Jim had slipped on the slick mud and twisted his ankle; he also developed blisters on the side of his foot. Because of the pain he had been very quiet. It is good to see the Gorilla man in good spirits and robustly attacking the abundant buffet, but it is short lived.

Chapter Six

March 21, 2002

L ast night Jim became sick with a bug similar to the one that attacked me the first few nights of our trip, so he stays in bed for a while. I go to the post office to pick up the package of food and other supplies Barbara sent me and send some things to her.

Evelyn is a friend of Jim's from the days when Jim lived in nearby Murphy, North Carolina. When I returned, Jim is feeling better and tells me that he called Evelyn and she agreed to drive us to a few places. Evelyn drives up in an old Lincoln Town Car that sounds like it could have mechanical trouble at any moment. Evelyn is a short, slightly overweight woman whose daughter had died, leaving Evelyn to raise her fifteen-year-old granddaughter. She also takes care of her son who is ill. Considering the cards life had dealt her, Evelyn displays a bruised pleasantness, and I immediately like her.

Jim needs to do something about the boots he had poured water out of the night before. I think Evelyn is going to drive us to an outfitter in Hiawassee. Instead, she drives weaving, winding roads through mountains and spring-greening valleys deep into the hinterland of North Carolina. We pull up in front of a one-story rambling store that looks as if it has been converted from another building. When Jim sees the pile of surplus army ammunition cans outside, he turns to Evelyn with disgust, "What kind of redneck place is this?"

"Carl" (Evelyn always used Jim's actual first name), "don't you make a scene like you did at the hardware store!"

"What's that all about?" I ask.

"Carl was barred for life from one of the chain hardware stores for causing a scene."

"What happened, Jim?"

"I wasn't barred for life—only for six months."

"Why?"

"I bought an attachment for a lawn edger. It didn't fit, so I took it back to the store. It had been awhile since I bought the gadget, so they said they'd have to send it back and couldn't give me my money right away. I just wanted my money back. I paid for it in cash and expected my money back in cash. They went on and on. I told them they had ten seconds to give me my money, and if they didn't give me my money, I was coming over the counter to get it. I counted the seconds out and they didn't give me the cash. So, I started over the counter. A woman customer cried out, 'He's crazy, oh my God!' The cashier said, 'He's nuts!' and pushed a button for security. A big guy and another man escorted me out the door to my car. They took down my information and told me I wasn't allowed in the store for six months."

Evelyn, Gorilla, and I walk up the steps and into the outfitter store. Several hundred feet of aisles are crowded with camouflage colored clothing and gear. Mixed olive drab, khaki, brown and black cover pants, shirts, jackets, vests, Vietnam War–era Boonie hats, underwear, rifles, and much more. As far as you could see there are camo-colored items to allow someone to blend in unseen into the woodlands.

The salesperson sells Jim an electrical device that would dry out his boots. It has two vertical pipes that blow warm air through the footgear. Jim picks out socks, pants, a shirt, gloves, and tan suspenders. Evelyn and I remind Jim that he would have to carry all the stuff he buys. It doesn't register. Jim just hurries down an aisle searching for more gear.

I tell one of the young men who works there that we're hiking the Appalachian Trail. He asks, "Are you going to be in Georgia on Saturday?"

"Why do you ask?"

"It's the beginin' of turkey huntin' season."

It doesn't make sense to me. "Don't turkeys usually hang out near fields and not up in the mountains?"

"No. Turkeys go where the acorns are."

I picture all the acorns we stepped on during the past week. "To prevent getting shot," I said, "we'll make noise and call out cadences."

Gorilla Jim is a former drill sergeant. I reminisce about the day I had told him I often sound out those rhythmic military songs in my mind to keep moving or to get me moving faster. "Hey, Jim," I had said. "Call out some army cadences."

Happy to return to the days when he drilled recruits—when he shouted out a verse in the rhythm of the march and the troops yelled it back to him— Sergeant Jim had delivered this to me in the singsong army way:

> I don't know,
> But I've been told—
> Eskimo pussy is mighty cold.
> I've been told,
> But I don't know—
> Eskimo pussy is cold as snow.
> Sound off 1 - 2
> Sound off 3 - 4
> Sound off 1 - 2...3, 4

That day I marched along the flat ground, keeping time with the tempo, yelling back each verse. At the end I shouted, "Give us another, Sarge."

> 1 ...
> 2, 3, 4, 5
> This sergeant...
> don't take no jive
> 6 ...
> 7, 8, 9, 10
> Back it up...
> let's do it again.
> My head aches, my back aches,
> my boots are laced too tight.
> And all I hear from this old Drill,
> is go to your left and right.
> Sound off, 1, 2
> Sound off, 3, 4

Cadence count 1, 2, 3, 4

1, 2...3, 4.

The sales clerk breaks through my daydream and asks me, "Anythin' else ya need?"

"Yes, twenty-one-year-old legs and lungs."

For a few seconds the clerk's ruddy face remained unchanged. Then he said dryly, "Oh yeah, I get it. That's funny."

"Not so funny. I really could use twenty-one-year-old legs and lungs."

"Well, hain't got 'em."

Evelyn is patient with us. She takes us to a supermarket and a few other places. We take her to lunch at a nearby restaurant. Jim and Evelyn both had hot platters that come with apple cobbler. I have a gigantic cheeseburger, and even though it doesn't come with my sandwich, the smiling waitress gave me an apple cobbler too.

During lunch and driving back from the outfitter, Evelyn talks about different things such as the bears that are waking up from hibernation. She says that "the female bears are green and mean because they're hungry." And, she brings up Eric Rudolph—the terrorist who killed several people and severely injured over a hundred others in Atlanta. She says he had been chased by the F.B.I. into the Nantahala Mountains—mountains and forests Jim and I are going to be hiking through. Although hundreds of F.B.I. agents were searching for Rudolph, he managed to walk into a supermarket in town and buy six months worth of supplies. In a matter of fact tone, Evelyn said of this terrorist hiding around the Appalachian Trail, "Bumper stickers say Eric Rudolph is the hide and seek champion of the world."

Eric Rudolph, looking like he is in his late twenties, could easily pass for one of the hikers out on the A.T.

Chapter Seven

Eric Rudolph

He took an olive green military-style knapsack, carefully packed it with three pipes filled with explosives surrounded by shrapnel of concrete piercing masonry nails, wires, a twelve-volt battery, and a detonating device. At forty pounds, it was one of the largest pipe bombs ever. An alarm clock counted off the minutes.

That evening in Atlanta, Georgia, fifty thousand people were celebrating the Atlanta Olympic Games. They gathered at the Centennial Olympic Park to hear an outdoor show by the R & B group Jack Mack and the Heart Attack. Tens of thousands cheered and yelled as they swayed to the music of the world-class bash.

He placed the heavy pack of explosives under a bench near the bandstand, and walked away.

A blue-white flash blasted a hurricane of pointed metal projectiles through the crowd. A nail penetrated the head of a forty-four year-old mother—her teenage daughter next to her was seriously injured. One hundred and eleven were wounded. They lay on the ground, some clutched bleeding arms and legs. Next to an overturned wooden bench, three men with POLICE across their black shirts knelt to help the writhing figure of a man sprawled on the ground; he turned his anguished face up to them and lifted one arm in a plea for deliverance from this butchery. Thousands, who had enjoyed the Olympic partying, now shrieked in terror.

With the explosion Eric Rudolph blasted himself into history.

Rudolph, medium build, brown hair, piercing blue eyes, and guy-next-door looks, knew the forests and mountains in the Nantahala area of western North Carolina near the border with Georgia. He grew up there. The difference between him and the guy next door is that Rudolph was a terrorist who:

- Bombed a family planning service, injuring seven people;
- Attacked a nightclub, injuring five; and
- Blew up a women's clinic, killing a police officer and tearing out a nurse's left eye.

The blasting of the women's clinic was his downfall. Witnesses provided his truck license number and his description to the authorities.

From his home in Murphy, Eric Rudolph had been chased by the FBI into the Nantahala National Forest where Jim and I would be hiking.

He knew the mountainous woodlands and trails well. In five locations he had stashed more than 250 pounds of explosives—orange-red sticks of dynamite—enough to blow up heaven knows what. The Department of Justice reported that dynamite was hidden "in the Nantahala National Forest in areas used by the public for recreation, such as hunting, *hiking and camping.*"[1] The feds were concerned that deteriorating unstable dynamite and unsuspecting hikers in the woods could be a deadly combination. A hiker digging a cat-hole to shit in might end up having the undertaker wipe his ass.

The U.S. Attorney General described Eric Rudolph as "the most notorious American fugitive on the 'FBI's Most Wanted' list." What followed was one of the largest manhunts in U.S. history.

Dozens of law enforcement agencies hunted for Rudolph in the Nantahala region. Search teams scoured the dense Appalachian wilderness with bloodhounds and sniper-scopes. They combed the rattlesnake and mosquito infested Appalachian deep woods. They crisscrossed the forest and mountains from above with helicopters and with heat-seeking devices. It is rough country. Macon County sheriff, Homer Holbrooks, said: "I've heard there are rattlesnakes back there that could swallow a half-grown deer."[2]

They could not find this outdoorsman skilled at surviving in wild country.

Heavily armed SWAT teams with search dogs scrambled across homeowners' yards and fields, distressing passive residents; low-flying helicopters' screaming engines rattled church windows, shattering peaceful

Sunday church services; government agents relentlessly questioned local residents. When it came to accusations about one of their own residents bombing innocent people, many locals formed a prove-it-to-me attitude. Maybe the invasion by two hundred federal agents to chase one of their neighbors brought out a desire among towns folk to favor the underdog.

One hunter put it this way: "People blame the FBI, which they say couldn't track a gut-shot buffalo through six feet of snow."[3] Rudolph cached a completed bomb near the National Guard armory where the Task Force command post was located!

Some in the community considered Rudolph a folk hero. A popular T-shirt was emblazoned: "Run Rudolph Run." Other tees were adorned with a variation of this theme: "Hide Rudy Hide." A restaurant sported a sign stating: "Rudolph eats here." Felecia Sanderson, wife of the police officer slain in the Alabama women's clinic bombing, felt much differently. She had T-shirts made up with Rudolph's picture and the wording: "FBI Most Wanted Fugitive and Million Dollar Garbage."[4]

Towns people spun this tale: Six months after his disappearance—so the local legend goes—with dozens of federal, state, and local agencies looking for him, Rudolph walked into a food store in Andrews, North Carolina (a town near Murphy), bought $500 worth of food, and walked away. More accurately: Rudolph went to the home of a friend who owned a food store, asked the man for needed supplies, including food and batteries. Several nights later, when his friend was out, Rudolph returned to the man's home near Murphy, taking a large supply of groceries from that person's house. Rudolph left $500, but took the man's pickup truck. The friend's watchdog was found dead behind this house—poisoned. [5]

Interestingly, Murphy, North Carolina, is the town Gorilla Jim lived in before he started hiking the A.T. Also, when Rudolph was in the army, he desperately wanted to go to Ranger School, the same elite corps in which Gorilla Jim served. Rudolph failed to get in.

Years before, Eric said he could use the Appalachian Trail to move "easily and anonymously."[6] Soft spoken, with clean cut "average Joe" appearance, some said Rudolph walked the same trails that hikers were trekking. One publication stated: "Mr. Rudolph may have been within 20 miles of Murphy the whole time; he may occasionally have traveled up and down the Appalachian Trail, unremarked by passing hikers."[7] Reporting on warnings to hikers, the *New York Times* stated that: "Fliers were tacked up at resupply points along the Appalachian Trail..."[8]

FBI Director, Louis Freeh, admitted that Rudolph "could have gotten on the Appalachian Trail and walked to Maine or Florida."[9] "Undercover agents posing as hikers walked the Appalachian Trail by day and camped at night, hoping Rudolph would approach them for food or help."[10] They warned that Eric was armed and dangerous—he owned a variety of rifles and pistols.

A local resident who frequented the A.T. said of Rudolph: "He might have been another hiker, just another bearded, dirty guy."[11] Eric Rudolph had turned the Appalachian Trail into a rogue's highway. A dangerous killer lurks in the same woods we're hiking through.

There are startling similarities between Eric Rudolph and Gorilla Jim:

- They both have blue eyes and similar medium builds.
- Both were born and, for a while, raised in Florida.
- Both had lived in Murphy, North Carolina—not even a block and a half away from each other.
- Both have four brothers.
- Both enjoy living in the wilderness.
- Both wanted to be in the U.S. Army Ranger Corps—Jim made it, Rudolph did not.
- Both had learned how to use explosives.

But what a huge difference between them. Jim would give you the shirt off his back and lay down his life for people. Rudolph blasted the shirt off police officer Sanderson in the Birmingham clinic bombing and stole the lives of several blast victims. Jim is outgoing, loves most people, and could talk the ears off a brass monkey. Rudolph was said to be a shy loner who lived for years in the backcountry without speaking to anyone.

Or did he?

His average-Joe description described dozens of guys we met during our A.T. trek. Because of the nature of the trail—using trail names, being completely isolated from society—anonymity is easy. He probably mingled with hikers for years. Who knows, we may have crossed his path.

Chapter Eight

March 22, 2002

Every time I see someone with a dog, I stop to pet it. I miss Jack, my Rhodesian Ridgeback hiking pal. By mid-morning we stop near the Plum Orchard Gap Shelter. Jim drops his backpack and walks two-tenths of a mile down an old forest road to the shelter to sign our names into the register. During our first days we did this even if we don't stay in the shelter. We log our journey in case someone needs to locate us.

I stay up near the trail with our packs, sit on a log, and take out my food bag to eat lunch. While spreading out my pita bread, peanut butter, and block of cheese, I notice an animal coming through the woods. As it comes closer I realize it is a friendly dog, a small brown-tan-black Rottweiler and Beagle mix. The pooch seems playful enough. He comes closer, catlike, slowly sneaks up on my Ziploc food bags, and the little rogue starts to pull one away. When I take it back he grabs my bag of pita bread. "You're a thief!" I say as he keeps snatching different plastic bags. His antics make me laugh too much to scold him. I shoo him away, and he goes off a few feet. Three girls who had stayed at the shelter walk toward me and say the dog doesn't belong to them, but they gave him some oatmeal for breakfast and now he is attached to them. The girls went off and the dog followed.

Today, we hiked eleven and a half torturous miles crossing into North Carolina. We climbed up and down mountains higher than Blood Mountain. It was the longest hike we had done in a day so far—a severe welcome to North Carolina. While the hike was a painful ordeal, it's gratifying to come into a new state—quite an accomplishment. I am having fun.

Tonight we are at the Muskrat Creek Shelter at forty-six-hundred-feet elevation. It is constructed of cedar logs and other building materials that had to be airlifted by helicopter to the remote site. This is a Nantahala-style shelter with three sides like the other shelters, but this one has an extended front roof that covers an open area to be used for cooking and eating, including a table with benches.

The weather is clear and cold. The day had started at a chilly twenty degrees. It warmed up somewhat as we hiked, but by now it is dropping sharply.

I set up the alcohol stove on the table where others are also making their evening meal. The idea is to boil water, pour it into a plastic bag of dehydrated food, seal it, and let it cook for five minutes. My stove won't boil the icy water. Finally, I pour the warmed up liquid into the bag, and it leaks all over the table. I rush to get my pot and quickly transfer the mess into it. The lukewarm water doesn't cook my dinner, and I end up eating soggy half-prepared food.

After dinner, the temperature is back down to a cussing-cold twenty frigid degrees.

There are many congenial people at the shelter. Three young women, Lee, Alex, and Nicole, had taken off a semester from college to hike the trail. Several other hikers here include John, Kevin, Blaise, and Morris. Before dinner Morris collected dead wood and made a leaping blaze in the fire pit near the front of the shelter, and keeps it going afterward. Having completed the Georgia part of the A.T. calls for a little celebration. We huddle around the orange flames, warm in the front, our backs chilly. It isn't long before everyone starts to shiver and retreats into their puffy sleeping bags.

The temperature is supposed to drop into the teens during the night. It is too cold for us to sleep in the shelter with its open front. We had pitched our tents earlier and are glad to be able to be inside them. I am usually very warm at night and only sleep in a T-shirt and hiking shorts. Tonight, even I feel Mother Nature's frostiness. It is backwoods wintry cold during the night. I put on a heavy fleece jacket. Snuggled into my thick down sleeping bag, I get warm during the night, remove the insulated jacket and sleep in a long underwear top—and love every cozy minute of it.

March 23, 2002

This morning Jim's thermometer reads eleven degrees. Outside, the air is heading toward freezer temperature. People in town have to snap their dogs off the fire hydrants. Inside my tent it's fifteen degrees colder than a refrigerator. I hate to get out of my snug sleeping sack. I force one arm out into marrow-chilling air; it gets goose bumps. The rest of me shudders; my body doesn't want to be that cold. I ponder what it will feel like on the open-air privy.

I pull my shirt, pants, and fleece lining into the sleeping bag and squirm to get dressed in the sack's warmth. Then, I grab my shell and in one quick movement I jump out of the bag and into my jacket, with a fast zip up.

One of my gloves had disappeared. Morris is making another fire this morning but I am busy looking for my glove, so I couldn't sit around the warming open flames with the others. I search through everything in my tent—the glove doesn't show up. Some hikers complain that the plastic tubes on their water bladders froze in the night. I am glad I kept my water bottle warm inside my sleeping bag, but I really want my glove.

The three girls who briefly had befriended the stray dog are now known as the Carnival Girls. Jim has been trying to think of names for them individually. He must have seen one of them eating a bagel because he is working on a name that had something to do with bagels.

"We'll call you Bagel Girl," Jim says as she finishes her breakfast.

Probably thinking what a crummy name to take back to college, she smiles graciously at Jim, but shakes her head *no.*

"Missy Bagel," Jim tries.

She walks away.

As legend has it, long, long ago a huge winged monster terrified the Cherokee Nation darkening the sky, swooping down, and steeling away their children. The Cherokee prayed to the Great Spirit for help in getting rid of the horrid monster. A brilliant bolt of lightning brighter than ten suns shot from the sky with a deafening thunderclap, killing the winged beast. A Cherokee warrior had been posted as a lookout but became afraid and fled from his post. For his cowardice, he was turned to stone on that mountain. The Cherokees call Standing Indian Mountain *Yunwitsule-nunyi,* which translates to "where the man stood."

Over the centuries the stone has worn away, but if you look carefully you can see the remnants of the Indian…if you believe this legend.

We hike to the top of Standing Indian Mountain. It is the first time we are over one mile high. My ears pop the same as when you go up in an airplane. It is the highest point on the A.T. south of the Smoky Mountains The views are spectacular. We have a clear view of one of my favorite mountains: Chunky Gal. According to folklore a chubby Cherokee maiden fell in love with a young man from another tribe. The plump Miss left her family and traveled across this mountain range to be with her lover. Chunky Gal's unusual name led to a famous newspaper headline about bawdy activity on this mountain:

Two Jailed For Lewd Conduct On Top Of Chunky Gal[12]

Looking east you see *Big Butt Mountain*—another fertile source for interesting headlines.

Gorilla Jim is showing signs of pain. He tells me he has very serious back problems, and one of his legs has developed a deadened feeling since we started. Thinking it is related to his back I ask him if he wanted to go to a doctor, but he doesn't want to get off the trail.

Standing here looking out at Chunky Gal and the other beautiful mountains, I said, "Hey, Jim, how'd you hurt your foot?"

A grin breaks across his face. "You won't believe this."

Knowing Jim, I reply, "With you I'd believe anything!"

The Gorilla man's grin widens. "It happened coming down a mountain, playing crazy. I took my son to the Presidential Peaks in Colorado. We were climbing the snowy crests." Jim pumps his arms as though he were climbing. "I said to the boy, 'Let's go ski boarding.' I told him, 'Use your coat for skis by tying a square knot in the arms of the coat, grab the coattails, jump off the mountain, and use the coat as a ski board. He thought I was nuts. I did it.

Coming down the hill I thought there were little stones ahead. Instead they turned out to be large boulders. The only way to stop was to lean to the side, but there was a deep ravine on that side. I put my foot out like a brake, I heard my ankle crack. My son said I looked like a slow motion cartoon flying over the rocks, bouncing down the hill. I cut my head, broke a finger, broke my wrist, and shattered the arch of my right foot. There were compound fractures of the arch with bones sticking through. I had to come the rest of the way down on my butt." Looking down at his boots, "There are two pins in my right foot."

We are probably hiking more miles per day than we should this early in our journey. We hiked over nine miles to the Beech Gap campsite, which is nothing more than a clear area at the base of what we would ordinarily call a valley; on the trail it is called a "gap." There aren't many suitable places where we can stop for the night. We can't camp along mountain sides that are sharply slanted upward and there is no water nearby.

Unlike in civilization at the end of each day, we have to set up our home—or camp—and stock it with our belongings in our backpacks. There's no faucet to turn on water. Unlike in civilization if we want a drink, we have to locate water—sometimes down steep ravines—filter it through a pump, and bring it back to camp.

When we set up camp, I unfurl my sleeping bag. Out falls my missing glove. It had been tucked into the sleeping bag's hood. In the woods, if you lose a precious article of clothing or piece of cookware, there is no store nearby at which you can replace it. And when you are tired and cold, there is no way to escape it. You only have your tent, sleeping mat, and sleeping bag, which you have to carry with you. Once everything is set up, it is time for dinner. The only food you have is the food you can carry—and now my stove works fine. It is a hard routine that brings great satisfaction. In civilization you generally don't have the gratification of conquering mountains on your own and in the company of great, hardy folks who are sharing a fantastic adventure. When you watch the magnificent mountain crests and stately towering trees on a large screen TV, it's almost like being there. When you hike the trail, you *are* there.

There is no closet for clothes, no drawers for utensils, no bedroom for the sleeping bag. It all ends up a jumbled mess on my 58 x 89-inch floor. You quickly learn that it's important to have a place for everything—especially in freezing temperatures when you are searching for your extra socks...with freezing hands. Everyone has to come up with their own system for handling the mess.

Ordinarily, I'm compulsively neat and require things to be put back where they belong. My tent is small and sort of oblong shaped with the zip up door on one narrow end. Over time I have found the best places for my gear:

- Nylon stuff sacks for the tent, sleeping bag, and sleeping pad are stored on the left side near my feet.
- Backpack goes on the floor on the left side.
- Sleeping bag and pad goes on the right side.
- Glasses, knife, photon flashlight, and whistle goes in the mesh pocket on the right near the front.
- Water bottle is on my left near the front.
- Clothes bag is my pillow.
- Boots go inside the zippered door because I don't have a vestibule.
- Hiking poles lie outside near the door—close if I need them to fend off an animal.

My tent is always in some disarray. Jim's tent is smaller than mine, and it's as neat as a surgical operating room. It's amazing that a portable nylon house, bed, clothing, food, water filter, and everything else needed fit into a backpack weighing forty-plus pounds and can be carried on a person's back, although not always comfortably.

By 7:00 p.m. I'm ready to go to sleep. We're all tired and face another strenuous day with ten miles of mountainous trails, including a near vertical climb. I'm not griping, though. After all, the experience is rocking my world. Just about everyone has turned in or is doing their final tasks before going to sleep.

It's hard to believe, but we are a two days hike from civilization—an unsettling thought if anything serious happens to us. Inside my tent, looking out through the doorway before I zip it shut for the night, watching for the North Star—any star that Barbara might also be looking at—cool damp night air seeps through my fleece jacket, trying to get at the part of my ears not covered by my blue fleece cap. In a remote nowhere, far from everything, I'm feeling lonesome and thinking of Barbara and Jack, our dog, warm in our house, warm in our bed, the left side of that bed empty next to the night table where I put my glasses every evening before I kiss Barbara goodnight.

March 24, 2002

After an evening down in the frigid twenties and lower, the days dawn cold—sometimes crisp, sometimes damp. Supposedly, it's ten degrees warmer in a tent—here that's still below freezing. My body rebels against the icy wall of air surrounding the sleeping bag. I tug the blue fleece hat snug around my ears, take a shallow breath against the cold, and start pulling clothes inside my sleeping bag to dress in the warmth of the goose down sack.

We start off the day's hike avoiding spots of ice. The sun is slowly turning them to small pools of water and muck, which coats our boots. The past few days have been sunny, warming in the afternoon to the mid sixties, a sharp contrast to the dark frozen nights.

The ten-mile hike up and down mountains seems demanding but doable. However, near the end of today's trek, at almost one mile above sea level, is slender Albert Mountain. It is a vertical climb followed by a sharp drop that, on the map's elevation profile, looks like Mother Nature giving us the finger. The trail goes straight up bulging rocks. Jim reaches for tree roots to pull himself upward. He takes off his pack in order to climb a vertical stone wall. I hand up his pack, then mine. Climbing using both your hands and feet is known as scrambling. I scramble skyward, grabbing roots of trees that clasp the shear rock face and use footholds in the stone to climb to join him. We are both panting for air, but Jim also has a slight wheeze.

Stopping to gulp more oxygen, I look straight down and see Michael and his dog Charlie advancing below us. Charlie is a talented Golden Retriever who can pick up the trail in woods and mountains and leads ahead of Michael. Charlie, his tail swishing, moves around the stone mountainside and climbs a near vertical ribbon of dirt in "four-paw" drive steadily moving up toward us. With each strenuous stride the small blue saddlebags on his back shift from side to side.

When Charlie reaches the boulder I'm standing on, his tongue hangs out, and he pants profusely. But he still smiles the way Golden Retrievers do no matter how difficult their task. He is enjoying being with his master, out for a six-month stroll in the mountains. As we wait for Michael to pull himself up, I look at the four-footed trekker. "Charlie," I say, "you're a hell of a guy."

He smiles back and seems to say, *So are you.* I pet his head and he nuzzles my leg with the side of his face, a slight bit of slobber from the edge of his mouth makes a nickel size damp spot on my pants leg. Charlie is a genuine member of the fraternity of A.T. hikers. Now, we stand together on the nasty ascent of Albert Mountain, which I will always remember because it is my first vertical climb, and I'm not yet in good enough condition to take it in stride.

When I started on the Appalachian Trail, I had little appetite because of being sick—and probably from excitement—and had to force myself to eat. We were told our appetites would improve by the second week. Not even into my third week I am eating two dinners a night. Even so, I lost weight. My pants are sliding down. I am glad I bought a pair of suspenders at the redneck outfitters outside of Hiawassee.

When we finally make it to the Big Spring Shelter, we are ecstatic. The shelter sleeps seven, and there are many tent sites nearby. When we camped in the woods Jim and I were the only ones around. It's nice to stay at a shelter and chat with fellow hikers. And it has a privy! The privies lack privacy, but they sure beat having to go in the woods. Remarkably, small things like that become important to people who previously would have expected a tiled bathroom with toilet and sink and now have to dig a hole in the ground. Another great feature of this shelter is the bear cables. We don't have to string a bear line to hang our food bags out of the reach of bears and other hungry marauders.

After dinner, with daylight fading away, some of the guys snap dead branches from huge rhododendron bushes, combine them with dried brushwood, and form a pyramid in the fire pit in front of the shelter. We light the twigs and kindling and as the flames grow, we add larger branches that will burn longer.

We sit around the campfire on logs and boulders, and enjoy the golden dancing flames. When the fire dies down one guy takes a stout limb, lays it across the sparkling golden coals, blows into the heart of glowing embers and the fire springs to life.

A high school student, who has been hiking with his older brother, says, "I wonder how many steps it's from Springer Mountain to Katahdin."

"Five million," the older boy answers smugly.

"Howda ya know?" the younger boy asks in a sharp tone. "Are you counting 'em?"

"No, smart ass. I read it somewhere."

A short girl wearing hefty mittens, her plump cheeks reddened from exposure to the wind and cold, says, "Weren't the vistas magnificent today?"

A guy in his thirties with bushy, brown, windblown hair pokes the fire and muses, "I could see for miles, range after range of mountains."

"You could look out to the edges of the world," the rosy cheeked girl responds in a dreamlike voice. "It somehow makes it all worthwhile."

An athletic-looking woman with dark hair speckled with silver and ashy highlights that are inconsistent with her ageless face leans back on a log. "We're all getting stronger. Even though we're hiking at higher elevations, we're not panting as much—but it's still exhausting."

Her companion, a tall and rugged man in his fifties drops a thick log on the fire, causing it to spark up. "We," pointing to those of us who have hit a certain age, whatever it is that separates us from the younger folks, "are hiking more miles than we should at this point." He pauses, then adds, "But, you just can't stop anywhere when you're on the side of a steep mountain… no place to camp and no spring."

A young woman, an emergency medical technician with her hair parted in the middle and pulled into two long braids, leans forward on her log. Fire light flickers across her face as she says, "It's easy to become obsessed with hiking huge mileage every day when you have Maine on the mind. But those obsessed with doing enormous mileage need to be careful you don't get shin splints, bloody feet, or sprains."

Gorilla Jim and I are averaging ten miles or more a day for the last few days. And we are feeling it. While some of the young campmates sit around the fire, tossing on more branches, we are ready to go to sleep, and it isn't even seven o'clock.

Most hikers keep a journal, an account of their A.T. hike. At night, before going to sleep, with a headlamp on a band around their foreheads, trekkers write notes about the day's happenings. I'm probably the only one using a small handheld microcassette recorder. I'll send the tapes to be transcribed by my secretary—also one of my dearest friends—Cindy. I use the machine far away from everyone so as not to disturb anyone.

Jim saw the little dictating machine, asked me about it, and decided he wanted one. When we were in town, he bought a recorder. Tonight I hear Jim in his tent twenty-five feet away loudly dictating and playing back. I may have created a literary monster. "Jim!"

"What?"

"Turn that thing down. Remember what I said before?" I had told him it disturbs people to see cell phones, or other electronic gadgets that remind them of civilization. They come out here on the A.T. to get away from all that. I said, "If you don't want to get lynched, don't show any electronic devices out here."

"Oh, okay. Hey, Avalanche, this is pretty neat!"

"Have fun." Maybe another Steinbeck in that tent.

Chapter Nine

March 25, 2002

Morris is in his mid-twenties, tall and slender. He has a dark beard, sun darkened skin, and a distant look in his eyes as if he shared time in both this world and another. He always wears a baseball cap, and his clothes look like donation box rejects. Morris certainly is different in his World War II vintage combat boots, but he is always cordial enough to me. Jim doesn't like him. It's a matter of trust. Jim doesn't like Morris' slightly hunched over posture, the secretive, walking-close-to-walls way he comes and goes, a vaporous man who is here one minute, quietly disappears only to later appear again. It unnerves Jim. It means nothing to me. I feel sorry for the guy, who apparently fell on hard times.

This morning, as we stand around a fire Morris had made in the fire pit outside a shelter, he tells me he has been out of work, lost his job as a dishwasher and is in no hurry to go back to that type of work.

Jim had spoken to Evelyn about picking us up at Winding Stair Gap where U.S. Route 64 crosses the Appalachian Trail, a nine-mile ramble from Big Spring Shelter. She would drive us to the city of Franklin, North Carolina, where I have a box of supplies coming into the post office. Somehow, Morris overhears us talking about our ride and hangs around us in the early morning dark.

Jim grumbles, "Why's he hangin' around?" icily looking at Morris who rarely returned direct eye contact and absently gazes toward the planet Mars over Jim's left shoulder. "He gives me the creeps," Jim says low and confidentially to me and himself.

Jim is eating his most beloved breakfast: hot oatmeal. I never make it because I don't like cooking with chilly hands and detest having to clean stuck cereal out of my pot. It is not a bother to Jim who eats with gusto so much of the hot cereal that he is down to his last two packets of adored oatmeal. By the time Gorilla and I are packed and ready to go, Morris has evaporated from the campsite. I notice Gorilla taking a quick look around as we walk toward the trail. He was trained to be wary of anyone sneaking up. Life survival depends entirely on sudden recognition of danger.

It is a magnificent day. The sun shines so bright you could feel the warm glow. My legs take pleasure in their repeated movement over the terrain. Jim and I hike for about an hour, talking—and not talking. This is so different than Jim's danger filled trooping through Vietnam. Yet, in the core of Jim's mind a sniper's bullet is possible with every step.

The trail is open, and I enjoy watching the tall trees cruise by as we head north. A drowsy song by Nat King Cole and Natalie Cole swims in and out of my mind:

> Un-forget-able…that's what you are …
> Like a…something…un-forgettable…

There is no warning. Someone is coming from behind us. Jim's protective instincts jump into full alert. Something far distant, long ago…

Back in a steamy hot Vietnam jungle, in the thick vegetation where a cadre of sniping VC conceal themselves, and an innocent jungle path conceals sharp spike lined pits covered so perfectly you don't realize the ambush below until stepping onto the hidden trap.

To Jim, there was no sleep, no letting down his guard—not if you wanted to stay alive. Jim listene d for that life-ending shot… the ping of a bullet… a deadly enemy quietly coming toward him…. Listened for the sound of a foot settling down and cracking a piece of dead bamboo foliage.

By experience, his reflexes heightened to spring at a glimpse of danger. "Soldier," he'd whisper to the rifleman near him. "Watch 'em," nodding up ahead… Turning his head sideways, then to the rear, "Now those bastards are on your flank. They're sneaking up from the rear just like…like this son-of-a-bitch coming up behind us…"

Gorilla's jungle instincts snap into place when he sees someone who had left camp before us strangely coming from our rear. Jim jabs his long wooden hiking pole at Morris, demanding, "What the hell are you doing back there?"

"Just walkin'."

"Bullshit! How'd you leave *before* us and wind up *behind* us?"

"I turned south when I got to the A.T. instead of goin' the other way is all. And when I knew I was goin' wrong, I turned around and went north. Then I was followin' you."

Jim studies Morris—unkempt, out of uniform, a strange look about him. Is he some sort of enemy sneaking up on us? It isn't clear. "Look," the field sergeant in Jim commands, "I don't like guys coming up from behind like that. Just get—get on your way." Using the javelin-sized Gorilla hiking stick, Jim waves Morris to hike ahead of us. Morris is a faster hiker, and the part of Gorilla Jim that never came home from war wants the potential sniper to be in front of us and not behind.

Morris, not knowing what to say, just shuffles north and out of sight.

"I don't like that guy. If he keeps doing this, he and I are goin' to Tent City!"

When the Gorilla man doesn't like what someone is doing and is getting into fighting mode, he calls it Tent City. I heard of a tent city prison in Arizona where the guard dogs eat $1.10 worth of food a day, but they only provide an inmate 90 cents worth of food. Gorilla was close to feeding Morris to the prison dogs.

Jim adds, "If that guy keeps bothering me, I'm gonna put his head in a shoe box!"

We reach the Rock Gap Shelter and stop to take a snack break. Jim is ready to dig into the bag of mixed nuts he loves so much. I take photos to show everyone at home. While we are there, Morris quietly, vaporously arrives in the same way he disappeared earlier in the morning. His knees are slightly bent. He shuffles his feet, hardly raising them from the ground and looks at the dirt as he walks rather than taking in the surrounding beauty and distant "purple mountain majesties," as the other hikers do.

Vietnam's worst flashed into Jim's mind. "What the fu—" Jim fumes so he couldn't complete the word. "What're you doin' here?"

Morris flinches, and around his dark brown beard the color drains from his face.

The part of Jim trapped in that war-torn land roars, "You went ahead of us! Now you come up behind us...*again*. What the hell you doin', man!"

"I just—"

"I told you before," Gorilla pokes his finger into Morris's face. "I don't like people slinking up behind me." Jim is red with anger.

"I wasn't hidin'—"

"How'd you get behind us again?" Jim demands, ready to go to Tent City.

"I went down to the next gap—it ain't far from here. Montana Max told me there was food left at this shelter." Indeed, there are a few cans of food on a shelf inside the shelter. "Look, man, I ain't eaten in several days."

Jim pauses, thinking of the enormous amounts of food we have to consume to keep up our strength. Morris did look lean and weak, knees buckling. Jim hops up the steps into the shelter, removes several cans from the shelf, and hands them to Morris without saying a word.

Morris takes a jackknife out of his pocket and fumbles with it as he nervously tries to pry open the can under Jim's glare. With the can on the picnic table, he hungrily pries at the tin lid, but it won't yield. Gorilla snatches the can and grabs the knife from Morris' hand. He replaces the bottle opener Morris had been using with the can opener blade and pries away at the can's lid, which quickly separates from the rest of the container. With a puppy-eyed look Morris dips his spoon into the beans with bacon and slowly, but hungrily, polishes off its contents.

As Morris is working on the second free can, Jim leans over from the opposite side of the table, looks Morris square in the eyes and says, "I don't like you being ahead of us, then behind us, then ahead of us. We ain't gonna have that." He does not break off his gaze.

Morris tries to avoid Jim's laser eyes and murmurs, "Didn't mean any harm by it."

Jim is not so sure and remains suspicious.

While I put my food bag away and hoist my pack, Jim goes into the shelter toward the shelf. He comes out, moves toward the trail, and we leave.

As we walk along the rest of that day I catch something in Jim's tight-faced and deliberate manner that makes me also frequently look up and search through the trees on the mountainsides. We do not see Morris again.

Thinking back on it, in those last seconds when we were moving away from the shelter, I caught Morris looking with surprise at the shelf holding the remaining two cans of free food. Except, now, leaning against the cans, were two packets of oatmeal, a package of Lipton's noodles, and a bag of mixed nuts, that weren't there before.

It is nine miles of baby blue sky and bright sunlight to Winding Stair Gap. We get there at midday, but Evelyn has not yet arrived. The temperature is up in the mid sixties. We take off our packs, set them on a grassy area, and settle down beside them to eat lunch until our trail angel driver arrives. Just as we are finishing, Evelyn's old Lincoln chugs up. She drives us to a local outfitter. I explain to the salesperson that my water pump has been pumping slower and slower. They take it in the back to examine it. The filter is clogged with stream sediment. They lubricate the pump and replace the clogged filter. Ever in search of lighter gear I browse the store, and find a penknife smaller than the one I had been using. I buy it and an odor-resistant T-shirt. Strenuously hiking four days in a row in the same shirt produces what we call on the trail a Toxic T-shirt.

"What else ya need?" asks the salesclerk, a middle-aged man with twinkly eyes and a broad smile.

"How about twenty-one-year-old legs and lungs?"

"Twenty-one year old—" he lets out a guffaw that spreads his grin to the limits of his face. "That's a thigh-slapper," he says as he strikes the palm of his hand on the upper part of his pant leg.

Today we reached the one-hundred-mile mark from Springer Mountain.

Chapter Ten

March 26, 2002

Last night, while eating dinner at an Italian restaurant, we were talking about Evelyn not being able to get us back to the trailhead. A woman who works at the restaurant overheard us talking and told us her father, Big Wiley, was a taxi driver and could take us. She called and made arrangements for us. Sure enough, this morning after turning in our motel key, we walk out front and a man weighing three hundred plus pounds climbs out of a taxi. Big Wiley is big in both size and heart, an altogether jolly guy.

As forecasted on TV at the motel, it starts to rain on the way to the trailhead. We have covers on our backpacks, and don't think much of it, until the drizzle builds into a steady rain. By the time I realize it is not going to be a mere drizzle, my shirt is soaked through. I put on my rain jacket. The rain continues, developing into a downpour. The trail becomes a riverbed, with water rushing down and us sloshing through it. I wait too long to put on my rain pants and my pants are soaked. Now I'm hiking in wet pants and wet T-shirt under my rain gear. The temperature is in the forties, but as long as I keep hiking I avoid getting cold. We had planned on hiking to Tellico Gap in three days, trekking about seven miles a day. We feel good enough early in the day—or is it that we just want to get the hell out of this rain—that we decide to do ten and a half miles instead.

Rain on my glasses looks like the rush of water on windows when you go through a carwash. The sky lights up with an amazing display of lightning. The woods are thick with brush and a few slender trees. We are nearing the summit of Siler Bald.

A *bald* is a mountaintop that has no trees. The balds we come across in North Carolina are mainly rounded, like giant fields covered with grass or shrubs. Some say the balds were caused by lightning-induced fires; others say grazing sheep and other livestock bared the mountaintops. Folklore says the devil got drunk one night and stomped on the mountaintops—nothing worthwhile can grow where the devil has trod. A few people think balds are landing strips for UFOs.

At Siler's summit the undergrowth opens to grassland. A lone grouping of mountaintop rocks has painted on it a white blaze with an arrow pointing the way. Brilliant lightning bolts land around us, with ear-assaulting crashes. We hesitate under a tree at the bald's edge, the rain leaking down on us through the sparse canopy. We stand there wondering whether or not to make a break for it across the open area. An enormous jagged lightning bolt strike on the open grassland directly in front of us is accompanied by a crash so loud it is beyond being heard. The ground trembles from the impact.

I'm desperately trying to think of everything I'd learned to do in case of lightning. The brilliance of light and roar disrupts thought…Something about avoiding ridges…stay away from trees, get to lower areas…It seems like everything we shouldn't be doing we are doing. The only words I think to yell to Jim are: "Let's get the hell out of here!" Chased by another lightning bolt we rush Siler's mountaintop, legs churning fast, and disappear into the woods on the side of the bald.

We barley make it. Hiking down the other side, with lightning and thunder bouncing around us, I keep thinking of the guy we met a week and a half earlier who said, in case of lightning say a prayer—or, try laying on the bagels. I snicker at that thought.

There is no one else on the trail for miles.

Nearing the end of today's hike, we come to yet another steep mountain; it is a struggle—hard even to lift our legs, especially with wet pants that might as well have been made of lead. Our sprightly step of 8:00 a.m. has turned into a foot-dragging crawl. "How much further do we have to go?" I ask over my shoulder to Jim.

Jim takes the map out of a deep pocket in his cargo pants, unfolds enough of it to size up the area where we are. "Only a couple clicks more." He hands me *The Appalachian Trail Official Map*, which asserts in bold: "Do not underestimate the difficulty of the terrain, however." A map of an earlier section of trail stated this part of the A.T. as: "some of the most challenging miles of the fourteen-state route. Do not underestimate the difficulty of the terrain and the possibility of sudden heavy rains."

No kidding!

In the Cherokee language, *Wayah* means wolf. Red wolves once roamed these mountains before bounties on them caused their extinction.

At 5,340 feet Waya Bald is the highest summit in the area. Waya's bare mountaintop has an observation tower built of stone by the Civilian Conservation Corps. Jim expected us to stay tonight on the structure's ground floor. This base floor of rock construction has a doorframe without a door. The floor slopes inward, is loaded with sideways blowing rainwater, and could not be used by us. I climb the outside masonry steps to see if the covered observation deck is dry. The deck has a cedar-shake roof, but except for a low wall, this top level is completely open sided and offers no protection against the forty-mile-an-hour wind blowing the rain like little darts. I had wondered what it was like to set up a tent in wild wind and rain. Today, I found out…it's a mess. Everything gets wet. The gale-force winds keep pulling the nylon ground cloth out of my grasp. I find some twigs, put them through the grommet holes in the corners of the ground cloth, and stab the twigs into the ground.

As the tent is assembled, water gets into it. By the time it is set up, there are pools of water on the tent floor. I pull in my soaked backpack. I use my camp towel to mop water from inside the tent and reach out through the small tent door to ring it out. My rain jacket and rain pants drip more water onto the tent floor. I wipe off my jacket and pants and mop up the floor again. My backpack is also draining water onto the floor. So I wipe that down as best I can then mop more water off the floor.

I know from extensive readings that you get cold and wet on the Appalachian Trail. That knowledge no more prepares you for the A.T. than saying *If you invest in the stock market, your stocks may go down* prepared this country for the Great Depression of 1929! You're still damp, wet, and coldly miserable.

By the time I finish mopping up it's 4:30. We had no lunch today—just stopped to grab snacks under leaky trees. It is impossible to cook at Wayah

Bald because of the driving rain. I sit hunched in my tent and eat what would have been today's cold lunch.

When it is dry enough in my tent, I take off my wet clothes, put on dry clothes, and get into my sleeping bag. The rain lets up some, but the wind continues to howl. The Appalachian temperatures are like a seesaw, and that night they drop again. All I can do is hope for sunshine the next day so we can dry out.

March 27, 2002

High up in the mountainous area along the North Carolina and Tennessee border the climate resembles parts of New England. Over a mile above sea level, cold blasts are common at this time of year and visited us during the night as the temperature plunges way below freezing.

In my tent I awaken to a winter wonderland. Ice crystals had formed on the inside of the nylon sides. The tent poles are encased in a solid sleeve of ice.

Because everything is so wet and cold, we want to get moving as quickly as possible. I begin taking down my tent and try to shake off the icy coating without success. The snowy icy crystals cling to the nylon as if glued to it. I give up and stuff the silvery snowy tent mess into my backpack as best I can. I try breaking down my icy poles with my gloved hands; the poles laugh at the effort and icily slip from my grasp. There is no giving up here. My poles are ten feet long and have to be broken down in order to fit in their tent bag. With bare hands I clutch the icy rods and tug until my fingers and palms are stinging and numb. Then, *thwack*, the ice breaks, and the sections finally come apart.

By three o'clock in the afternoon, we arrive at the Tellico Gap Hiker's Hostel*, a lovely house perched on a hill. The hostel is surrounded by mountains, the closer ranges are dark blue. The furthest ranges are tinged in purple, fading into a softened sky of robin's egg blue. The hostel has a large

---

* At a much later time we heard that the Tellico Gap Hiker's Hostel may no longer be in existence.

wood-planked deck that overlooks a valley that is beginning to turn green with budding spring.

Ron Vaughn, who runs this hostel, is not here. He left a note on the door saying he went to shuttle someone and will be back at 4:30. Jim and I string up our bear lines to the wooden posts supporting an upper deck. Our gear is thawing. We hang up our wet tents and sleeping bags on the line and drape our ground cloths, pack covers and other damp items on the wooden railings that surround the deck. The sunny, cool, breezy afternoon is a welcome change from the recent rains.

Ron Vaughn is average height, slightly more than medium build. He has a dark beard, and a carefree gait. He shows up with a slender woman who has a blonde ponytail. She wears glasses with lenses that change color in the sun and khaki hiking pants with zip-off legs similar to mine. After brief introductions, Jim and I leave our muddy boots on the deck, and we all go inside.

The hostel is warmly decorated, more like someone's home: tan drapes on the windows, a dried floral arrangement on the table, a quilted wall hanging on the wall. One room sports wallpaper with a small whimsical pattern of a person in front of village cottages.

We settle into comfortable chairs. "I'm Avalanche. What's your trail name?" I ask the blonde woman.

"Frishe Luft," she replies with a slight German accent. I remember from my high school German class that *Frishe Luft* means "fresh air." She goes on to explain that she has done the A.T. in sections.

When Jim hears that she is German, he proceeds to regale her with an accounting of his prior wives. "My first wife and fourth wife were German, you know. The second wife was Danish. The third was from Tennessee… finally married an American girl. Now I'm married for the fifth time. Wedded a woman from Colorado, and this marriage is for keeps."

Frishe Luft is interested. "Your first wife was from Germany?"

"Let me tell you about her," Jim says with animated gusto.

Frishe Luft and I look at each other and realize there is no way we're going to avoid hearing it. I slump into the comfortable chair and put one leg up over the arm.

"I was in the army in Berlin in the sixties when I met the first future Mrs. Saxton. I wanted to impress her. Didn't own a suit, so I borrow one from a buddy. It was one of them shiny cloth suits, real shiny—you could see it a mile away." Jim talks in an accent bordering on hillbilly; he sometimes uses it to show his early years naiveté.

"I take her to a nice restaurant," Jim continues, warming to the task of entertaining. "The waiter comes to the table with a towel over his arm, and I'm thinking that's kinda odd. The waiter half-bows and asks what wine we want. I don't know anythin' 'bout wine. Never had any in my life, so I say, 'The lady will order.' She tells the waiter what kind of wine to bring. The waiter brings a bottle and shows me the bottle. Now, this looks just like any bottle, so I don't know why he's showin' it to me. He's pointing toward the label, but I don't know what's going on, particularly since the label's not in English. So, I sort of push the waiter off. The waiter opens the bottle and gives me the cork. 'What the heck is that?' I say. 'I don't want the cork!' The lady I'm with says, 'No. He wants you to smell the cork.' I say, 'Where I come from, we don't smell corks!'

"The waiter pours a little bit of the wine in a glass and hands it to me. That really ticks me off. I say to him, 'First, you bring me a bottle and ask me to read a label I can't understand. Then you give me a cork to sniff. Now you pour a little bitty bit of wine in the glass!' My future wife looks at me like, *Man are you dumb*, and she says, 'He wants you to taste it.' I gulp it down like a beer while the waiter is saying things in German, such as me being a dummy."

Jim pauses for only a moment. "She was real pretty and married me anyhow."

Frishe Luft's blonde ponytail bounces as she laughs at Jim's story. She removes her glasses and wipes them off then goes into the kitchen to make a pie.

A physically fit gentleman arrives. He has graying hair, deeply receding hairline, ruddy complexion, firm handshake. Several lines—the result of much weather exposure—crease his face, particularly when he smiles. We all talk. His name is Lindy, and he is a *Triple Crowner*, someone who hiked the entire three long trails in the U.S.: Appalachian, Continental Divide, and Pacific Crest, each trail well over two thousand miles long. Lindy once hiked the entire Appalachian Trail from April to June—almost impossible to our way of thinking. He averaged about thirty miles a day.

"How'd you do it?" Gorilla Jim asks.

"I keep my backpack weight down to about ten pounds."

I'm amazed. "What's in your pack?"

"A forty-degree sleeping bag."

My bag is rated to fifteen degrees, and I still get cold. I had to ask, "What do you do when it gets really cold?"

Lindy looks at me with his cool blue eyes. "Suffer," he says. (Lindy would go on to set a record, hiking in thirty-two days the more than one-thousand-mile Ice Age Trail, covering thirty to forty miles a day through remnants of the Ice Age in Wisconsin. He would later describe that experience as "kind of walking home.")

Ron has hiked the A.T. several times, among other lengthy trails. He chimes in, "You can continue to hike to keep warm." Of course, he is half my age. I couldn't conceive of hiking any farther than we did yesterday in the rain and cold.

Apparently, Lindy is there on official business. Not only is he a Triple Crowner, but he is also the awards coordinator for the American Long Distance Hiking Association-West (ALDHA-W) that awards the Triple Crown designation to hikers. After dinner, he unwraps a wooden plaque with a large bronze plate on it stating TRIPLE CROWN, honoring Ron for completing the three extensive trails. Ron's full face is all smiles. He beams as he holds the gleaming plaque with his left hand and shakes hands with Lindy. I take photos of the rare occurrence of a hiker being honored for finishing over seven thousand miles of rough mountain and desert hiking.

With two accomplished Triple Crowners in our midst, Jim and I spend the evening eagerly talking about hiking, equipment, and how to lighten our packs.

It's wonderful to sleep in a real bed in a dry room.

March 28, 2002

Ron's trail name is Waffle King, and for good reason—he makes great waffles. Ron makes a large batch for us this morning. I have two large helpings of the sweet breakfast confection dripping with melted butter and thick, slow-pouring maple syrup, a fragrance of tropical islands with the taste of sweetest northeastern maple trees.

After breakfast, Jim brings his backpack into the dining room and spreads its contents on the table. The purpose is for Ron to go through each item and tell Jim what should be thrown out or sent home to lighten his pack. Waffle King looks professorial, stroking his full but trimmed dark beard, looking through the untidy heap on the table. He takes a maroon plastic pail and fills it with items that Jim could do without, such as a raccoon cap, extra pan, large Buck knife, space blanket, plastic bottle, sacks, ski mask, several articles of clothing, and a container of insect repellant. Ron takes a folding saw for cutting trees out of Jim's pile. He asks, "What's this for?"

Jim answers, "For making a teepee." Everyone laughs.

Each time Ron says an item should go in the bucket, Jim moans, "It don't weigh anything." Ron picks up a small mosquito net Jim brought to put over his head. Jim says, "Now, that doesn't weigh anything."

Ron lifts the lightweight mesh item several feet above the table, lets go of it, and when it reaches the tabletop, Ron says, "It must weigh something, otherwise it would have floated."

Then comes the weigh-in. Jim's disposable items weighed *nine pounds.*

I'm the next victim. Ron searches through my stuff, fills the same bucket and part of my plastic water collection bucket. When I weigh all of my disposable items, they come to *ten pounds.* The message was clear. When we get to the Nantahala Outdoor Center I'll have to ship home unnecessary items to lighten my backpack.

Frishe Luft, whose real name is Anna-Lisa, shows me how to best load my backpack. When I finish repacking, she asks me to put it on and come out to the deck. It's a warm sun-drenched day, but Anna-Lisa isn't outside to enjoy the beautiful low sixties North Carolina weather. She cocks her head slightly, observing my backpack from the side. "It doesn't look right." She lightly tugs the dark olive green pack and moves it around. "Ron. Look at this."

Ron opens the sliding glass door and comes out onto the deck. He shakes his head. "Something's wrong with this pack, Avalanche." Ron and Anna-Lisa work together pulling and releasing the shoulder straps, hip belt stabilizer straps, shoulder stabilizer. For some reason it doesn't fit right.

The top of my pack hangs too far away from my shoulders. Lindy joins us on the porch, tossing advice from the sidelines. I remove the backpack, and they take the entire thing apart and reworked the adjustments on the suspension system—for two hours! If we can get our packs weight down and the adjustments make our packs more comfortable to carry, we can get more miles in each day.

We're finally ready to leave at 1:00 p.m. Ron calls the Nantahala Outdoor Center (known as *the NOC*) to arrange for us to have a place to sleep. They tell him the office closes at five o'clock. We have only four hours to travel eight miles over mountains. We quickly thank Ron, Anna-Lisa, and Lindy for all their help and jump into high gear.

Jim and I climb to Wesser Bald and finally get views of other famous balds that rain and mist previously concealed from us. We briefly stop, clang up the metal steps of a former fire tower—now an observation deck—for magnificent views of the Great Smoky Mountains, Fontana Lake, and the Nantahala Mountains. These are not craggy mountains. They are among the oldest mountains in the world, smooth and somewhat rounded, having been weathered by time. The nearby brown brush is a stark contrast to slate-blue mountain ranges, the spray of far off misty vapors, and a vivid sky decorated with fluffy white clouds. The wind plays roughly with the metal tower's framework, sounding like rattling huge wrapping paper. We decide it's time to get going.

Even though it's mainly downhill for the six and a half miles to the Nantahala Outdoor Center, we couldn't get there by 5:00 p.m. The office was closed when we arrived. White letter-size envelopes are taped to the outside of the office window for late arriving hikers. I pull off the envelope addressed to us and rip it open; it contains our key and instructions on how to get to our cabin.

We find our cabin, small and simple with two beds. Previously, Evelyn had agreed to bring two boxes of food and gear she was holding for us, and we arranged to take Evelyn and her granddaughter, Danielle, to dinner. Without Evelyn driving us, there was no way to get to the restaurant, which was many miles from the Nantahala Outdoor Center. I don't know how far she lives from the NOC, but Evelyn loves to drive and is happy to oblige, and we all are grateful for our hot sit-down meal.

We get back to the NOC and before going to bed I want to call Barbara. My cell phone doesn't work; I have to use a pay telephone in a remote darkened area of the compound. With my little flashlight, I stumble in the dark, then up steps, moving toward a voice having a one-sided conversation in the blackness. As I wait to use the phone, I listen to the chatter of a high school girl repeatedly saying, "okay," "ah ha," "alright," in a monotonous tone. I could only see the dim figure of this person in the gloom; her voice is condescending, bordering on irritating. This one-sided conversation drones on for at least a quarter hour with her repeating each word over fifty times. She finally hangs up the phone, turns to me, says, "Overprotective parents!" and walks away.

The telephone service out here is horrendous. My call won't go through as dialed. Reading the numbers off my credit card in the dim light of my flashlight, I try several other long distance carriers and none of them are able to connect my call. Someone else comes up, so I let him use the telephone. I sit on a small bench nearby and endure another lengthy conversation that begins with, "What's new?" and includes "What did you have for dinner?" When this call mercifully ends, I am so eager to use the phone I drop my credit card. Another man comes up to use the telephone, and helps me search around in the dark with his flashlight until I find the card.

Finally, I get through to a supervisor who tells me to dial "00" before the number and the call goes through. Now, Barbara's line is busy!

Another person comes up to use the phone. My mind runs through my inventory of curse words—it's an ample supply. I sit in the darkness trying not to listen to another inane telephone conversation. Weary and irritated, but determined, I wait it out for another twenty minutes. Half asleep, I eventually get through. Barbara and I talk about things Jim and I need, calls she has made for us, and her visiting us when we reach Gatlinburg, Tennessee. Why Gatlinburg? It's supposed to be a fun place, and we're ready for a little R and R from the trail, a little party time!

March 29, 2002

The Appalachian Trail goes through the heart of the Nantahala Outdoor Center, a natural adventure playground on a river in the midst of the Nantahala National Forest. It's a hiker friendly village with lodging facilities from lavish suites to the sparse cell-like room Gorilla and I shared. An outfitter provides kayaks, personal flotation devices, cloth and straw hats, hiking gear, and books on river sports. Mainly, the NOC is dedicated to kayaking and whitewater rafting from its fleet of paddled watercraft, with a smattering of biking and other outdoor activities thrown in. The NOC is a haven for Eric Rudolph look-a-likes: slender but athletic men in their twenties and thirties, some with beards of two weeks hiking growth. Hard bodies are enjoying the mild, late March sun, sporting shorts and backpacks or red life jackets and water helmets.

The movie Deliverance was filmed close by. If you're hiking in deep woods and you hear a banjo, move fast as you can.

I take a box of gear and supplies Evelyn returned to us with me when I go to the outfitters to pick up boxes Barbara sent there. At the outfitters a hundred cartons line a stairway leading to the second floor. I look through the odd assortment and pick out two boxes Barbara sent us. Juggling the three sizable cardboard containers, I stop a clerk. "Is there some place where I can go through all this stuff?" He takes me to a spot near the fly fishing department. While people around me shop for rods, reels, waders, and fly tying materials, I spread everything from my boxes out on the floor.

Sorting the deluge of food is a confusing jumble. In order to get my pack weight down, I select a few items for the next three day's breakfasts, lunches, and dinners, enough to get us to Fontana Dam. Since food is one of the heaviest things we carry, instead of cans of chicken and turkey, we opt for the lighter Raman noodles and Lipton rice or noodles mixes, to which we'll add nuts, dried carrots, and peas.

I fill Box #1 with things to bounce (send) to a future destination—far enough up the trail to be assured it will get delivered before Jim and I arrive. I'm lightening up. In box #2 I place many items that I'll send home. In cardboard box #3 I place items that I removed from my backpack on a temporary basis, to see if I can do without them. I'll send them to Hot Springs. If I don't need them, I'll send box #3 items home permanently.

In the process of getting lighter, I decide to buy the same kind of knife that Lindy carries on his thru-hikes. It's a small knife that has a blade, screwdriver, nail file, and small scissors and weighs the same as the knife I recently bought, which has only a blade.

Through the hubbub of hikers, kayakers, and bikers, we spot Lindy walking around the Nantahala Outdoor Center. "I hiked here to see if both of you were still around and wanted to have lunch." In less than three hours Lindy did the same hike that took Jim and me four hours and twenty minutes to do yesterday.

The NOC restaurant—open-sided to underscore the warm spring air and sunshine—overlooks the high spirited Nantahala River that is splashing foam like an out of control electric mixer sloshing whipped cream in every direction. Below us are kayaks of every primary color and silver-gray inflatable rafts. People laugh at each other as they are sprayed going through the rocky rapids. One woman yells as she navigates around a partly submerged boulder, dips into thousands of bubbles, and rises up at the down-river side, wet and happy. The sun tosses silver sparkles off splashing water and reflects shimmering golden light through the mountains, trees, and buildings of this outdoor recreational paradise.

Almost noontime, the restaurant is packed with outdoor enthusiasts. Lindy notices a tanned middle-aged woman, book in one hand and the last quarter of a club sandwich in the other, sitting at a table with six chairs. In his most mannerly style, Lindy asks if we could join her since there are no other tables available. She slowly looks us over, smiles, and in her soft Chattanooga accent says, "Why, of course. I'd be delighted."

Gorilla and I order juicy burgers, the last real meat for a while. The woman from Tennessee joins in pleasant conversation, finishes, takes her check, and leaves as our meal arrives. We chow down, relishing the medium-well done concoctions and watching the river—and its passengers—flow by. When our check arrives, Lindy grabs it, and we protest, explaining that he was so helpful to us the day before, it seems appropriate that we buy lunch. Despite that, true champion that he is, Lindy insists on buying lunch.

We go outside in bright March sun, drop our packs, and sit on a bench by the Nantahala River to listen to the gurgling water rushing by and watch the flotilla of oar-powered craft bob past us. Lindy says, "I'm interested in knowing how you make out. Keep in touch." As we speak, a woman strikes up a conversation with us. She is from Boiling Springs, Pennsylvania, shapely for her fifth decade of life, lively in her mannerisms, and laughs easily. She tells me she lives very close to the Appalachian Trail and that we should try some tavern when we get there. With the noise of a rushing river and yelling of the rafters and kayakers, I don't catch the restaurant's name. Lindy makes room for her on the bench next to him, looks directly into her eyes as he speaks, his face close to hers. He waves goodbye to us, only briefly looking away from his new acquaintance. As we climb out of the river area, and for as long as they are in view, Lindy is actively chatting with her.

Chapter Eleven

We are approaching the blue-and steel-colored Great Smoky Mountains. It's a tremendous hike upward, a quad-busting six-mile climb without a break—the greatest elevation gain since starting the Appalachian Trail. All afternoon we steadily go up. There are no slight dips as when we ascended other mountains. We are teased by a slight break when the trail levels off, but then it steepens up to the eight-mile mark. We look up through the trees as far ahead as we can. There is no end to it. "Doesn't this mountain have a top to it?" Jim says. It's a mantra I hear throughout the afternoon. We started at 1:00 p.m., a late start for such a vigorous hike. Pack straps dig into our shoulders, and we stop only once to adjust backpacks. Wearing the packs continuously for five hours is a record.

We're climbing an endless ladder into the sky. Late in the afternoon, it's as if a hundred pounds of iron has been attached to each leg. The tops of our thighs ache.

We finally reach a steep descent going down to the Sassafras Gap Shelter. Jim and I take our final tired steps to today's destination. The shelter is filled up with weary hikers. One girl sits on the shelter floor using her knife to cut squares of moleskin, which she places on the red and blistered heels of her feet.

We set up tents on sloping ground, making sure that our heads are high and our feet low. Otherwise, you get a headache, probably because blood rushes to the head.

In one afternoon we accomplished what ordinarily takes an entire day for such a strenuous stretch—what an extraordinary accomplishment.

At 10:00 p.m., I'm awakened out of deep sleep by a roaring noise, and then quiet. Miles in the distance, I hear a moderate sweep of wind begin again. Gathering speed down the steep slopes, rolling faster, crashing through trees, breaking down branches and throwing them into the forests, the wind raucously races toward us. I brace for it as it approaches. Thunderous, deafening, it hits the side of my tent violently shaking it. I reach for the small keychain light hanging from a loop above my head. It waves frantically, and I can't catch hold of it in the dark to turn it on. The buffeting of the tent slows down. It is momentarily at a standstill. Miles away it begins again, the sound building, rushing toward us—there is no stopping it. The roar of wind comes back along the mountainside and rocks the tent again. In a brief motionless interval, I turn on the little flashlight.

Though not fully awake, I remember that the tent can tear apart if not properly lashed to the ground. I don't want to go out into the cold gale-force wind, but I have to tie down my tent's sides. I grope for my pants and a fleece to put on, place the headlight band around my fleece cap, and yank on my boots, but don't bother to lace them all the way up.

As I step out into the storm a blast of air shoves me back through the tent's doorway. I push against it, out into the blustery weather. Wind swirls around. Dark clouds above rush across the sky. I use a rock to pound a stake into the ground and tie down the windward side. I grab some sticks to use as stakes and tie down the other side. Checking the remaining tent pegs, I use the rock to pound loose ones farther into the earth.

As quickly as I can I climb back inside my tent, pull off my outer clothes, get back into the down bag, and return to sleep. An hour or so later I'm awakened by a seeming barrage of cannon fire shaking the ground. The roaring thunder is earsplitting. A brilliant light display outside stabs through the tent's thin material, lighting up the interior. My sleep numbed mind tries to recall how to calculate the distance of a lightning strike. Is it five seconds per mile? Some gaps between flashes and violent ground-shaking booms are only a second, which means the strikes are close…and loud. Since I don't have any bagels to lie on, there is nothing much to do but wait it out. The storm is in high gear. The rain beats on the tent. Although I'm concerned about heavy debris or violent wind ripping the tent, I keep falling asleep between bouts of thunder.

March 30, 2002

In the morning the rain strengthens, violently attacking the tent. I'm tired from the night's broken sleep; decide there is no sense in getting up and getting soaked, so I sleep a little longer.

With the rain still coming down we decide to eat in our tents. My tent's highest point is merely forty-three inches high, just enough for me to eat sitting up.

We're determined to get more mileage in today to make up for the shortened hiking day yesterday. Also, I want to make sure we get to Gatlinburg in time to meet Barbara, who I had not seen for over three weeks.

We climb to the top of Cheoah Bald with its campsites on the ridge. There, camping in the rain are the Carnival Girls (Lee, Nicole, and Alex) a guy we had met earlier named Michael, his dog Charlie, and a few others. The Carnival Girls and I talk in a cold drizzle at Cheoah Bald's summit. They tell me of their startling experience in the rainstorm and lightning, and I tell them about having to secure my tent in the wind.

Michael, wiping light rain from his face, walks up to the group, and with a mischievous grin says, "What a magnificent sunrise we saw. And last night was beautiful, filled with bright stars. Did you have any rain, Avalanche?"

"Right." I say, and everyone laughs hysterically at this.

The rain broke for a few minutes. Charlie comes up to me with a stick. I throw it, and he chases it across the wet grass.

Jim and Lee are talking nearby, and he notices blue leggings over her calves and boot tops. "Great pair of gaiters," he says.

Lee is taller than the others, roundish face, outgoing with a lively sense of humor. She looks down at her new gaiters and says, "One of the guys is getting rid of stuff to make his pack lighter and gave me his gaiters."

Looking at Lee and with mock seriousness I say, "Around here, if a guy gives a girl gaiters, it's a sign of great romantic interest."

"Is it like receiving roses?"

"It's even better. You can wear the gaiters, but you can't wear roses. You know, Lee, if a guy gives a girl his platypus,* it means they're engaged, and she should call her parents to arrange a wedding." Lee and the others giggle.

We still had much climbing and hiking to do, so we get on our way. Stopping to take a break, others pass us, and when they stop for a break, we pass them.

The hike up the mountains is intense because it's so slippery. Everyone thought the rain would stop. Instead, it gets worse. The trail turns into a brook of slippery mud and water. By the time we reach Brown Fork Gap Shelter, nine miles from where we started, the rain had been intense for a long time. My pants are soaked through.

Periwinkle, Salamander, the Carnival Girls, Cooperstown Kid, and others are already at the shelter. To keep warm, I put rain pants on over my wet hiking pants and pull on a fleece jacket. The shelter sits on a high point sloping off in all directions. It is difficult to find a good place to set up our tents. Gorilla manages to find a couple sites that will do. We leave our backpacks in the shelter while we set up our tents on the sloping muddy ground in unrelenting rainfall. Before I can get the rain fly over my tent, the inside gets soaked. We stay in our wet things while we walk back and forth from the shelter to the tents.

We cook dinner under the protection of the shelter's roof. One of the guys was eating mac-and-cheese with cutup spicy beef jerky in it. Between bites he asks, "Hey, Avalanche, you're a lawyer, aren't you?"

"Yes, I am." I have finished my dinner and am sitting on the edge of the shelter floor eating chocolate chip cookies

"Ever lose a case?"

"Every lawyer—even the best of them—loses a case now and then. Attorneys have a saying: 'The lawyer who never lost a case, never tried a case.'"

"Yeah, but when the judge doesn't get it, doesn't it piss you off?"

"A lawyer is required to respect the legal system, and that includes judges. A case should always be presented with energy and passion for your client's cause. Nevertheless, when you are sharp on the law—and the judge clearly isn't and exasperatingly balls up the facts, making you want to

*A plastic drinking container with a tube attached to it so a hiker can drink from it while walking.

say: "Dammit, what the hell's the matter with you? Aren't you listening?—when the arguing is over and a ruling is made against you, there is only one appropriate answer to the court: 'Yes, Your Honor.' You wait until you leave the courtroom before muttering: '*Go screw yourself!*'"

March 31, 2002

Yesterday's clothes are still damp. Everything in the tent is wet, either from rain or from condensation from the wet things in my tent. The only thing that's dry is the inside of my sleeping bag, and my shirt that was kept in my sleeping bag. I have no choice but to put on my refrigerator-cold, wet pants —a creepy icy feeling against my skin with every movement of my legs.

The privy at the shelter has a toilet with only two walls: the back and one side. It's open on the other side and open in front. Doing what Gorilla calls "the morning push-out," with wind blowing cold rain into your face and bare legs from the open front and side, is an experience to be missed.

The storm shower dies down. I try to shake the water off my tent, but most of it is imbedded in the fabric. I think, *Oh crap! All this wet stuff is adding five pounds to my backpack.*

During the morning, we reach the top of a mountain. I call Barbara to discuss plans for meeting in Gatlinburg. As we speak, fog rolls in and the rain starts again. I cut short the phone conversation because I still have to make reservations for tonight at Fontana Dam. I call the Hike Inn. They're filled up. They recommend the Fontana Village. I call and make a reservation. The woman says to give them a call when we reach the highway, and they'll pick us up.

We hike all day, mostly in the rain. The trail is mud and rain-slicked rocks. It's like walking on hundreds of marbles. My feet slip out from under me. Several times I plant my hiking pole to catch myself falling, which jars my shoulder. I know that when I sleep on my shoulder tonight, I'll remember the slippery rocks. Later in the day, several twenty-somethings tell us they slid and fell to the ground numerous times. That makes me feel a little better—not because they fell, but because it wasn't only me.

Our goal is to reach Fontana Dam, hiking eleven and a half miles today. It's a new record for us, made more difficult by climbing the slippery mud and wet rocks.

When we arrive at the highway I call Fontana Village; the shuttle van is being repaired and is unavailable. As if we didn't have enough exercise today, we start walking two miles to Fontana Village Resort.

A pickup truck approaches from our rear. I hold up my thumb. A couple in the truck stops. She is lively, opens the passenger door and in mild Appalachian tones asks, "Where you fixin' to go?"

"Fontana Village Resort, ma'am." I sound tired...it isn't an act. At this point, about 50 percent of the people who started hiking at Springer Mountain have dropped out.

"We'll be glad to take you there directly." She looks back. A large crate covered by a black tarp fills the cargo area of the pickup. "If'n you don't mind sittin' on the box. We'll drive slow."

Gorilla and I lift our packs onto the vehicle's cargo area, jam them into the little space between the truck's sides and the large box, pull ourselves up over the cargo area's sides, and sit on the crate. The pickup takes off and is doing fifty miles an hour on a hilly, twisting road. White knuckled, our hands grab the wooden crate and the ropes tying down the tarps. The slipstream rocks us on our shaky perch.

"Her idea of *slow* is a lot different from mine," I yell to Jim over the speeding air current.

Before he could answer, Jim's khaki, olive and black camo-colored Boonie hat blows off his head, flying away behind the truck. By instinct Jim starts to rise off the box to grab for it, the blast of air almost takes him off his feet, and unsteadily he sits back down. "Damn! I loved that hat. I wore that hat in Vietnam."

He watches it bouncing at crazy angles along the asphalt.

Jim mumbles about his loss for the rest of the truck ride, and into the evening.

Fontana Village Resort, in the Nantahala Forest, provides outdoor recreation of all types—biking, hiking, horseback riding. It's the gateway to the Great Smoky Mountains. Fontana Village is a sprawling facility with an outfitter, a lodge, suites, and cabins. The extensive dining room has a hiker's favorite food: *buffet*. While I fill my plate for the first time, some of the guys we met hiking join me at the all-you-can-eat feast. One of them says with a laugh, "We got Gorilla Jim's hat. Saw it flyin' off the back of the truck. It hopped all over the road."

I return to our table where gloomy faced Jim is quietly assaulting a plate of salad, fruit, breads, with a second plate of meats and vegetables waiting next to it.

"The guys got your hat. They saw it fly off the pickup."

The glum face brightens. "Hot dog! I love that hat." Wide grinned, "Won't have to go to the outfitter and get another."

The boys come to our table whooping it up, teasing Jim, calling his hat an "old piece of crap," and present it to Jim. Gorilla is happy as if he won the lottery. Reunited with his dear old friend, he touches it, rolls the brim, puts it on and takes it off, examines the material, flicking off tiny specks of leaf remnants.

Don and Cooperstown Kid eat dinner with us. Don is twenty-one years old and goes to an Ivy League School. Cooperstown is eighteen and will be starting college at the end of this summer. I love talking to younger people who are having such a fantastic experience so early in their lives. We talk about the merits of using a lightweight tarp instead of a tent, and how some thru-hikers, so called "shelter rats," prefer to stay at shelters all the time.

Don tells us that he spent the previous night at a shelter nicknamed the "Fontana Hilton," because it has the luxury of a restroom and shower facilities. Don had the shelter to himself except for a guy named Trouble. Trouble had hassled people at other shelters. Don tells us that one night Trouble was up on a shelter roof howling at the moon; he bothered some of the girls and was smoking pot. Don continued, saying complaints had been made about Trouble before he arrived at the Fontana Hilton. A third man showed up, said he was staying at the shelter and would be going fishing the next day. Trouble started to smoke pot, and the other man made a deal to buy a joint for twenty bucks. When the transaction was completed, the man arrested Trouble. The excitement of that moment returned to Don's face. "That's the first time I saw a drug bust!"

We tell Don and Cooperstown Kid that we had heard about pot smoking at a few shelters. "That's one reason we're not interested in sleeping at the shelters—but mainly because of mice running all over us as we sleep," I say.

The few shelters we have slept at had no evidence of any drug use. Gorilla makes it clear that that's something he wouldn't tolerate.

The Carnival Girls also got a lift by a pickup truck. They sit at a table next to us, and we chat back and forth. The food is good and we all make multiple trips to the buffet. The thru-hiker's ravenous appetite is hitting us big time.

Many backpackers complain that coming down the mountain is tough on their knees and feet. At dinner, some hikers walk around stiff legged as if they just finished a long horseback ride.

Watching them rub sore joints and talk about knee braces, I think back to late in the afternoon when we were exhausted after weeks of struggling up mountains. It had been our longest day yet. Often we had looked at the trail—so steep above it seemed incapable of being climbed—thinking we can't tote heavy packs on our backs one step higher, can't raise a leg one lung-busting step more. As we neared the last mountain summit of the day, frantically trying to catch my breath, I turned to Jim and gave him a "What the hell are we doing here?" look.

Jim had leaned on his hiking pole with his head down, gasping for air. He looked up and said, "I'm paying four thousand dollars to be tortured like this!"

That made me laugh. I remember thinking how preposterous it was— two grown men working so hard and suffering for something, and I didn't know what. He laughed and we both got backslapping hilarious with laughter.

I waved one pole out through the mist to the distant world, and yelled: "To the men sitting with their feet up this Sunday afternoon watching a game and drinking beer—fuck you!"

Jim raised the Gorilla stick high above his head and shouted louder, "To the people who already hiked the Appalachian Trail and know how tough it is and are sitting around this afternoon knowing we're out here struggling— fuck you!"

Gorilla bent forward, convulsed with laughter.

Tears of hilarity ran down my face. I took off my glasses and dabbed at them with my bandana. My sides hurt.

April 1, 2002

How could we turn down staying another day at the Fontana Village Resort? The facilities are great, hiker's rate only fifteen dollars a day for a good room with two double beds and a balcony. Buffet breakfast is $6.95, and a good and plentiful dinner buffet is $9.95.

Fontana Village is a village spread out over a mile or two. Most people drive in by car. We didn't. So, we have to walk the steep terrain. At the Laundromat we put some clothes in a washer. My food drop box has been delivered to the admissions office about a mile away, so I start off to pick it up. We got to know Brandy, the banquet manager and a server in the dining room. She drives by. I wave, and she stops. "Where you going, Avalanche?"

"To the Admissions office to get my food drop."

"It's a long walk. Hop in and I'll drive you." On the way Brandy asks about the Appalachian Trail and how we were doing. She waits while I pick up the box and then drives me back to the Laundromat.

"Thanks," I say holding the heavy box with both hands and closing the door with my hip. "You saved me a lot of time and my weary feet say thanks."

"No problem." She smiles. Her openness and wholesomeness are not seen often enough these days.

As I wait for the clothes to dry, I strike up a conversation with a college-age woman, medium height, short dark red hair, willowy body, and large brown thoughtful eyes. Her name is Melissa and she doesn't have a trail name. She seems like she's not having a good day, but speaks in a warm alto voice. "I'm going to school to become a massage therapist."

At this point Jim, who had been outside yakking with some of the guys, came in and heard the last few words. "Did you say you're a massage therapist?"

"Not yet. I'm still going to school for massage therapy."

"Got a trail name?"

"No."

Jim thinks a few seconds. "Now you do. It's Soft Touch." Jim grins. "That's a good trail name, Soft Touch," he says as he looks at the dryer, sees the clothes are not done, and goes back out.

"I've been up here for a week or so with a boy I know." There is a hint of downheartedness in her voice.

I was about to ask, How are things going?

She reads my face and, without answering, her body language says, The relationship with this guy isn't going well.

Me sitting on the folding table, she leaning against a dryer, straight, athletically slender, we talk amidst the washers and driers whirring and humming in the background, the smell of Tide in the air. Soft Touch's face brightened, the conversation turned pleasant and we had a great chat. I tell her a joke. "A guy once told me: 'My wife said, "If you go hiking one more time I'm going to leave you"... I'm sure going to miss her.'"

Soft Touch responds with her own:

"What sort of shoes do frogs wear?"

"Open toad!"

We laugh at that one.

She wears tan shorts, light brown shirt, the top three buttons undone, soft braless movements beneath. This makes me wonder, What's wrong with the guy she's with? Here's a good-looking girl, pleasant to speak with, intelligent. When I was their age, if I was with such a pretty young woman at a resort, I could think of ways to make us both very happy.

It's a steep, half-mile trek from the Laundromat to the lodge. Soft Touch offers to drive me back. She finishes her laundry and is outside at her car when I come out. She is struggling to get her trunk open. Several guys walk by and Soft Touch tells them: "There's a bottle of whiskey in the trunk. You can have it if you can get the trunk open." They did.

Jim wants to go to the arts and craft shop and asked me to take his laundry back to our room. I climb in the car with Soft Touch and we are off. She tells me, "Avalanche, someday I'd like to do the Appalachian Trail."

I glance at her youthful profile. She is a picture of beauty and health. "Do it before you get old as Gorilla Jim and me." But at that moment I felt young, sitting next to very attractive twenty-year-old girl, telling me her dreams. We pull up to my building. A box and bundles of laundry in my hands, I watch as she drives away.

Then I feel my age again...grateful that two people saved me from walking several miles carrying arms full of stuff.

❖ ❖ ❖ ❖ ❖

Back at our room I check the parts of our tents that we had hung over the balcony to dry. There isn't room to spread everything out at once, so I switch out the dried parts with wet parts. Even the tent poles had to be dried.

Jim needs a new watch so we head to the outfitters. The store has a sitting area with overstuffed easy chairs and a television showing an old sitcom. I drop into one of the comfortable chairs and talk to Ryan, a hiker sitting with his leg extended, massaging his knee.

"I've got knee problems," he explains. When Ryan moves his leg, his knee sounds like a kid popping bubble wrap. "I got it coming down into Fontana."

"Yeah, that's a steep descent. Don't like the sound of that knee."

He slowly lifts himself out of the chair, and, putting weight mostly on his good leg, pops and limps away.

It's a lazy afternoon, a *zero day,* a day when you don't hike. Very restful. We need this day to recover from the fatigue built up during the last few weeks.

Tomorrow we start to trek the Great Smoky Mountains.

Chapter Twelve

April 2, 2002

This morning at breakfast one of the thru-hikers got a local weather report. He tells us, "The weatherman said the month of March had the highest rainfall this area had since 1917: *10.7 inches*. All of it in the second part of the month…And all ten inches fell on my head." This confirmed the miserable weather we had. Of the seventeen days we had hiked, fourteen of them must have been in rain. It's no wonder. According to the National Parks Service information about the Great Smoky Mountains: "In the Smokies, the average annual rainfall varies from approximately 55 inches in the valleys to over 85 inches on some peaks—more than anywhere else in the country except the Pacific Northwest. During wet years, over *eight feet of rain* falls in the high country."

In the last nine years, Circuit Rider (Bill Newman) trekked more than ten thousand miles of the A.T. in his job as a minister to those hiking the trail. This experienced Appalachian Trail backpacker discusses the wretchedness of constant cold rain:

> Anyone who has endured a hike through the Great Smoky Mountain National Park in early April knows from hardened experience that "sunny and warm" is, by and large, a pipe dream, reserved for those yet dreaming of hiking all the way from Georgia to Maine as they sit in front of a cozy fireplace peering out their window at the falling January snow. The Smokies, which are surpassed in annual moisture only by the notorious Pacific Northwest, are most prone to

less than ideal conditions during the month that is famous for Spring "showers." Of course, April showers everyplace else bring promise of May flowers. In the Smokies, you are only promised misery![13]

This is the last chance to load up at the morning buffet. We sit at the same table as Just Do It, a sixty-five-year-old gentleman with silvery hair and beard who had been in the "Foreign Service" and is now retired. He has a metal cup attached to the rear of his backpack with a carabiner. On the trail the cup shakes from side to side, striking the backpack and hitting branches, making a clanging sound like a cowbell.

Fontana Dam, towering at 480 feet in height is the highest dam in the East and is almost a half mile long. The hiking trail goes along the top of this high-water barrier. The concrete thoroughfare across the dam's summit is wide enough to handle vehicles side-by-side plus pedestrian walkways. Jim and I look down at the Little Tennessee River; it's like looking downward from a skyscraper. This monumental barrier holds back a reservoir of water twenty-nine miles long.

The day is as clear and sunny as glistening Eden. Sun beats bright—shadows black and sharp. The wildly fluctuating temperature rises to a sweaty ninety-two degrees.

This is the gateway to the Great Smoky Mountains. Out there, beyond the water and budding vegetation, the misty Smokies straddle the border between North Carolina and Tennessee. The Cherokees referred to the Blue Ridge Mountains' hazy color when seen from a distance, a bluish mist hugging the mountainsides.

A permit is needed to backpack in Great Smoky Mountains National Park. Self-registration facilities are provided when entering the so-called "park," actually mountains and jungle-like forests so huge the A.T. extends seventy-one miles through it. We fill out the paperwork and attach our group permit to my backpack. National Park regulations include: backpackers must stay overnight in a shelter; three spaces in each shelter are reserved for thru-hikers; if no space is left in a shelter, you must tent close by; and use the provided bear-proof cables to hang up food bags. There are hundreds of bears living in this national park—and they love human food.

We reach the site of the former Birch Spring Shelter, which had been torn down, leaving splintered wood and debris. We had already hiked nine miles and maybe we should have considered setting up our tents here, but we decided to move on to the next shelter.

Jim and I trudge to Mollies Ridge Shelter another five miles away, altogether about fourteen miles for the day—mostly upward. The usual group of people is here: the Carnival Girls, Just Do It, Pick Up (who is section hiking going south), Salamander and Periwinkle. I don't like the shelters because of the mice and crowded conditions. There are stiff fines for violating the *no tenting rule*, so we all pack in here. This is a two-tiered shelter. We stay on the bottom, my sleeping bag spread out on the wooden floor. As I lay on the floor, the upper tier is less than three feet above my nose.

The topsy-turvy weather turns cold at night. When we went to sleep, Chestnut was on my right side. One of the girls who I thought was Alex was on my left side. During the night I felt something move on my left side and I preferred it to be her, not a bear. It was actually Nicole sleeping on that side—they are sisters and with their wool ski caps pulled down covering most of their faces it is hard to tell who is who, especially since it gets dark early at this time of year.

People sleep close to each other, within a foot or so. One guy told me during the night he turned over and found his hand was on Alex's face—he withdrew it pronto.

April 3, 2002

Jim is his bubbly self this morning, describing breakfast as "a beautiful thing" and declaring "it's a good day to hike." On the trail, though, he turns strangely quiet. Three quarters of an hour go by and he doesn't say a word. I look down at the trail at what I think might be bear droppings. Excited at this discovery, I say, "Bear scat?"

Jim glances down. "Dog shit!"

I don't hear from him again for a half hour, when we take a break.

Temperature starts to drop and wind picks up; fog is coming in. Not a good sign. Today will be another long day of hiking—about eleven and a half miles—particularly tiring after yesterday's lengthy trek. The temperature keeps falling and the Gorilla man struggles along.

Jim says to me, "Did you ever have the feeling you can't take another step?"

"Yes, every twenty minutes."

Climbing mountains carrying forty pounds is fatiguing—sometimes you have to force yourself to do it. Yesterday's hike was like that. We had to reach deep inside and with pure determination I tell myself "I can't stop. I'm exhausted and hate it at this moment, but I must do it anyhow."

Today seems easier to me, although not to Jim who looks tired. He shuffles his feet, shoulders bent forward, head down, searching the ground as if looking for an end to this torturous journey. This isn't like Gorilla Jim, a former army ranger.

"You okay, Jim?"

"Very tired." Highly unusual for the Gorilla man to say.

In the woods everywhere is a bathroom. If you have to go, you just walk off the trail and do your thing next to a tree or bush. Drinking so much water to keep from getting dehydrated, people pee often. Jim doesn't. He goes only several times a day, and when he goes he disappears for some time. One day I ask, "Hey, Gorilla. Where you been?

He explains, "When I urinate I need some seclusion because I got to use a catheter."

I am surprised. "Why do you use a *catheter*?"

Jim pauses. "After I got out of the service I worked as an ambulance driver. Ramp in the back of the ambulance didn't have safety straps to keep a wheelchair or gurney from falling backward. I was putting a lady in the back of the van," Jim gestures like he is pushing a stretcher into the ambulance. "She was rigid, but the lady grabbed hold of the bar and she pushed back, driving me backward. I fell off the ambulance. The vehicle was on a hill, parked on gravel and rocks. The center of my back hit a rock...some pieces of my backbone broke off. I got nerve damage and a neurogenic bladder. For four years I've had to catheterize...you know, stick a tube up my penis into my bladder to urinate."

Jim looks pale, washed out, lethargic. Jim's head is down, and he says in a slow, weak voice, "Al, I think I'm getting sick. Maybe it's my catheter problem."

I got a flashback—a case I had in the mid-1980s.

One filthy toilet has a hand printed cardboard sign over it: "PISS HERE." The second foul toilet has a sign over it: "SHIT HERE." The room—smaller than a two car garage—is dim, only a low wattage bulb in an overhead ceiling fixture. Jammed into this tight space are nine beds, plus four mattresses on the floor. One toilet is cracked, leaking watery sewage onto the concrete floor. Up to thirteen men are squeezed into this small county jail cell twenty-four hours a day, day after day, sometimes for months. The men are not allowed out. Not to go to meals--the room has a table with benches. They don't leave to exercise–there is no recreation.

No place to move around…no leg room, one man's elbow in another's face. In this explosive atmosphere hardened criminals bump into each other—and fight. When men aren't battling, they stand around hating. Each is in cell 208 for a different reason: terroristic threats, kidnapping, aggravated criminal sexual contact. Tim Ryan is in this county jail cell for only a traffic offense–he has not been able to post bail.

At breakfast an inmate couldn't eat his doughnut and offered it to Tim. Maurice Scott was a vicious inmate who kept his powerful physique by lifting a broomstick with water-filled trash bags tied to each end. Scott wants the doughnut. Before the slender built Tim could hand it over, Scott blares at him, "I'm gonna fuck you up!" He grabbed Tim in a neck hold, and threw him to the concrete floor. There was a sickening cracking sound as Tim's neck broke—his spinal cord was severed. The life seeped out of Tim's body forever--he was now a head on a corpse.

As a lawyer, I usually represent construction workers who suffer life-altering injuries on the job. People came to me when they were severely hurt by the collapsing steel structure of a building under construction; or, defective products maimed workers; or, for any catastrophic injury. Tim

Ryan's case was different. Here was an innocent guy in the hands of jail officials who were responsible for his safety, but we had to prove they were legally liable for his injuries, which were caused by another inmate. This required detailed investigation by a former Philadelphia police detective, now a private investigator who had worked with me in other major cases. He went to the county jail. One guard told him the inmates do nothing but beat each other. In the three weeks before Tim Ryan was assaulted, in the jail there had been fractured jaws and black eyes. One inmate talked about the jammed and hostile conditions, saying, "It makes you want to kill." The assailant, Scott—confined in cell 208 almost continuously for 84 days—had viciously beaten others, breaking one inmate's nose.

Not only were there overcrowded conditions, there was no effective classification system to separate dangerous inmates from nonviolent offenders. We discovered records of an earlier federal court case that required:

- No more than 117 inmates to be housed in the entire jail at any given day—Instead, there were up to *170 inmates* in this small jail.
- A maximum of eight inmates to be placed in cell 208—instead there were about a *dozen*.

I am admitted to practice law in Pennsylvania and needed to associate myself with a lawyer who practices in New Jersey. I had the great fortune to get highly skilled attorney, Joseph Goldberg—an expert on civil rights and municipal liability issues—involved to work with me on this case. A great deal of evidence was amassed. There were twenty-one defendants, including the county, county freeholders, jail administrator, those who operated the jail, county solicitor, and New Jersey Department of Correction officials. Even before trial, the defendants twice appealed this matter to the U.S. Court of Appeals for the Third Circuit and to the United States Supreme Court.

During the several years I represented him, Tim was in ten different hospitals, nursing homes and rehabilitation facilities. In preparation for trial, I studied Tim's voluminous medical records and met with each doctor who would be testifying for us. Barbara, my secretary Cindy and I took a personal interest in Tim. Through 14 surgeries to repair severe decubitus ulcer damage to his body, infections, high fevers--ordeals no person should have to endure--he never complained to us.

Eventually the case was settled for *$9.7 million*—believed to be the highest reported settlement of a personal injury case in New Jersey at that time. With the aid of caretakers, Tim could live in a home of his own fitted up to the needs of a person in his quadriplegic condition.

And now, this case's relationship to our hike of the Appalachian Trail.

One day, while he was still my client, I received a call that Tim was gravely ill. I rushed to the hospital. Tim was asleep, fever spiking to 104. He was down below 100 pounds. While I stood at the bedside looking at my emaciated client, medical equipment hooked up to him beeping in the background, the attending physician came by. "I'm Al Dragon, Tim's lawyer," I said.

The doctor took me aside in the hallway. "You've got a very sick client."

"What do you mean?"

"You know, Tim's spinal cord injury made him quadriplegic and he needs a catheter to urinate—a condition known as a *neurogenic bladder*. The brain tells bladder muscles when to hold urine in and when to release urine. These messages from the brain go down the spinal cord to nerves that tell the bladder muscles when to release. If the spinal cord is injured, the message doesn't get through--bladder muscles don't discharge the urine. This poses a serious problem: if urine stays too long in the bladder, it backs up causing pressure that damages the kidneys."

"So, what's a person with neurogenic bladder to do?"

"A catheter, a thin hollow tube, is inserted into the penis," a slight motion indicating sliding the slender tube up into the bladder to let urine flow out. "Using the catheter can cause an infection. That's what Tim's got."

"How bad's the infection?"

"Between Tim's infected decubitus ulcers and a possible kidney infection, he's a sick pup. *He could die.*" I was told the symptoms of an infection: high spiking fever, shaking chills—and *fatigue*.

Before starting the Appalachian Trail, Jim catheterized himself three times a day without any difficulty. Because we're sweating a lot from the physical activity, we have to drink more water, which increases the urine in the bladder, requiring Jim to catheterize more often. Jim's physician told him not to hike the trail because lack of sanitary conditions when inserting the tube could cause an infection.

Several times my client almost died from bladder and kidney infections—and his catheter was inserted in much more sterile conditions. He would get a high fever with violent shaking. They were emergency—possibly life-threatening—situations, requiring antibiotics. One symptom of such an infection is fatigue! It takes all your energy to lift the lightest object, great effort just to keep your eyes open. Jim is exhausted and saying, "Maybe it's my catheter problem."

"You got a fever, Jim?"

He puts a hand on his forehead. "I don't know."

Jim falters; my concern heightens. We're in remote nowhere, and the air temperature is dropping. Fog rolling in—visibility in the bleak grayness is about forty feet, and we have to keep going. Around us is rocky landscape or steep dense woods and no water source. We can't set up camp. There is nothing else to do but stay directly on the trail, go up mountain after mountain, and Jim struggles to do so. We stop often. Jim's not eating. At one rest stop, I reach into my backpack, unwrap an energy bar, break it in two, and Jim forces down half.

Salamander and Periwinkle come from behind us. Jim whispers to me, "Don't say anything to them about my condition."

Periwinkle says, "I'm having trouble with my knees." There are steep descents in these mountains. Carrying body weight, plus an additional forty pounds, knees suffer the jolts of each steep step down. Everyone complains their knees hurt, including Jim.

This area is covered with damp, deepening mist. We watch the two young women hike away ahead of us, going up a mountain. It's weird seeing them walk into the fog. A short distance into the cloudbank they become a smudge and suddenly disappear.

Later, we reach Derrick Knob Shelter. Jim is completely depleted—looks like he might fall into the shelter. We had hiked so slowly that all spaces on the first level are already taken. In a commanding voice I tell those on the lower tier we needed two places because Jim is sick and can't climb up and down the ladder. I'm not sure who moved for us, but I am able to get Jim situated near Just Do It. I quietly ask around if anyone has medical skills, but nobody does. Jim originally brought the antibacterial compound sulfa with him, but when he lightened his pack, he sent it home because he was feeling good at that time.

The air temperature hovers around freezing. One guy mutters, "Yesterday ninety-two degrees, today thirty-two."

As cold as it is, we are required to cook meals outside the shelter. Most likely so bears won't be attracted to the inside of the shelter by the smell of food, and to keep people from burning down the shelter. Cooking with cold, numb hands is quite an experience. My usually supple fingers freeze up, and it is difficult to get them to do what you want. What I really want to do is put my fingers in my warm pocket, but hot food tastes great. I make sure Jim eats some.

While dictating my notes I don't want to disturb anyone, so I stand far away from the shelter. The wind blows hard, like a baby blizzard, and sticks its cold fingers up the back of my jacket. It's so cold my face is starting to burn. I look at the shelter's stone walls and corrugated metal roof supported by log beams. There are dozens of names and dates carved into the lumber. It's 6:30 and Jim is sleeping soundly. Everyone is burrowed into their sleeping bags, wool or fleece caps pulled down over foreheads and sides of faces. They look like a row of mummies. Some are buried so deeply, all that shows is the top of a warm cap. I'm about to do the same thing because it's glacial out here.

Temperature drops during the evening. In the middle of the night I get up, worried about Jim. He says he's feeling better and falls back asleep. I had come to depend on Jim—now I'm trying to return the favor by helping him.

To keep bears away, a chain-link fence covers the entire front of the shelter. There is a door in the middle through which we can enter or leave. I open the door and go out. It's cold. The wind has died down. I shine my small flashlight in different directions. Hazy all around, my breath adds mist to the air.

Still, quiet. An out of focus partial moon gives otherworldly light to the surrounding woodland. Part of the sky opens, and I glimpse a few stars sparkling in deep black. I'm grateful Gorilla is not as sick as he had first thought. I feel happy, glad to be part of a great universe, to be alive on this frosty April evening. My happiness had been locked up in a dream of hiking the A.T., and now it is being fulfilled. For the moment I'm not worried about Jim's condition. I'm not even concerned about the breathing problems I've had. I am perfectly content.

Standing outside it occurs to me: I'm on the bear's side of the chain-link fence. Feeling so good, it really doesn't matter. I return, close the door, latch it, check Jim again, and go back to sleep.

April 4, 2002

Yesterday, when I was busy tending to Jim, the Carnival Girls, Periwinkle, and Salamander borrowed my fold-up elastic water bucket. Salamander took it to the spring and brought back enough water for all of us to filter. I had put a plastic bottle of water inside my sleeping bag so the water wouldn't freeze. It's a good thing I did. This morning the temperature is below thirty-two degrees.

Jim gets up; I watch his movements. They are slower than usual, but stronger than yesterday.

"How you feeling, Gorilla?"

"Better, but still a little sick." His voice is quieter than normal, and he rubs his forehead to ward off remnants of his ailment.

"Want to stay here for the day?"

The Gorilla man looks around. "I can hike. How far we going?"

"Short day; we'll only hike seven miles."

Gorilla Jim is slower than usual, and for the first time I get my stuff together before him. If he had an onset of some illness, he is rapidly beating it away.

Every tree branch is a glazed alabaster of ice and frost. The forest floor is covered with hoarfrost, an early morning swan-white carpet. We walk into a frozen white and silver fairyland. A rising sun catches the sides and tops of icy limbs and lights them up like a mall's sparkling winter holiday display.

The terrain is a gentle incline. As we hike, the temperature rises above freezing. Jim is getting back to his old self. By the time we are ready for lunch, it is a great day, around forty degrees.

We stop at the Silers Bald Shelter for lunch. Jim is much better, but can use a hot meal. Ordinarily, I don't like to cook lunch because it takes time—and it's a pain in the ass to scrub the messy pot without a sink and hot water. Today is an exception. It's a short trip; we have plenty of time to make a cooked lunch instead of the customary tuna or peanut butter on pita bread. I cook ramen noodles, and put peanut butter in it.

Slick arrives. Thirty-three years old, slightly built, he has dark hair parted in the middle, eyes so deep set you can't tell their color, and a rough voice. Slick carries an old, long black-handled knife in a scraped-up leather sheath. The knife sheath hangs from a worn-out leather belt that's too big for his narrow waist. Slick used a rock to drive a thin nail through its leather, punching an extra hole to make it fit.

I first met Slick in the Laundromat at the Fontana Village where he tried talking to Soft Touch. In his coarse voice Slick said he wanted to find someone like her to share his life. He told her how he had found religion and read the Bible for an hour every day. She saw his grim mouth, stealthy movements, and showed no interest in him.

Slick, Gorilla, and I are alone at Silers Bald. I'm sitting outside the shelter on a fallen tree, eating a snack of gorp. Slick stands above me gnawing what I presume to be remnants of a strip of beef jerky.

I turn to Slick and the book with the dark cover he has in one hand, "You still read the Bible every day?"

"I do." He looks up at the sky, reverently, and back at me. "I found something …because I had to. My life was bad. I traveled with people who did lotsa *terrible things.*" Remembering, his eyes go down, his face becomes cloudy for a moment, then with a certain piety in his voice, he tells us he was "born again."

In his hand, as if for proof, he holds a worn black volume, inscribed in faded gold leaf on the cover: *Holy Bible.* Three things Slick keeps close to him: the raggedy olive green backpack he bought at a flea market, the large knife with the black handle, and his Bible.

"What do you mean by 'terrible things'?" I ask. I know some people turn to religion because of a horrendous life, usually involving drugs. In my experience as a lawyer, when many people tell me they are born again, I am in for an earful of former sins that even the Ten Commandments don't cover.

Slick doesn't miss any. He had a life of stealing, dealing drugs, taking drugs, violence, and murder. As Slick puts it, "I was in with a bad bunch who didn't give a damn about anyone or anything. They'd take their fingers," he stares directly into my face, "rip your heart out soon as look at you...walk away, blood dripping from their hands...never look back."

Many souls are reborn shortly after they hear the crash of a heavy barred steel door slam shut on them. If it is a true rebirth for the better, well and good. However, despite Slick's alleged reading of the Good Book, and occasional references to religion, we learned from others that this guy, who walked with the Bible in the curl of one hand, wrote bad checks with the other hand, and passed them up and down the Appalachian Trail.

Chapter Thirteen

April 5, 2002

We wake up to temperatures in the upper twenties. It is difficult to get my freezing fingers to do anything. I stuff my backpack with the coordination of a one-year-old.

Gorilla and I are going to Gatlinburg today. Most of the others are moving on past there. By the time we get back on the trail, they will be days ahead of us, and we might never see them again. With nostalgia, Gorilla and I say goodbye to people we lived with for the past three weeks.

It takes a while to get our legs moving; once we do, we rush to keep warm. We planned on a short day, only going seven miles to the next shelter.

Jim and I are going through thick forests of spruce fir trees. We trek up the trail to Clingmans Dome, over a mile high, the *highest point on the Appalachian Trail*—loftier than the A.T.'s mountains in New Hampshire. Think of it: Katahdin in Maine isn't this high. At Clingmans, a steep ramp leads to a five-story-high concrete column with a circular observation deck. On a clear day views are over a hundred miles; you can see seven states. That's on a clear day. Today, as usual, the 360-degree panorama is hindered by visibility of only about twenty to thirty miles.

Sightseers drive on a road to the concrete ramp. Before leaving their cars, they encase themselves in thick jackets, mufflers, and wool hats to insulate themselves from the cold, whistling wind. A few rotund tourists stop part way up the ramp, puffing, try to look over the side, and head back down. Those who trudge up the ramp see grubby thru-hikers, sporting backpacks of different sizes bursting with gear. Many of the male trekkers now display three weeks of whiskers and some wear shorts, and goose bumps. Excitedly, the day-trippers ask us about our hike. "Where you going?" "Do you carry all your food?" "Where do you sleep?"

Some of the hikers from the last shelter join us. There is a blustery cold airstream at this elevation. Wearing hats and gloves, mountains in the background, we huddle at the observation tower's low wall for photos; a visitor takes our group picture. Each hiker hands her their camera in turn. Jim—back to his old self—poses for a photo, holding the Gorilla hiking pole, wearing his large backpack, behind him range after range of distant olive green peaks become blended into the sky-blue haze of the Blue Ridge Mountains. One of the girls takes Jim's Gorilla stick and smiles broadly.

We say goodbye again to our fellow hikers and trek to the Mt. Collins Shelter, marking *two hundred miles* we have hiked so far. It's five more miles to access a road into Gatlinburg. Jim wants to move on even though we had agreed to make this an easy day. I think of a hot, bubbly mushroom pizza waiting for me in town and agree to push on. We start out fast and reach the Newfound Gap parking area in less than three hours. Now, how do we get to Gatlinburg, fifteen miles away?

Earlier, I had a conversation with a former pilot for Northwest Airlines. His trail name is Longshot because he is sixty-one years of age and his wife didn't think he would make this trip. Longshot said his wife was going to pick him up at Newfound Gap. When we reach the Newfound Gap parking area, Longshot is putting his backpack in the trunk of an automobile. Near the car a woman comes up to us and offers me a bag of Oreo cookies and a bag of peanuts. We put two and two together and realize it is Longshot's wife, Kay. We tell them of our dilemma and find out that Longshot is waiting for Pilgrim to arrive. Pilgrim is a young woman with the group with whom we had spent time. Gorilla and I had passed her earlier on the trail. She told us she had ankle problems from slipping and falling and was moving slowly. Kay offers to drive us while Longshot waits for Pilgrim.

In town Kay drops us off at the Grand Prix Motel. Later, she brings Pilgrim to the same motel because she figured if we were staying here it must be a decent place. (You can't always bet on that.)

After getting settled in our rooms I go to the motel's laundry area. While loading clothes into the washer, a woman comes in to wash clothes. She is in her late thirties or early forties, walks and talks in animated gestures. She wears a sleeveless yellow and rose flowered dress, cut deep in the front. "You hiking?" she asks.

"Yeah, doing the Appalachian Trail."

"I met other guys hiking the trail who stayed here." Her voice and mannerism is unpolished, with a slightly suggestive edge to it.

"You been here awhile?"

"My house got flooded out and I been here since—"Just then the washer starts filling, and I don't catch how long she's been at the motel. I pick up my clothing bag and start to leave.

"I got a car here." She looks me over. "If you need a ride to get supplies, or anywhere, I'll be glad to take you. My name's Linda. Just ask at the front desk…they know me."

"Thanks. My wife is coming tomorrow with a car."

"If you need a ride in the meantime, just call…Ask at the office for my number, they know me."

Pilgrim arrives and calls our room. "Pretty nice place here." She sounds happy and relieved.

"Yeah, it's okay. Gorilla Jim and I are going to Pizza Hut for pizza and beer. That was my motivation for hiking this far today. You interested?"

"Pizza and beer, you bet!"

Pizza Hut is five or six blocks from the motel. We need pizza, and I need plenty of it. They bring me a medium mushroom pizza, cheese bubbling, mushrooms sweet and tender, beautifully seasoned red sauce rich with tomatoey taste. I lift the first slice, the mozzarella cheese stretches from the sides, hangs, and then breaks. I eat every loving slice, savoring each bite. Jim and Pilgrim share one of the large pizzas with everything on it: pepperoni, beef and pork toppings, green peppers, red onions, mushrooms, and, because Gorilla likes pineapple, they add on some of that tropical fruit.

The beer is cold; it quenches a built up three-week-long thirst. We drain a couple pitchers, laugh, and talk about the trail. Pilgrim tells us about the time she slipped on the trail and fell on her back. She had an extremely heavy backpack, and she couldn't get up. She called it "turtling," and demonstrates it by flailing around like a turtle on its back. She had to release the straps and wriggle out of her backpack.

Later, I reach Barbara by phone and tell her we are in Gatlinburg. She has dropped our Rhodesian Ridgeback, Jack, off with the people who will take care of him. They say absence makes the heart grow fonder. Take it from me—my heart is about as fond as it's going to get.

April 6, 2002

There's a hikers box at the motel. It's similar to the leave a penny, take a penny container that sits by some cash registers. I make a deposit of a few things I don't need, and Gorilla makes a withdrawal. Jim and I meander around town, going to an outfitter and the mini-mart, picking up a few items. It's a lazy day accented by the anticipation of Barbara's arrival. She should be here by 3:00 p.m.

Around 2:00 I look for a florist, and finally find one on a side street. By the time I get someone to ring up my order and walk back to the motel, Barbara is already there—early as usual. It's wonderful to see her, and we embrace each other as if I've returned from the ten-year Trojan War. Jim takes a picture of her holding the bouquet of long-stemmed crimson roses wrapped together by a wide red ribbon fashioned into many bows. She stands there, head coming up to my chin, with sparkling, bright brown eyes, the same beautiful smile as the day I married her.

The three of us enjoy an excellent steak dinner at the Peddler, a large restaurant decorated in a rustic style with carefully crafted wood walls and ceiling, wood beams and columns everywhere. Like schoolboys telling their teacher about summer vacation, Jim and I gush forth, interrupting each other to tell Barb what we've been doing for the past three weeks. "Beautiful views...nearly froze my ass off...rained almost every day... great people on the trail...hiked over two hundred miles...listen to this trail name..."

When I look into Barb's bright brown eyes and see her enthusiastic response to all of our blabber, I know one of the greatest parts of this trip is having her with us for these few days. Don't get me wrong. Being away in the backwoods is great—better than great. Fabulous! *Except...*

April 7, 2002

The weather gods smile on us today. It's sunny, going up to seventy degrees.

Gatlinburg, Tennessee, is a fun-filled, honky-tonk Atlantic City of the South. A gently swaying, glass-enclosed gondola carries visitors up to Mt. Harrison to see the vistas of the city and surrounding green mountains that fade into far distant pearly vapor. We ride the Space Needle's glass elevator 342 feet above the city to an observation deck for a panoramic view of the town and surrounding Smoky Mountains.

Walking along Parkway, the main street, tourists go in and out of arts and crafts shops. There's Hillbilly Golf, thrill rides, fun museums, an aquarium, and village-style shops.

Fresh faced young women in billowing white wedding gowns they just rented, on arms of grooms feeling awkward in tuxedos and ties they hired for a few hours, are walking to or coming from more wedding chapels than I thought existed in the entire U.S.A. This is the South's wedding and honeymoon mecca. If a chapel is not your style, you can arrange to get married in a Smoky Mountain cabin or chalet. There is no blood test and no waiting period. Can't wait? One nearby chapel provides a drive-thru ceremony. Just pull your car or truck up to the window, and a minister performs the service while you remain seated in your vehicle.

Jim, Barbara, and I walk arm-in-arm along streets reminiscent of a carnival. There are aromas of cotton candy and hot dogs; a mother walks by holding two plastic cups of smoothie, a straw sticking up from each lid, as her kids dash ahead to look in the doorway of a candy store at displays of jars filled with gold foil–wrapped chocolates, multicolored hard candies, and clear bags filled with pastel colored confections.

We enjoy the weekend in Gatlinburg, roaming the town and laughing. Jim teases Barbara because she doesn't have a trail name. Our final dinner is at Calhoun's, an eating place with a large waterwheel out front—good steaks and ribs.

April 8, 2002

The roses still look beautiful, but Barbara can't take them on the plane. I take them to the front desk and say to the clerk, "Would you give these to Linda? You know her."

Barbara drives us back toward Newfound Gap in the mountains where the A.T. resumes. Driving to the cloud-capped peak, it begins to get foggy. The further up we go the thicker the fog gets. By the time Barbara drops us off in the almost mile-high parking area, the fog is so dense we can hardly see the sign that reads:

Tennessee

North Carolina

State Line

Elevation 5048

Great Smoky Mountains

National Park

Jim takes a picture of Barb and me, both of us with our hoods up, and looking eerie in the dark cloud bank. Barbara is eager to leave because she has to drive down the mountain road in bad visibility. We watch her rental car rapidly vanish—and so has the Appalachian Trail. I turn around 360 degrees and don't see it. Jim searches the perimeter of the parking lot and yells through the thick mist, "I found it."

"Keep talking," I shout back and move through smoky dampness toward his voice. He materializes out of the fog, and we resume hiking along the border between North Carolina and Tennessee.

All morning we trek through chowder-thick haze. The temperature drops, the wind picks up, and it starts to rain. Stiff, face-whipping air currents get worse along the ridge, gusting up to sixty miles an hour. Trying to keep his footing on the slim crest, Jim yells above the roaring, "They're trying to blow us off this damn mountain!" As we cross on top of one ridge, I feel a shoving of my backpack as if Gorilla is pushing me from behind. I turn around. It is the wind.

Although there are ups and downs, this section of trail is easy compared to terrain we had been through in the past few weeks. We hike about eleven miles, including a half-mile trek from the A.T. to the Pecks Corner Shelter. This shelter is down in a valley where all of us staying here are relieved of wild airflow that howled and screamed most of the day. The rain stops as we finish an early dinner, and a bit of sunlight breaks through.

April 9, 2002

I was the first person to start moving in the morning. Having stuffed earplugs in my ears to drown out the snoring, I didn't hear rain on the tin roof until I awoke and removed the plugs. Jim, still in his sleeping bag, eyes half closed, stares out at the water pounding the ground into mud and mutters, "Heck, I ain't gettin' up." He turns to his side, pulls the sleeping bag over his head and goes back to sleep.

After breakfast and almost fully packed, I realize the Gorilla man is still in his sack. Many of the others have already gone. "Hey, Jim. How about it? Ready to get up?"

He grumbles. But I tell you—half asleep, irritated by the weather, and moving slower than usual—no one could get his stuff together, eat, and get going as quickly as Gorilla.

The rainstorm is relentless. No one seeing my photos will ever know how crappy this weather is because I don't want to ruin the camera by using it in the driving downpour.

Other than rain induced flooding, the trails in the Smokies are a pleasure to travel. Unlike the tough climbs in Georgia and the rough parts of North Carolina, the trails in this part of Tennessee are a moderate grade and easy terrain. Because the Smokies attract so many tourists the trails can't be too steep. The weather eases up; Jim is way behind me somewhere watching a large hawk up in a tree. I don't realize I am singing to myself until, rounding a bend, I walk into a man hiking south. Often, I sing when I'm happy hiking and no one is around. I'm not conscious of it until someone crosses my path and smiles at my animated voice.

The fog isn't as thick as yesterday's. After the rain dies down, we're able to see for miles, beautiful scenes sprayed with a light milky haze.

There are supposed to be hundreds of bears around here. We haven't seen any and neither has anybody I spoke to. If the bruins are around, they're keeping very quiet. Maybe bears don't like all this rain and fog anymore than we do.

Everyone at the Cosby Knob Shelter wants to get to Davenport Gap tomorrow. Then we'll be out of the Smokies and free of the regulations against tenting, and thus free from the sardine-jammed shelters.

April 10, 2002

The terrain is relatively easy for the eight-mile hike to Davenport Gap. Some people complain that the six mile—often sharp—descent causes their feet to rub and burn, but it doesn't bother me. However, I've been having some difficulty breathing.

In the Smokies we passed the point marking completion of one-tenth of the Appalachian Trail. We have trekked over 235 miles

Our next stop is Mountain Momma's, a country store, hostel, and short order grill. Mountain Mommas is best known for its large burgers and being the only resupply point for the next thirty-six miles. As we trek, I'm singing to myself part of John Denver's song, *Take Me Home, Country Roads* that refers to "mountain momma."

At these lower elevations flowers are in bloom. Jim is pointing out Trillium, a white flower on large heart-shaped leaves. I am thinking of a large juicy burger with catsup on a large bun.

At the Davenport Gap there is a road so small you have to closely scrutinize the map to find it. We were told it's easy to catch a ride to take us one and a half miles over steep hills to Momma's. No vehicles are on the road. We wait, look up and down the narrow stretch, and suspect no one uses this remote lane. Deep in these mountain gaps, as usual, there is no cell phone service to call for someone to come pick us up. Gadget, a hiker who spent last night in the shelter with us, sits on a large rock, shoes and socks off. We join him. No cars come by. About ten minutes later Colt, a twenty-year-old comes out of the woods and talks to us. He doesn't' want to wait for a car and starts hiking to Mountain Momma's. We yell after him, "Send somebody back to pick us up."

Another fifteen minutes goes by. Jo and Ranger come down the trail and set out for their burgers, with a promise they'll ask someone to come pick us up. More time slips by. We realize no one is going to come and get us, and we start to walk.

Not five hundred yards into our hike we hear the sound of a pickup truck behind us. I give them the thumbs-up. They stop. "Goin' to Mountain Momma's?"

"We sure are."

"Hop in." They drive us to Mountain Momma's.

Mountain Momma's décor is large metal cigarette signs out front, along with old tires, cars, and assorted junk. The small building was formerly a fine old schoolhouse. Inside on the left is a limited assortment of groceries, along with many shelves loaded with cartons of cigarettes; and going from the middle to the right is the grill and some tables and booths.

As we come inside we run into Teetotaler and Maybe Muscles. We haven't seen them for a while. Maybe Muscles gives me a big hug. "We're waiting for Moxie to be delivered." There's a fretful tone to her voice and her forehead takes a wrinkled appearance when she talks anxiously of their adored Jack Russell Terrier.

Dogs are not allowed on the trails in the Great Smoky Mountains National Park. Thru-hikers with dogs to be boarded drop them off at Fontana Dam. I'm glad for Moxie that she didn't have to endure the horrendous weather, although these trails were much easier than we had for the first three weeks. Maybe Muscles and Teetotaler leave.

I listen to those ordering ahead of me and hear things like: "How you wan choo burgah, boy?" It's Appalachian music to my ears. I bite into a hefty hot cheeseburger and let the juices run over my fingers and chin. Instead of French fries I opt for potato chips and crunch them with such zest you would think they were tiny toasted pumpernickels piled with Beluga caviar delivered from the Caspian Sea. Today, I don't have to use the back of my hand to wipe my face, I have a paper napkin. We sit and have lunch with Colt who spent one year in college and would like to go back and become an art teacher. Jo and Ranger are friends from school. Ranger is on his way to see his fiancé but spent the week hiking. Ranger is looking for a ride to Fontana Dam where he apparently left his car.

While we eat lunch a woman comes in and asks, "Who belongs to Moxie?" Maybe Muscles and Teetotaler are at the river nearby having lunch, so I take the woman down there, Moxie skipping along behind. At the sight of their much-loved "youngster," their impatient expectant faces transform into an explosion of glee and tears—as though a kidnapped child has been safely returned to its parents. They laugh, cry, kiss, and hold tight the small, joyful tail-wagging terrier, smiles as wide as the Grand Canyon.

The guy giving us a ride back up to the Gap is ready to leave. He charges us a buck a piece. We haul our backpacks to a light blue Ford

Ranger pickup truck on the gravel parking lot. Tailgate down, six of us put our packs in the cargo bed, climb in after them and make ourselves fit into the remaining space on the floor; Teetotaler sits on the wheel well, cradling Moxie in her arms. Jim pulls his hat down and wedges the rear part of his brim against his backpack as insurance. "I'm not takin' a chance it'll blow off this time."

Climbing out of Davenport Gap the weather is beautiful, but hot at eighty-two degrees. As we clamber higher and higher, the trail goes back and forth, crisscrossing a picturesque creek, tumbling its way from one terrace of rocks onto rock outcroppings below it. We have five more miles to cover on a trail so steep it often stares us in the face. Our foreheads spill water. I'm becoming more aware of pain in my lungs as they are seemingly busting, trying to get enough air.

Jim is red-faced. "I'm getting dehydrated," he says and starts sucking down water.

"Okay. We'll take a short break."

"No, Avalanche. Go on."

"I'm not leaving you here."

"I'll be all right, drink some, repack my pack and catch up with you later." The "Sergeant" is speaking, finality in his voice like: That's the *end* of the conversation!

"I don't mind waiting." I get a long unbroken stare. "Okay. I'll find a campsite, filter water, and have it ready when you get there."

Eventually I get to a level area with a stream, see Teetotaler and Maybe Muscles off to the side, and stop to talk. I leave my backpack with them and continue up the trail to see if I can find the Painter Branch campsite. Not too far up, looking from the trail, I spot a fairly level area near the stream. I'm dawdling, checking it out. Along comes Jim who also left his backpack with the women. He looks much better.

"What do you think, Jim?"

"Got water close by." Probing the soft ground with his hiking pole, "Good places to setup tents."

I survey the horizon, mountains all around. "Look at this view…listen to that babbling brook." Water is gliding over rocks somewhere above, the stream spilling down toward us on its journey to a gap.

We erect our tents, filter water, and make dinner. While we cook, a white flash runs on short fast legs the five hundred feet between Teetotaler's campsite and ours. It is Moxie. This pooch is good at begging for food. Jim gives her tuna, and I give her some of the cheese I'm putting into my dinner concoction. She hangs around while we eat, hoping we'll give her more. Teetotaler comes up to our camp to see how Moxie is doing. When she finds out that Moxie has gotten tuna and cheese, Teetotaler says, "Moxie is eating better than I am!"

This evening when I dictate notes of the day's happenings, I walk up about a quarter mile so I don't disturb Jim and the other hikers. We have been doing thirteen miles a day. It's rough at times and maybe more than we should be hiking at this point. All of us have gotten stronger. Several weeks ago we never could have done the mileage we did today. Yesterday was our four-week anniversary. Though we complain about how difficult some climbs are, considering everything, we're having fun.

It's been a good, although exhausting, day, and I'm grateful to be in this part of paradise. The night is clear. Almost moonless. Only a tiny, barely perceptible, crescent sliver of light defines the dark moon's left edge. Standing, looking up at inky black sky with brilliant stars, I finish, turn off the little recorder, hold it in my hand, for the moment secluded in darkness. Air is soft and gentle. My headlamp lights up nearby trees and bushes. I breathe in the surroundings, beautiful and primitive, something lost to our civilized world—that only exists out here. A pleasant, tingling sensation spills through me. There is happiness almost bordering on euphoria. I feel strong, independent. I feel like yelling out: "I'm Avalanche, the damned rugged woodsman!"

Back to my tent, I clean up as best I can—my T-shirt stinks as if two skunks had a fight with each other. Sometimes I think, *What is that horrible smell? It's me! If only I could wash some things.*

April 11, 2002

Weather is warm, a little over eighty degrees. The Appalachian Trail is directly on the border between two states. We walk mountain ridges along this line, often with one foot in North Carolina and the other in Tennessee. Again we climb for almost the entire day. At lunchtime Gorilla and I stop at a shelter and eat with Teetotaler and Maybe Muscles. Maybe Muscles, trying to keep cool by sitting in the shade, looks at me sweating, eyes my long pants, and says, "Unzip the legs from the pants and wear them as shorts."

I check out the flimsy zipper, very lightweight plastic. "I never unzipped them before and don't know if they'll re-zip." I fumble with the zipper pull. "What the heck will I do if the damn things don't go back together?" I picture being stuck with a pair of shorts in freezing weather.

"It's too hot," she says, like a sister would. "Just do it!"

I unzip the legs, stuff them into the backpack, and walk in great comfort all afternoon.

Jim and I are exhausted climbing the almost vertical trail to the summit of Snowbird Mountain. Looking directly in front of us the footpath is at eye level. I turn back to Jim and say, "Don't let your nose bump into the trail." This is known as PUDs: Pointless Up and Downs. When a trail is constructed, it can be built steeply, going directly up and over the mountain—exhausting; or it can be constructed at a more reasonable grade zigzagging up the mountain.

We finally make it to the creek at the base of Max Patch. Maybe Muscles and Teetotaler are lying on the ground, dead tired—and they are half our age. They're not sure if they want to climb to the top of Max Patch, another mile—straight up. They decide to get it over with, and we all pump water here; there is no water at the top. Now, we each have to lug six more pounds, enough filtered water to carry us through dinner tonight, breakfast tomorrow, and until we find more water.

Max Patch is a bald, wide and grassy. At the top we are treated to the most magnificent 360-degree view. With incomparable vistas of royal blue and purple mountains forty to sixty miles away, this place is in a class by itself. It's like the scene in *Sound of Music* where Julie Andrews, arms open, runs, twirling across a high grassy alpine field, mountains in the background. Breathtaking. This may be one of the most beautiful places in the world.

Unfortunately, winds up here are about forty miles an hour. With a little effort I zip the legs back onto my pants. My hat is blowing off even with the chin strap tightened. We take photos, trying to keep our hands steady in the squall, and move on. Jim and I expected to camp at the top of this mountain. However, we previously read it can be extremely windy on Max Patch—as we now know—and we're not about to try pitching flailing tents in robust wind. We walk about a mile down the mountain to an area that is not so blustery.

Jim searches in vain for a level spot. We finally find places where we can sleep without constantly sliding off our sleeping pads. It's 8:15 p.m. I'm in my tent dictating notes. There is so much howling and banging noise from the wind, I don't have to take a walk to avoid being heard.

During the night the wind grows stronger, and becomes ferocious. My tent shudders; a tiny keychain light hanging inside my tent dances madly. The rustling of several leaves is one thing. Nearby tens of thousands of leaves and branches slamming into each other sound like a tornado. The wind gets so bad it seems like my tent will tear loose. I tie down each side, which I usually don't have to do.

Oh well, soon we'll be in one of the best trail towns on the Appalachian Trail.

Chapter Fourteen

April 12, 2002

This morning the wind is calm. The weather is in the lower seventies. It's overcast, but it isn't raining. There is a light breeze. It's a good day for hiking.

People come into and go out of our lives like strangers you meet at a party. We hear the scrape of boots on the trail behind us, turn to see her approaching—slightly less than average height, dark black hair in bangs, which frame flawless skin, dark eyes so soft and interesting that you overlook her extra wide hips. We all stop. She takes a clear plastic water bottle from the side of her backpack and between sips tells us, "…attending college…" mentioning the name of a university not too far away, "…want to be a marine biologist…" takes another drag on the water bottle, unwraps an energy bar and offers it but we shake our heads "no." Between bites she continues, "…off from school a few days hiking and trying to clear my mind…" mentions something about a guy she knows, but at that moment I'm swatting mosquitoes, so I don't hear it. She puts the bottle back into a sleeve at the side of her purple backpack. We all start walking, she moves at a faster pace, waves back at us, climbs a rise as she moves away, rounds a bend of boulders and is gone.

"What was her name?" Jim asks.

"I don't know. She didn't say."

In dense woods, we come across two logs stretched over a stream. On the other side I step off carefully, trying to avoid an old tree's wet roots, which I know will be slippery as if ice covered. Instead, I put my foot down into poison ivy which I've been trying to avoid, but it was unseen, mingled in with other ground plants.

Across the forest floor comes the sound like someone starting up a large diesel engine. The deep thumping noise increases in rhythm: trummmmm… trummmm…**trummm…trumm trumm trumm** purrrrrr.

I stop hiking—wanting to stick my fingers in my ears—and shout, "Where is somebody starting up a huge lawn mower out here?"

Gorilla looks out toward the blaring noise and yells back, "That's no motor."

"What the hell is it?"

"Grouse."

"Get out!" I can't believe it. "A bird's making a racket like that?"

Jim heard that sound before. "There's a male grouse out there, a large chicken-size bird on a stump or big log, beating his wings against the air. That's what makes the sound like an engine starting up."

"Man, it's so loud I can feel it as well as hear it. Why's he making all this ear-splitting racket?"

"Best reason in the world. He's attracting a hen who wants to mate."

I'm trying to recall…something like that before…oh, yes, the damn Barred Owl!

Later in the day, I'm walking in a state of half attention, daydreaming about food, thinking about what I'll eat for dinner. Should I have Lipton's beef rice or pasta with cashews and dehydrated meat? Maybe for dessert, a Hershey bar. Wonder if I have any chocolate chip—BAM! There is an explosion from the brush in front of me; dead leaves and twigs go flying. It jolts me backward. A hefty-brown object blasts into the air, wings flurrying as it takes flight. Gorilla laughs at the sight of me lurching backward, one arm and a hiking pole up guarding my face. I hadn't yet started breathing again.

Gorilla stops laughing long enough to say, "Remember the male grouse making noise to attract a hen? That was her!"

Today we cover more miles than ever before. Jim starts walking stiff legged, says to me, "My knees and feet are killing me." He stops at a downed large tree fallen next to the trail, leans his pack against it, and sits on the trunk. "Ah, that's better," he says, massaging both of his knees enough to bend forward and remove his heavy leather boots and put them on the ground. "That does feel better." He pulls off a wool sock.

"Hey, Gorilla. Look at that blister on the side of your foot, near the big toe. How long you had that baby?" Gorilla examines the almond-sized bubble bursting from the side of his foot. "Didn't have it this morning—I can fix this." The Gorilla man takes a jackknife out of his pants pocket, opens the blade, presses the tip against his thumb to test its sharpness. "This should do it." He plunges the point of the knife into the flesh bulge, clear liquid oozes onto the knife blade, and when he withdraws the knife, drips onto the ground.

I wonder if Gorilla is going to clean the blade before using it to prepare dinner tonight. "Need a Band-Aid for your toe?"

"I got 'em." He wipes the blade on the side of his pants and puts the knife away, turns, and rummages around in his pack.

"That's okay. I can get my first-aid kit," and I easily reach into the top compartment of my backpack and hand Jim a small bandage to put on the thin saggy blister bag that now looks like a teeny used condom. Jim puts his boot back on and we hike the rest of the way to the Deer Park Mountain Shelter.

We trekked *sixteen miles*, the longest distance we ever backpacked in a day. Toward the end—out of desperation to get it over with—I hike as hastily as weary legs will take me. Jim wants to walk an additional three miles to Hot Springs. I am beat and I wonder if he would have made it.

Staying at the shelter are Maybe Muscles, Teetotaler, a guy named Cowboy, who's wearing a western hat, and several other people. Jim and I take off torturous boots and put on light, comfortable camp shoes or sandals. Someone collects wood and builds a campfire. We all cook and eat our dinners, sitting around talking to each other. Moxie, the little Jack Russell Terrier, comes by and I feed her some of my dinner of Ramen noodles with cheese.

This is an old log shelter with an overhang in the front supported by log posts. Pilgrim, still wearing her wide-brimmed khaki hat, sits on the ground leaning back against a post, using a spoon to eat out of a metal cook pot. Small cook stoves, plastic water bottles, green and blue nylon food bags are scattered about. Teetotaler sits on a log, her long legs stretched out in front of her. Moxie, now fully fed and tired by the long hike, curls up on Teetotaler's thighs and sleeps while her master eats from a shiny metal container.

What was once a parade of hikers is now reduced to a more intimate group. Everyone is friendly, like cousins. No one is obnoxious or annoying. We exchange information and try to be helpful to each other. Talk about our equipment, our lives, why we are out here.

Today, I spoke to a man who was a financial analyst in the stock market. He is considering a career change. Though he has two children in college and one in high school, he is out here to think about what he wants to do in the future. Many college students and graduates take time off to hike the A.T. but few financial analysts do.

I'm sitting on a rock, talking about my gripe. "When they build these trails, they can run them at a slight grade up the mountain. Instead, why do they make them go straight up, turning a hike into an ordeal?"

A guy inside the shelter comes out and says, "My friend, that's known as 'huff and up'."

One of the women asks, "What's that?"

"When they make you hike a steep mountain without the help of switchbacks, it's 'huff and up'."

Puzzled, one of the guys asks, "What's a *switchback*?"

"You've seen it. They zigzag the trail up the side of the mountain so it's less steep than going directly up and over."

This is a small shelter with a full house tonight. Cowboy is on one side of me and Jim is on the other side. Before we retire to our sleeping bags, we build a large fire in the stone-rimmed fire pit out front. In our sleeping bags, on our stomachs, we look out at flames and sparks from the fire blown up by the breeze, and everyone in the shelter talks as though we are at a family reunion.

Today, we went sixteen miles and I'm still alive and not aching too much. The old Appalachian Mountains have got me. I'm on a hiker's high.

We've been on the trail for a month; hiked 267 miles. Still, over nineteen hundred miles to Katahdin.

April 13, 2002

It's an easy hike downhill to Hot Springs, named for its healing natural one-hundred-plus-degree mineral springs. The A.T. goes through this North Carolina town, smack down Hot Springs' main street. That's where you'll find a large, rambling, entirely white Victorian mansion, porches all around with gingerbread railings, white columns, chimneys sticking out of peaked roofs, long sash windows with curtains pulled open to let in the morning sunshine. We enter this 1800s era inn through the kitchen, where a large black stove's backsplash curls up to form a shelf loaded with assorted bottles of spices. Above an island in the kitchen, huge pots hang from hooks. This is Sunnybank Inn, known to hikers as "Elmer's," named after its owner, Elmer Hall. He is a gourmet vegetarian chef whose meals are coveted by camp-food-weary thru-hikers.

Elmer, gray haired, grandfatherly, thin-rimmed glasses, looks at some papers and tells us, "There's a waiting list of people. I don't know if you'll get in." He welcomes us to leave our backpacks there while we go to the post office and the outfitter to get boxes that were shipped to us.

At the post office, two boxes have arrived. The outfitter also received a box of our supplies. We take all these things back to Elmer's Victorian mansion with its throng of thru-hikers.

Three boxes are getting to be a pain in the ass to go through. I want to straighten everything out once and for all. On Elmer's back porch I lay out rows and rows of stuff. People come by to chat with me and comment, "Where'd you get all this stuff?" "Opening your own store?" "I don't think you can carry all this to Katahdin."

"Yeah, tell me about it!"

I set aside five days worth of food to use until we reach Erwin, Tennessee. I sort through the rest and decide what to send to Nolichucky; and what excess food and unneeded gear to send home—and put those items in boxes. After an hour of sorting and resorting, the post office has closed. I take the two boxes to the outfitter to ship home and to Nolichucky.

Elmer's stately manor house has a large living room and music room and is loaded with antiques that lend an Old-World charm to the large sprawling dwelling. He tells us there will be room for us, if we don't mind sharing a room with other people. Train is a tall, slender young man with abundant light brown curly hair. He is handsome enough to be on a daytime soap opera, but soft-spoken. He is working here until the local version of Trail Days, which is a huge gathering of backpackers. Elmer tells him to show us to our accommodations.

The place is jammed, so we take what we can get: an upstairs attic type room for Jim, which he is to share with Train, and I will share a room with a hiker named Rainbird, whose gear is strewn all over the four-poster bed in the room. There is a small dark wooden desk with an antique lamp and other small items on it. The dark drapes are pulled aside and sunlight streams in.

I look around. "Hey, Train. Where do I sleep?"

In his easy mannered way, Train points and says, "There."

There is a small flat sofa, slightly wider than my shoulders, with maroon bedding on it. As I try to figure out where to put my stuff, in comes Rainbird, a twenty-something hiker whose most immediately noticeable attribute is his small dog, Lucy. He opens a door to a large porch off the bedroom that extends the length of the huge house. Lucy is relegated to sleep out on the porch on a small mat next to the door. Considering where Lucy has to sleep, I don't feel so bad.

We amble down the main street, past a few stores and pizzeria and turn into the outfitters—a place easily recognized by backpacks leaning against the front wall and hikers visible through the big glass front window. Near the cash register at the front counter, a lanky boy fresh out of high school tries to capture the attention of the salesperson who is ringing up the sale of a tent and new lightweight spork—a spoon with slits cut into the front to make tines to spear food. The spindle-legged lad asks, "Can I borrow a scissors?"

The salesman ignores the request, saying, "I'll be with you in a minute." He resumes the conversation with a customer: "Directions for setting it up are in the box." He shakes the customer's hand, and turns his attention to the gangly boy leaning toward him.

"I need a scissors."

"Yeah, sure." Fishing around in a drawer behind the counter, the salesclerk says, "They're in here somewhere." Moving a scotch tape dispenser, he pulls out the scissors, hands them to the gangly hiker and without breaking stride says to a woman standing behind the boy, "May I help you?"

Gangly boy takes steps toward the sunlight coming through the store's front window, produces an empty Pepsi can from his side pocket, looks it over, opens the scissors wide, selects the part of the scissors with the pointed end, and plunges it into the can. He tries to cut off the bottom to make a soda can stove. He curses under his breath as he struggles to cut through the metal, realizing this is more difficult than he had expected. A small group drifts toward him to watch the transformation of a soda can to a stove.

The commotion draws the salesman's attention, and he looks wide eyed as the boy is systematically dulling his scissors. "What're you doing?"

"I'm makin' a soda can stove, sir."

"Not with our scissors, you're not!"

"Gotta cut through the side of the can to make it. That's how it's done."

"Get a hacksaw or sheet metal shears or use *your* knife, but don't ruin our scissors." He steps out from behind the counter, takes the cutter from the lad who sheepishly looks down at his shoes. Returning behind the counter, the salesclerk drops the scissors into the drawer and says to the next customer, "Some nerve."

I find Jim walking the aisles. He looks like a buyer for a retail chain as he examines the merchandise, feeling the material, holding garments up, looking at them with a critical eye, and giving his "expert" opinion about each. "Did you see this, Al?" Holding up an item I can't identify, "This, we could use."

I'm much more methodical. I have a list. I hunt for the first item, find it, check the list, and then search out the next item.

There is a tent set up on the floor that looks like my tent, only smaller. Pilgrim also looks at it and each of us considers buying one to save about two pounds.

The temperature is in the nineties, and I'm sweating with all this walking around outside. Late in the afternoon I take a shower, the first clean up I had from Monday until this late Saturday afternoon. It's good to shower and put on fresh clothes we had washed at the Laundromat.

Elmer is busy in the Victorian kitchen preparing a gourmet vegetarian meal. "What's on the menu tonight, Elmer?" I ask. He goes through the courses, including curry broccoli. I can't eat any raw vegetables, and any

quantity of cooked vegetables makes me sick. Curry and my digestive tract
have never gotten along. This meal is not for me.

Jim sniffs the air like a yellow lab in a butcher shop, looks into the kitchen
at the goodies being prepared. "Jim, you'll like this dinner. I'm going to the
restaurant up the street."

On the way out I look in the dining room: patterned wallpaper; long
windows with cream colored drapes held back by wide ribbons of cloth, each
window separated from the other by medium brown-toned woodwork; two
long tables beautifully set with candles. Elmer is going to have one of his
biggest crowds for dinner: twenty-four people. It's depressing not to be able
to join them. When they rang the bell for dinner, I was gone.

I walk out of Elmer's, turn right, and go up Bridge Street, the main
street in town, cross a small bridge over Spring Creek, and go into a neat
restaurant nestled next to the ambling water. They seat me at a table outside,
overlooking the creek. There is practically no traffic on the street so it's as if
I'm eating at a backcountry inn. There is no one to talk to. I order a beer, have
another, and start to feel blue but mellow. Feeling an urge to write a letter to
Barbara. I borrow a pen; the only paper available is a notice of Trail Days in
Damascus, Virginia—I write on the back of it. While writing, they serve me
French bread, mozzarella cheese, sun-dried tomatoes, black olives (which I
only nibble), and olive oil (which I dig into). While writing, the paper gets
spotted with olive oil, but I don't care.

While waiting for the check Jim comes walking up the street. He sees
me and joins me on the patio. I snap out of my funk and pay the check. We
saunter up Bridge Street, the sound of bluegrass music and laughter draws us
into the Paddler's Pub. Several thru-hikers (including Cowboy, who stayed
at the shelter with us the previous night, and Ron, who I had never seen
before) join us at the table, and we kid each other, whoop it up as live music
plays in the background. Too many glasses of suds lubricate our vocal cords
and the words roll out. In a surreal moment in this small-town pub, I listen
to my overly loud voice, almost detached, as if I'm someone else sitting at
the table.

Between sips, we watch foot stomping clog dancing on the dance floor.
At the next table is a tall girl, about six two, with a more gigantic boyfriend.
Cowboy, who is kind of short, is eyeing her up and down. She's wearing tight

jeans that show off her shapely rear end as she leans across the table to speak to another woman sitting with them. With a slight slur, I say to the entranced Cowboy, "Hey! Go ask her to dance—and have her boyfriend punch you all the way to Erwin, Tennessee. Save yourself a hard five-day hike."

Everyone laughs.

Ron is dressed in a black shirt and dark pants. He does some heavy-duty drinking, tosses back pint after pint of beer, leaving wet rings on the table. Then he loudly orders an Irish whiskey. It arrives in an oversized shot glass, which he lifts with two fingers and a thumb, throws the drink down his throat, and yells, "Let it burn!" He shakily stands, approaches a woman who is just returning to her table from dancing, and asks, "May I have the honor?" He unsteadily leads her to the dance floor. It's an amusing scene in which she dances by herself while he holds his hands out close to the outline of her body, slowly lowers himself until he's sitting on his heels, all the time his hands are gradually following the contours of her body without touching it.

Jim and I weave our way back to Elmer's, and I manage to find my room without waking everyone in the quiet mansion. In the middle of the night I get up to give back some of the beer, walk down a hallway of dark wood and antique furnishings, and listen to a clock making century-old sounds.

Chapter Fifteen

April 14, 2002

It's Sunday morning and we dawdle over breakfast.

Jim and I stop by the outfitter before getting back on the trail. The teenaged salesperson says to me, "You need anything else?"

"Yes. Twenty-one-year-old legs and lungs."

She giggles, and we leave. We don't get to hiking until 11:30 a.m.

We cross the French Broad River and start climbing, hauling the heaviest load of food we had ever carried, enough for the five and a half day trip to Erwin, Tennessee. It's overcast, the high today is eight-one degrees. Uphill all day, and with the excessive weight it's a major grind day I'll never forget.

After eight miles we stop at the Rich Mountain fire tower and camp with Ishmael, Dharma, and others. I am tired. More tired than I should be and I've been having trouble breathing.

April 15, 2002

These are tough miles, steep ups and downs, a tremendous elevation gain brings us almost a mile high.

At such heights, views to the horizon—across valley after valley, mountain in front of mountain—are glorious sights. Trees sixty to eighty feet tall, Birch with light bark peeling in thin, curly strips; maples' dark brown bark in vertical grooves, leaf buds swelling; on drier ridges the impressive oaks have dropped acorns along the trail. Trees are not greened up yet. With little vegetation on them, we can see the contours of valleys and rising mountains in the distance between the towering trunks.

We hike through massive growths of rhododendron, forming a high canopy over the trail, a long green tunnel filtering out major sunlight, thick green leaves, and in season, large pink and pale violet flowers. Closely clustered branches of dark jade leaves so dense and tangled they are known as "rhododendron *hells*." Exasperating snarls, impassable were it not for a passage cut through it.

Each morning greets me with a cough that does not want to go away until we've hiked several hours. Deep in my lungs a pesky congestion does not want to free itself, despite hours of hacking. I'm paying a price for being here.

My arms have become blistered—red, itchy, swollen. They weep a clear liquid—extensive poison ivy. We're hiking and tenting in all kinds of vegetation. Poison ivy plants are easy to identify: *Leaves of three, let them be! Hairy vine, no friend of mine.* This saying refers to the exasperating plant's three leaflets. Picture the lower case letter **t** as a stem, with a leaf growing out of the top and a leaf growing out each end of the crossbar. The leaves are almond shaped, mostly two to four inches in length, light green to dark green turning to shades of yellow, orange, or red in autumn. Climbing a tree trunk, the vine is hairy, appearing like a fuzzy rope.

This benign-looking plant deceives. Within its leaves, stems, and vines lurks a nasty colorless, oily sap called *urushiol*. Urushiol spreads easily and causes skin rashes, fluid-filled blisters, weeping sores that leak fluid onto clothing. The itching is maddening; makes a person border on insanity. There can be swelling of arms, legs, and face. Eyelids may inflate until they are closed.

Unknowingly, you step on a poison ivy plant, later remove your boots—it's now on your hands. Or brush against a plant with your bare arms. You try to avoid it, but the plant mingles with innocent forest vegetation. The poisonous liquid gets onto hiking poles or may be on wood for a fire—even spread into the air by the fire itself. So potent is this infuriating chemical, that 1 billionth of a gram can cause a rash. Only a quarter of an ounce could cause a rash in *every person on earth!* Poison ivy's urushiol can ravage the skin even after the plant has died, even after several centuries.

Temperature today is way up in the high eighties. I don't sweat easily, but wetness now builds up under my arms, soaking my shirt. The humid air has a thickness that makes breathing for me even more difficult.

On the way to the Little Laurel Shelter we climb for several hours, as on a steep stairway. Lugging the heavy load on our backs in the extreme heat bleeds energy out of us. Sweat drips. Out of water, feeling beet red, and unsteady on my feet, I sit on a rock and Jim gives me a drink.

"How much further, Jim?"

"Only a few more clicks."

Each time I ask how far we have to go, Jim responds, "Only a few more clicks."

I didn't know what a *click* is. Jim never says, I never ask. All I know is it always turns out to be much farther than the Gorilla man lets on. The climb to Camp Creek Bald is sharply upward. My mind wants me to keep climbing higher. The heavy pack on my back and gravity drag me down, saying: "Stay where you are."

Deep within I start to despise these strenuous and unnecessarily steep climbs—trouble breathing. Possibly it's a voice inside trying to tell me something as I'm beginning to feel tightness in my chest. Nothing is said to Jim, maybe it will pass. We struggle higher, and Jim says, "We're almost at the top." I know we are far from it. Earlier, I calculated it would take an hour more to climb to the top and we are far from that point. We reach one false summit after another. Each time Jim says, "We're almost at the top."

Weary, the third or fourth time Jim repeats it, I blast him: "Bullshit! We're nowhere near it."

Today, we hiked thirteen and a half miles to a campsite between Camp Creek Bald and White Rock Cliffs. Everybody is tired, griping about the elevation. The heat and humidity has also gotten to them.

April 16, 2002

Another day of constant ups and downs. I detest *climbing* the mountains. I don't mind coming down, which almost everyone else dislikes because it hurts their knees. It doesn't affect mine. The strain of dragging myself up, difficulty breathing, and vague tightness in my chest is disturbing, causing an increasing realization I might have to stop hiking.

Around lunchtime we arrive at Jerry Cabin Shelter. Two men are cleaning up the grounds. One of them is a school teacher who is off for the day. He volunteers to take care of the shelter and nearby parts of the A.T. He says, "As the weather gets warmer and vegetation starts to grow, I'll go along with a weed whacker and cut back weeds along the trail." He explains he usually only cuts one side so the trail moves to the side. It's a conservation measure, so the path is not constantly walked on in only one place.

"I'm amazed the privy is almost filled," he continues. He says it was constructed four years ago and is called a "gazebo." To me it is one of the ugliest privies I've seen on the trail, but I keep this observation to myself. Instead, I tell him, genuinely, "We appreciate everything the trail maintainers are doing."

I hoped the tired feeling and the discomfort in my chest would go away. It didn't. Thought seriously of asking these two guys to drive me to a nearby town so I can end the hike. However, resting makes me feel better at the moment, I think I'll try again. We get back on the trail, start climbing, and almost immediately I struggle breathing. Should have asked those guys to take me with them. Just don't want to leave Jim so abruptly. It would be best if we could make it to Erwin, Tennessee, and I could say goodbye to Jim there. I hike along and continue feeling terrible. Something has to be done.

According to some people, the Native American word *Appalachian* means "endless." To me this has become an endless struggle.

We hiked about twelve miles today. Late in the day we search around in the mountains and find a good spot. Jim is singing as he sets up his tent. I have a growing suspicion this is the last time I will be tenting. There is a steep mountain ahead, and the *Thru-hiker's Handbook* says, "Many thru-hikers find that the stretch from here to Sams Gap is a little *tougher* than it looks on the profile map." On the map I notice a road before the steep mountain. I make my decision, but can't bring myself to say anything yet and spoil Jim's joy of this forest campsite. I try to keep things light, though I know this is the last time Jim and I will cook dinner with each other.

It starts to get dark. I go to my tent. The final night I'll be sleeping in mountainous backcountry.

My morning cough is not any better, neither is the problem in my chest—nor is my itchy, inflamed, fluid-filled, poison-ivy-covered arms and body. I'm a determined person, but sometimes determination has to shake hands with reality.

I have argued against seasoned lawyers, sometimes four or more on the other side. I have been up against tough opponents who represented the largest corporations and governmental agencies. Negotiated settlements with hardened insurance company officials, involving multiple millions of dollars, but you can't negotiate with a steep mountain, can't compromise with a bitter wind to make it milder, can't coerce oxygen into lungs that are clogged and want to cough, can't will away chest discomfort, and can't ignore the miserable itching of your own weeping, sore red flesh. I am losing hold of my dream.

It's the saddest I have been in a long time—mixed with a sense of relief.

April 17, 2002

I'm up before Gorilla, unzip the door to my tent. A thinning morning mist shows sunlight angling through trees. The woods are quiet. A distant fox cautiously crosses the forest floor like an actor in a silent movie. The air is warming. Soon it will be sunny and pleasant. Spring is arriving like a pink blossom opening its petals.

I feel heartsick.

We trudge down the mountain, I'm looking into the valley below for a road. If there is a highway with traffic, you can hear it from miles away. There is no traffic sound, just crickets and a bird whistling. Around mid-morning we come off the mountain and head toward a country lane. Seeing it is bittersweet. This ends what has become a great ordeal. This terminates my dream of completing the A.T., a vicious disappointment.

Walking far ahead I call back to Jim, "Come on down to the road."

We walk downhill to the deserted narrow two-lane road. I take off my backpack and lean it against a tree. Jim catches an anguish in my face he'd never seen before. "I can't go any further. I really detest having to climb these damn mountains day after day. I've been having tightness in my chest—I don't know if it's a sign of my resentment or maybe it's something more significant." As I explain this to Jim, welling despair makes it difficult to form the words—years of dreaming, months of hard exercise and detailed preparation, mammoth expectations—and now, crushing disappointment. I hear myself saying, "I'm just not going any further." It *hits me full blast.* I try to preserve a mask of composure but can't. I take out my red bandana and wipe at my eyes. "It's disappointing." My voice cracks, "I wanted to do this all my life."

It takes the hardened Gorilla man only an instant to softly respond. "I understand. What about your chest symptoms? You think it's anything serious?"

"It's probably nothing. I'm in great health. Had a thorough physical exam before I left. Just hate this damned continuous climbing of mountains—it's not what I expected. I expected this to be a *trail,* like a trail in the woods. Sure, some ups and downs but never strenuous, and certainly not continuously, without a break. I'm really concerned about leaving you, buddy."

"Don't give it another thought. I'll be okay." Jim is kind as a social worker—a part of him I'd seen at times when he offered to help someone. Gorilla continues, "In fact, now I'll be able to do some night hikes—I know you never wanted to hike in the dark, and now I can do it."

"This makes me feel like shit. I never like to give up something I start."

"Be proud of what you've done. You hiked more than three hundred miles over some rough mountains. That's a hell of an achievement."

I had hiked *305 miles* and it all abruptly stopped at Devil Fork Gap, North Carolina.

I expect Gorilla to cross the road and continue on up the Appalachian Trail. Instead, he insists on going into town with me. I tell him it isn't necessary. I think, to some extent, he, too, wants to get off the trail for a while.

We're standing on the border between North Carolina and Tennessee as we had in so many places on our journey along the A.T.'s boundary between the two states. I want to thumb a ride to Erwin, Tennessee. Twenty minutes pass; no vehicles come by. We start walking toward Erwin. This is rural, open area. There are scarcely any houses. The first home we come to, two dogs roam in a field nearby. They bark at us. One is brown, a bloodhound.

We knock on the door. A man, pale, wearing pajamas and a robe, answers. I explain the situation. He responds slow and listless, "Many hikers knock on my door 'cause they can't continue on the trail, and some have medical problems. I'd like to help you guys, but I'm sick myself." He looks terrible. "If I wasn't ailin', I'd drive you to town." He tells us a man farther up the road would probably be home and available to drive us to Erwin.

We continue hiking the small road, and come to a place where men are repairing trucks outside. Several people stand around. I tell one of them the situation and that I'd be glad to pay someone to take us to town. He points to a slender woman close by and says, "Wilma will drive you to Erwin." We thank him.

Wilma is a slender middle-aged woman. Her car looks something like an AMC Gremlin. She opens the trunk, and after Jim puts in his backpack, there's no room for mine.

Wilma, for all her kindness and decency, has allowed the backseat of her car to become a junk bin. "Just move that stuff to one side," she says in an agreeable tone, "and put your pack on top of it."

I shove armfuls of junk to the side and sit on a cleared spot on the backseat. Jim sits up front with Wilma. I have no idea that Erwin is so far away. It takes about twenty-five minutes to drive to the Super 8 Motel.

"You're a lifesaver, Wilma." She beams. "Now, I want to compensate you for helping us out. What would be appropriate?"

"Nothing."

I take out $35.00 and hand it to her for the drive up and back.

"I can't take this."

"You've spent your time and gas. Please take what you want." She reluctantly takes some of the money. We thank her profusely, but she seems a bit uncomfortable about so much praise.

The man who operates the motel introduces himself as C. P. Patel. I call him "Mr. Patel." Jim calls him "C. P." Mr. Patel tells us the closest airport is Tri-City in Kingsport. I call about flights. Jim says he'll call Evelyn to drive us to the airport. I tell him it's not necessary (especially when he told me Evelyn had to travel about three hours to get here). Jim insists and calls her. Evelyn says someone else would charge a hundred dollars to take me to the airport, and she'd be glad to do it for less, and take Jim back to the A.T. I don't like her traveling so far, but she insists.

It's sunny, and the temperature is rapidly rising. It must be in the nineties when we start walking to the Pizza Hut for dinner. Someone had told us it was close—close for them because they're driving. Far for us, walking almost four miles round trip in this hot as hell day. We stop at a convenience store on the way. The guy behind the counter tells us about an Italian restaurant that will deliver to the motel. He offers his phone. We call in an order, buy some beer, and by the time we reach the motel, our food is there. Jim and I drink a few brews, eat dinner at a small table in the room, and talk. About 8:30 Evelyn arrives. She has had a long day, working and driving to Erwin. We talk for a little bit, and then she goes to her room to sleep.

April 18, 2002

We drive to the Tri-City Airport and chat while waiting for my plane. I give Evelyn what she says is very generous compensation for driving me to the airport, taking Jim back to the trailhead, and arranging to have the box of supplies that I sent to the Nolichucky Hostel delivered to my home.

I have mixed up feelings seeing Jim wearing hiking clothes for resuming his hike today. "I'll meet you on the trail in Pennsylvania," I say. "Bring drinks and do some of the things trail angels did for us. Keep in touch so I'll know where you are."

The Gorilla man's face, which was always animated, loses expression. For the moment he is far away, looking over his past life, there is the slightest mist in his eyes. He puts his hands on both my shoulders, his eyes searching me as if he wanted to remember this moment. "You're a great friend—my best friend."

It is like saying goodbye to a brother I might never see again. Standing there in the airport I take hold of Jim's hand to shake it. "This is like the end of the movie Casablanca. This has been the start of a beautiful friendship." I smile. "And, we'll always have Gatlinburg!"

Jim grins, looks at me for a long moment, then slowly says, "It's time to go." We all hug. "When I sign the shelter registers I'll put down 'Gorilla Jim and Avalanche in spirit'." Gorilla looks out the windows at the distant mountains. "I'm determined to make it all the way to Katahdin."

"Do it for both of us," I say, and we turn and walk away.

I sit in the airport, watch them load the plane and think about the last month. I trekked 305 miles and had truly experienced the wilderness. It was a question of how much oozing scratchy poison ivy all over myself could I stand, how many days of putting on cold wet clothes could I tolerate, and how much relentless physical exertion that I had come to detest could I endure, with my breathing problems and chest tightness.

Sure, I went farther than over 50 percent of those who started at Springer Mountain, and only 20 percent make it to Katahdin, Maine. It still hurts.

Sitting and waiting for the plane, I think back to a question Jim asked earlier, "Will you and me ever hike together again?"

I wonder. Will I ever achieve my dream?

April 28, 2002

I return to the office and to practice law. It has been ten days since I last saw Gorilla Jim. He calls at 8:00 a.m. Jim is in the Kincora Hiker's Hostel. The Gorilla man had fallen, injured his knee, and is wearing a brace. Cowboy had also slipped and injured himself. Gorilla tried hiking with several partners, but it didn't work out. He asks, "Do you want to come back to the trail? I'll wait for you to catch up, if you do."

A big part of me aches to return to the trail, but I find myself saying, "I'm not coming back."

What is physically wrong with me? I have to find out and so I go to a pulmonary physician at one of Philadelphia's large university hospitals. They call my condition *dyspnea,* and *DOE* (dyspnea on exertion). They examine me, make me blow into equipment with things that bob up and down with each lungful of air and record the results. They give me pulmonary function tests with flow volume loop, spirometry with bronchodilator response, lung volumes, diffusion capacity, walking oximetry, methacholine challenge, and a thalium stress test. I breeze through everything and pass with flying colors. The exercise test report states for exercise capacity: *Excellent.*

There is no explanation for my symptoms.

So, if I'm so damn healthy—if I exercise for a half hour every morning of my life, if I use gym exercise machines several days a week, if I can bike fifty miles—what the hell is causing *dyspnea* and a tightening in my chest when I hike long distances in the mountain?

I have to know so I do research and find that coal-fired power plants, large factories, and automobiles that burn oil and gas as far away as Chicago, Detroit, Indianapolis, St. Louis, and other cities create sooty air loaded with sulphur dioxide and nitrogen oxide—particles in the air that make for a haze of pollution. Winds blowing into the Appalachians carry these pollutants from the cities of the Midwest, the Southeast, and sometimes the Northeast. This human-made airborne waste is trapped by the mountains and settles into air masses in these high areas. Smog is so impenetrable, it cuts down average visibility in the southern Appalachians by 40 percent in the winter and 80 percent in the summer. In natural conditions visibility is 113 miles; air pollution reduces it to an annual average of 25 miles. During severe conditions, the views are so smudged that visibility is reduced to *under one mile*. This is not natural mist-clouds for which the Smoky Mountains were originally named.

The Great Smoky Mountains have the worst overall air quality of any national park, and with the Shenandoahs has the highest ozone-pollution levels in our national park system.

Even worse for hikers, ozone concentrations are greatest at *higher* elevations.

During the summer of 2002, the year we trekked through the Smokies, they recorded forty-two unhealthy air days—and that surpassed large cities such as Atlanta, Georgia. It was healthier to hike through bus fumes in downtown Atlanta than it was to hike the Appalachian Trail in the Smokies.

Investigators checked the breathing of hikers along a four mile section of the A.T. The hikers filled out questionnaires and blew into breath measuring equipment.

The National Park Service tells us ozone pollution in the Smokies "threatens human health." NPS explains: "Ozone is a powerful respiratory irritant for humans. Research shows that ozone can cause *coughing...chest pains*...even permanent damage to lung tissue...and active adults are most vulnerable."[14]

My conclusion: get the hell away from the Smokies. [Much later I'd find another, easier solution to breathing problems.]

Chapter Sixteen

Gorilla Jim continued his journey northward on the A.T. Occasionally he calls, and I'm glad to hear of his progress. After hanging up I feel sad and empty because I'm not still on the trail. Jim hooked up with a wonderful family from Daleville, Virginia, Homer and Therese Witcher who were hiking the A.T. with their two children, Taylor, eleven, and Bennett, eight years old. The Witcher's progress was being reported by their local newspaper, which put reports and photos on the internet, making it easy for me to follow Jim's progress.

Summer 2002

Jim reaches Pennsylvania and is ready to take a few days off. I arrange to meet him at a crossroad of the A.T. and do trail magic while waiting for him. I hand out energy bars, bottles of Gatorade, soda and water, packages of Lipton's and other foods—I had plenty of it left over. Some hikers I had met when I was on the trail come by, we hug, and I get a huge lump in my throat.

A dark van drives up, the side door slides open, Jim comes out as two other guys exit from the driver's side and passenger side doors.

I yell to Jim, "How are you, you old son-of-a-bitch!"

Jim nods his head toward the two guys getting out of the van, puts his index finger in front of his lips, and quietly hushes me with, "These are church people."

"Oh…How are you?"

Jim had met up with Circuit Rider and Sherlock. Circuit Rider is a minister who hike's the A.T., ministering to hikers.

I drive Jim to our house at the seashore. Barbara eyes him, "You look thin." She attempts to fix that problem with a big meal and ice cream for dessert.

Jim lolls in the sun. He is the only person I know who turned a kayak over and got dumped in a calm cove. He regales us with his adventures on the Appalachian Trail.

At night, he and I sit on the upper deck of our house looking out at the waves of the Atlantic Ocean rolling in, me on my third vodka on the rocks and Jim on his umpteenth beer.

Gorilla looks at me without speaking. Then, "Avalanche. You ever coming back to the trail?"

For a few seconds I couldn't catch my breath. This time it wasn't because of polluted air. I recall warm sunny days atop a bald, looking down on a valley, feeling the success of having climbed, the almost religious experience of reaching a height nearer to whatever we believe in. The evenings cooking pasta with nuts and cheese in it that tasted like dining at the Four Seasons; freedom from the rat race; meeting fantastic people who shared the same dream of getting to a mountain in Maine. "Yeah, someday."

"When you come back, I'll hike it with you."

The same primal urge that originally set me trekking now welled up in me. There was nothing I could say. The waves out on the ocean were blurring.

Late August 2002

Gorilla phones to tell me he is in New Jersey recovering from several broken ribs. Circuit Rider took Jim to his mother's home to recuperate. I drive up to north Jersey to see Jim. Walking gingerly down a step, the Gorilla man winces, but is stoic as ever. I take him to lunch, and driving in my car ask, "What the hell happened to you?"

"We were in New York State. Circuit Rider, Sherlock, and I were taking a group of kids backpacking. We had some free time after lunch. You know I love rock climbing; I saw this great wall of rock and started up. Good handholds and places for my feet. You're not supposed to go higher than twelve to fifteen feet without a mat or belay person. The kids wanted me to climb higher, so I did it."

Jim points up as he relives the moment. "The top of the ledge was about thirty feet. I grabbed one of the rocks and it broke off—I fell backward and hit the side of the ledge, dropped and hit the edge of another ledge. One of the guys tried to catch me; I bounced a little off him, went down a gorge, and stopped when I hit a boulder. Fractured two ribs in front. On the back, near the kidney area, I broke ribs all the way through. They wanted to bring in a medevac chopper, but I said absolutely not. I'd hike out. They said there's no way, you can hike. Finally, they got me up to walk. It hurt with every breath.

"The guys carried my pack, and I hiked out. They had someone meet us at the highway. At the hospital they told me I'd be off the trail for at least twenty-one days. I said I had to be on the trail by Monday, three days away. The doctor laughed. He said, 'All I can do is fix you. You break it, I fix it. I tell you right now, you're crazy! You can never go out in three days.'

Jim shifts uncomfortably in the seat. "That's when Circuit Rider came up with the idea that I go to his mother's house. She doctored me and took care of me because I couldn't lie down."

Watching him involuntarily flinch in pain as he enters the restaurant, I ask, "Think you'll get back on the trail?"

He is walking with slow careful steps. Gorilla stops and looks at me with those solid determined eyes. "You know me. I'll be back in a few days."

Jim did resume hiking shortly afterward. He couldn't lie down. For a while, friends tied Gorilla to a tree at night to keep him from falling over.

Gorilla Jim went all the way to Katahdin, summited it in October 2002.

PART THREE

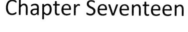

Chapter Seventeen

2003

She is tall, extremely tall. Alluring as she stands, thinly veiled in almost see-through silver mist, revealing enough erotic curves to fire the imagination. Light comes from behind and streaks her edges—bright highlights on suggestions of tresses, breasts, hips. She has gradually awakened and in half-sleep slowly, seductively beckons. It is the pull of a perfectly figured woman—a sex goddess. I hate her. She scorned me before. Trashed my heart—and now she wants me back. Like a crazed dog in heat I rush, blindly, unthinking.

Sure the A.T. is physical—mountains, soil, crushed leaves—but it's also a fantasy, an imagining—a conjured dream, an emotional longing.

During the last several months like a passionate lover overlooks his loved one's faults, her flaws have become invisible to me. As when a person closes their eyes to kiss, my mind shuts off the memory of exhaustingly steep mountains, bitter cold blasting wind, energy-robbing heat, and poison ivy that spit its dermatologic poison on me.

I only recall heart-quickening, sun-drenched mountain high views floating into crystal blue skies.

As I can't resist the pull of gravity tugging me to the face of this planet, so I'm drawn to the Appalachian Trail. I must conquer the A.T.! It is more than a spark. It's flames singe my insides. My thoughts frequently turn to the backcountry, to getting newer and lighter equipment. I must hike smarter—*jettison everything heavy*. In the middle of the night I come out of troubled sleep, thinking of ways to lighten my pack, weighty gear and foods to do without.

I research equipment and read about ultralight backpacking. I order gear: lighter backpack (which fits better than the old pack); lighter tent; combination sleeping bag-pad; headlamp with a tiny battery and headband; insulating layer with fewer ounces; my boots bother me, so I buy lighter footwear that fit a little better.

Using a scale I weigh everything—food and equipment—down to tenths of an ounce. I knocked off more pounds than a pudgy person on a Weight Watchers diet.

Out come the maps. I call Jim in Oklahoma. The quiet winter must have been a big letdown for him. He is eager to hit the trail again. We plan our spring adventure. My buddy, Lou Shane, agrees to drive us to Tennessee where we will pick up where I left off. Jim flies in and we are on our way.

March 21–23, 2003

In the morning we hunt around and find Devil Fork Gap where I left the trail last spring. Jim and I watch Lou drive off. Immediately, we are confronted with a steep mountain. It is extraordinary exertion for my first day back, but I don't have any problems. In sun-sparkling, sixty-degree weather, we trek the ups and downs and along ridges.

Jim and I hike eleven miles for each of the first two days and twelve miles the third day, arriving at the Nolichucky River.

I call the popular Miss Janet's House, a hostel in Erwin, Tennessee. On the trail Miss Janet is revered for her kindness. She has taken in injured hikers and allowed them to stay at her home, some without charge until they heal. Miss Janet is often out shuttling or picking up hikers to bring to her hostel.

She says she'd be along soon to pick us up. We wait at the Chestoa Bridge along with several hikers who had slack packed (hiking without your backpack, which is sent ahead by vehicle) twenty miles. Miss Janet drives up, a large woman with chestnut brownish hair and an easygoing manner. All of us pile in with our gear.

In Erwin on a residential street is a wood-sided house. At the corner of the furniture-scattered lawn is a huge tree with ivy growing up its wide trunk, old boots are used as flower pots with blue, pink, and green vegetation growing out of the age-worn footgear. Hikers love to come up the walk, along this lawn alive with flowers and ivy, onto the green-railed porch with hanging baskets of plants, and into an atmosphere that whispers "homey." Inside, a well-worn living room is filled to capacity, slender bearded distance hikers, legs over the arms of furniture, others sprawled on the floor watching TV, eating pizza out of the boxes, sucking drinks from straws stuck into large plastic cups.

Miss Janet is a laughing, fun-loving person who provides a very hiker-friendly home away from home and treats us like kinfolk. To the younger hikers she is like a trail mom.

She meanders through the house and shows Gorilla and me to one of the many bunk rooms. It is an average-sized bedroom. Along the wall are two bunks made of unfinished lumber. Miss Janet's hostel is overloaded with all kinds of possessions. The room we are in has a heap of blankets in one corner and one of the beds has piles of pillows on it. There are things everywhere—books, tin cans, plastic containers.

In the kitchen, Miss Janet gives one guy a mohawk haircut using a scissors and razor. As she cuts along both sides of his head, brown hair drops all around, the kitchen floor becomes furry.

This evening's entertainment involves several thru-hikers making camp stoves out of beer cans and cat food cans. The workbench is the cream colored Formica kitchen table. Miss J pushes aside paperback books, a white cardboard box, and a glass vase of flowers, produces an electric drill and a pair of scissors. Several hikers excitedly cut and reshape Pabst Blue Ribbon cans into mini-stoves. Then, to test their stoves, they have a contest to see how fast water can be boiled with these homemade burners. In hiking circles, the standard is: How fast a cup of water can be heated to bubbling. There is no measuring cup; someone finds a wine glass to use as a measure. The stoves are set on the Formica kitchen table. Alcohol is poured into them, some of it dripping onto the tabletop. Small camping cook pots are filled with water, the stoves are lit, and the timing begins. During the loud cheering and high-spirited experiment, the lights in the kitchen are sometimes turned off so competitors and onlookers can view the light blue flames in the dark.

There is no door to our room. A piece of cloth is strung across the doorway and periodically someone peeks in—no matter what we are doing—to say hello or ask us a question. At a drowsy 11:30 p.m., four hours later than we usually retire for the night on the trail, half a dozen hikers are still lying around the living room amid pizza boxes, food wrappers, soft drink containers, and other mess. They are watching a sci-fi movie, yelling at the TV screen, screaming at times. This place is like Animal House meets the Appalachian Trail. It's a little too Bohemian and quirky for a pinstriped guy like me, but I have to admit, I'm glad to be here.

March 24, 2003

In the morning Miss Janet makes breakfast: a fruit bowl of strawberries and bananas, scrambled eggs with mushrooms, grits, and bagels. It is delicious.

When he is not on the A.T., Sasquatch—about six feet five inches tall— helps run a program for wayward kids that teaches them how to survive in the woods in all kinds of weather. He drives us to the post office where Jim sends a box of things home to lighten his pack, and I mail to Barbara my extra telephone battery to recharge and a few other items in a large padded envelope.

Sasquatch drives us to the trailhead. We hike uphill out of the Nolichucky River area. It is brilliantly sunny, temperature in the mid sixties. After nine miles, we camp in the woods.

March 25, 2003

Gorilla Jim and I climb lofty mountains this day, including Unaka, which is fifty-two hundred feet. We stop at Beauty spot, an open grass bald with spectacular 360-degree views of Roan Mountain and other grand Tennessee and North Carolina high mountains. This is where hikers watch layers of bluish-pewter sky over distant mountains light up red and purple at sunrise and sunset. Jim and I rest and take in the spectacular scenery.

So far the weather has been perfect, reaching the high sixties. We hike eleven and a half miles and camp in the woods near Iron Mountain Gap.

Jim and I feel good and look forward to a tough climb as we start the ascent to Roan Mountain, the last time we'll trek up above six thousand feet until we reach New Hampshire. According to one guide book, Roan is reputed to be the coldest place year-round on the southern Appalachian Trail.

March 26, 2003

Our typical daily routine: I get up at 5:45 a.m. and Jim gets up at 6:00 a.m. Jim usually eats outside his tent because he likes to cook a hot breakfast. I eat a cold breakfast in my tent, go out and brush my teeth, and then we pack up our stuff. We look at the map and handbook, then decide where we can stop for water. We carry as little water as possible because each quart of water weighs over two pounds, and we want to be light. On this part of the Appalachian Trail there are many springs and streams to get water.

We typically seek a shelter to stop at for lunch and rest or nap for twenty minutes. Then we eat lunch. If there is a spring or stream at the shelter—and if we need it—we filter water, then get on our way.

We try to find a place to camp by 4:00 to 5:00 p.m. At the camping spot, we unload our gear, set up our tents, cook dinner, and clean up from dinner—use baby wipes to clean ourselves. Then I dictate my notes on what happened today. It's a hard thirteen-hour day.

We know very little about what is going on in the outside world. For example, we don't know how the war is going in Iraq. I have a little radio, but it's tough to get reception out here.

Gorilla and I have not seen any hikers for days. By midday it drizzles, mist rolling in. Visibility drops to about one hundred feet.

Temperatures fluctuate and today's winter-cold rain runs down inside my jacket, wetting my skin and giving me a chill. As I slog along, the thing keeping me moving is the thought of what I'll be eating for dinner tonight.

A pad goes on the freezing ground beneath the sleeping bag; otherwise, it's like sleeping on ice. The several-inch-thick air pad should insulate me, but it won't inflate. For three-quarters of an hour I try to inflate it. It stubbornly refuses and only accepts a tiny bit of air. Finally, I put my fleece and mid-layer under the sleeping bag for a small thin area of insulation. During the night every part of me becomes frigid—what little air that was in the pad leaks out. I sit—my butt on a stinging, cussing-cold tent floor—in the dark trying to inflate the pad. I am literally freezing my ass. My flashlight broke the first night we were on the trail. My headlight won't stay on. I try working in the dark, but can't. I put on my fleece to keep from becoming rigidly frozen and sit on my clothing bag for insulation. Eventually, the headlight stays on, and I get enough air in the slender mattress pad to keep some of the cold from getting through to my already marrow-chilled body.

The pad gradually leaks air until I lay on frigid ground. Too tired to do anything else, I'm resigned to be scrunched in the fetal position on the frozen ground.

March 27, 2003

With very little sleep, I wake in a cold, stiff, evil mood. Outside, Gorilla doesn't make it any better by proclaiming, "Got a real *tough hike* ahead of us."

"I don't want to hear about it," I snarl. The night's cold has gotten into the core of my body; my joints are achy and fight against bending. My knees seem frozen and locked.

"Roan's the third highest mountain on the Appalachian Trail. Rough as can be."

I shoot Gorilla a burning glance. "*I don't want to hear about it!*"

The Gorilla man has the map out. "Rough climb—"

"What part of '*I don't want to hear about it*' don't you understand?" My back jolts with every stiff achy movement, and I massage the pain along my spine.

"Hey, Avalanche. Just look at the profile on this map," thrusting the map in my face. "Look here. Highest mountain since Clingman's Dome."

"Do you want to take that map and stick it up—"

"Now, now, I'm just preparing you for the tough climb today."

Walking around in stiff jerky motions, "I don't need to hear how *tough* today's lousy climb is."

The only thing I want is to soak in a hot tub and melt the ice that has fused my joints. After breakfast and packing my gear, I am almost resigned to the ordeal. We start our ascent of Roan. I hear Jim mumbling to himself, "Rough mountain…over sixty-two hundred feet up…a bad climb…"

I just close my ears to it and put one foot in front of the other.

Roan is a strenuous aerobic test. The rugged mountain pathway goes almost straight up about a half mile, with only a brief break at a tiny gap. Then it's "huff and up" again.

The day is cold and windy. A fresh snap of frigid air hits my face, but it does not blow away the sleep deprivation. At the higher elevations there is snow on the ground. Only several inches, enough to make the mountain peaks look like a postcard, and just enough to add to our trudging.

Jim has been muttering, mostly to himself, "This is one bad old mountain...I told you it would be rough." He breathes heavily and gasps for air. Red-faced around his salt-and-pepper beard, he looks at me and says, "Let's take a water break."

Heart pounding, I had been gulping lungs full of air and moving solely on the energy surge you get when you are thoroughly pissed. My own face must be beet red, and I gratefully grab for the water bottle on the front of my backpack. When we both stop, leaning over and panting wildly, Gorilla tears open a package of peanut butter crackers and offers them to me. I hesitate, then take one. I pull out my bag of gorp, hold it out to him; he removes a glove, and I pour some into his hand.

"Rough hike, huh?" he says.

Smiling to myself. "I don't think so!"

We both laugh.

It takes hours to complete the long steep climb to the crest, but we did it. The shelter atop Roan, at 6,285 feet, is the highest shelter on the A.T.

We continue hiking and arrive at the Overmountain Shelter, a large old former hay barn reconstructed with a sleeping loft and spectacular views of beautiful Roaring Creek Valley—range after range of mountains sloping down to a green forest floor. The barn's red exterior boards are cut away in places, providing panoramic views of the mountain and valley.

Gorilla takes one look at the barn and says, "It's loaded with mice. I ain't sleeping here."

"Let's camp over here," I say, eying straw-like weeds growing nearby. I select a spot, drop my backpack, and start pulling up straw to make a thick bed to insulate me if my sleeping pad fails again tonight. The tent is set up over the straw mat.

Four guys on spring break from a University in North Carolina are camped about four hundred feet from us.

The young men come over for a cheerful chat as we eat dinner. They normally like to sleep later, but in this breathtaking location, overlooking majestic mountains and valleys that roll on and on, they want to see the sun come up. The guys ask me to wake them early.

It is 7:20 p.m. The sun has gone. It will be an early night, and I look forward to a good night's sleep. Hopefully, the mattress will stay inflated all night. I'm wearing long underwear because the wind and cold are fierce. All night the wind roars through the valley. The tent shakes with each blast that rushes up at us or comes from mountains above and races down to antagonize anything in the endless gorge below.

March 28, 2003

During the night cloud banks settled around us. I awake early and come out of my tent into a heavy fog. I cannot see seventy-five feet in front of me, so there is no sense in waking the college guys immediately. After we are packed and ready to leave, Jim and I go to their camp. I had told the guys I'd blow my whistle to rouse them. I sound the shrill instrument and say, "The good news is it's first light. The bad news is you can't see anything."

The guys groan either in disappointment about the poor visibility or because they had been awakened so early.

The wind keeps blowing as Gorilla and I start out. Temporarily, the fog thins. We go to the top of mile-high Hump Mountain, which consists of two balds: Little Hump and Big Hump. Each bald has grassy vegetation. The trail is a groove through the undergrowth created by years of trekking boots.

Clouds rush in, darkening vapor cutting our visibility to little more than arm's length. The smothering thick moisture coats my glasses. "Jim, I can't see."

Seventy–mile-an-hour wind is roaring. "What'd you say?" he yells above the gale.

"I can't see ahead." I remove my foggy glasses and wipe them with gloved fingers.

Gorilla could see well enough without his glasses, puts them in his pocket, steps ahead of me, is saying something about taking the lead, but his words are lost in the howling wind. I know this: Gorilla could find the trail blindfolded.

We lean into the wind. I try to stay one step behind Jim. If he gets more than several feet in front of me, he becomes a ghostly Rorschach inkblot and disappears into the madly racing cloud bank.

There are no trees. White blazes are on four by four posts driven into the ground. The winds increase with screaming gusts up to ninety miles an hour now. Jim tries to step over a post blown out of its mooring. He lifts his left leg and, like a top, starts to spin on his right leg. Other posts are thrust to the side at weird angles. I couldn't believe how strong the winds are. It's impossible to stay in the trail's groove. A sideway blast tackles me and I fight to stay on the path. An enormous wind surge throws Jim backward, and I hold out my hands to keep him from falling while bracing to keep us both upright.

These are hurricane-force winds, but this is not Florida. The wind chill is down at fourteen degrees. We are out in the open, no shelter, and we're being shoved around like toys. As I usually do, I'm hiking wearing only a T-shirt, a lightweight polyester shirt, and a thin shell jacket. The cold air runs around the inside of my shirt. I shake with a chill and quickly pull the hood tighter around my head. The coldness chews on my fingertips freezing inside my gloves. Once we are in the storm, and crossing the mountain, we have to go on no matter what.

For over an hour we struggle to keep upright. Around midday we start to descend, and as we drop to lower levels the weather improves. By the time we get down to the highway that will take us to Elk Park, it turns into a decent day. Jim and I pause, look up at the dark clouds blowing across the mountains we had just trekked. What a wild experience; it's too bad we didn't get to see the awesome views from those high balds.

We thumb a ride to a motel in Elk Park. Feeling we're entitled to a really good dinner, I ask the guy if there are any great restaurants around, and he points out one along the way. After checking in at the motel, we hitch a ride to the restaurant in the back of a pickup truck. While waiting for our dinners, three women at the next table, a mother and two daughters, strike up a conversation. The mother says she drove thirty minutes to this restaurant because the food is so good. The waitress brings me the most enormous steak I ever saw. It covers the entire plate. Jim has the same thing: salad, steak, and huge baked potato. The whole meal is only $10.95 a piece.

After dinner, the mother is kind enough to drive us to the motel as they go on their way to an auction. During the drive they tell us snow is expected on Sunday. We ignore this information. Today is Friday.

March 29, 2003

Jim didn't sleep well last night. He was disturbed by people having a fight in the next room. A husband and wife were separating and having a dispute about dividing up their property. The wife called her boyfriend who came and joined in the fray. This went on until 3:00 a.m. With plugs in my ears, I didn't hear any of it.

What a beautiful day. On the trail I can eat like a pig because we are burning thousands of calories every day. Even stuffing myself at buffets like this motel's breakfast, I'm losing weight and have a flat belly.

It's a beautiful thing!

Outside, we talk to Champ, an eighty-year-old gentleman, who offers to drive us to the trailhead, which is very helpful since the trailhead is two and a half miles from the motel. Champ is in some kind of business where they dig bushes, trees, and vegetation and sell them. He is waiting for someone to arrive to work with him today. We wait with Champ, our backpacks leaning against the motel wall. The other guy pulls into the parking area driving erratically, wobbles out of his car, and staggers over to Champ. With watery eyes and a scraggly beard, he challenges Champ in a slurring voice, "I hain't gonna shave 'til the firsht of April."

We put our things in the back of Champ's pickup truck and get into the cab. As we move down the highway, Champ says, "He's been drinking. I don't wanna work with him today. I'll just lose him," and puts the accelerator to the floor, shooting the truck away from the other vehicle.

❖ ❖ ❖ ❖ ❖

We hike through a former pasture, vast sloping grasslands, grass rippling with warm wispy breezes, making the meadow alternately darker or lighter depending on how the sun hits the waving blades of pasture coverage. Our pathway is a mere indentation in the swaying green, an occasional distant small white mark on a tree or post to aim for. In places, stones are piled into a gigantic rock garden. I amble through the meadow, lazily thinking of black and white cows that had grazed here. A flight of birds chirping overhead, leisurely circle and alight in the branches of a far away tree. The pasture rises in the direction we're hiking. On the rise's high point, we look back across emerald and jade land and up to mountains we crossed in yesterday's fog.

The air has a slight mowed grass essence, clear, sparkling. It's the kind of day you expect nature to fan out its blossoms in a rush of colorful spring flowers. Unlike early yesterday, the sky is now a scrubbed clean baby blue. Today the sun bathes distant mountains with golden light. We take our packs off and sit in broad warm sunshine. Jim drinks heartily—gulp after gulp—from a plastic water container. I take photos of the pastoral scene.

As we hike to higher elevation, the day turns dark, wet, and cooler.

We come to a relocation—a part of the trail that was moved to a different location. A sign informs us they added four miles to the Appalachian Trail, part running along the Elk River.

Because of the relocation we're not certain how far we trekked today; we went anywhere from twelve to fourteen miles. We set up camp in the woods in a cold drizzle. While Jim is bending his main tent pole down to the ground, it breaks. For twenty minutes we try to figure out how to fix it—otherwise, Jim has no tent! The problem is solved when Gorilla makes a splint for the broken pole out of an aluminum tent stake. He bends the stake to match the curve in the tent pole and duct tapes it firmly to the pole. Did you know most hikers carry a strip of duct tape wrapped around a water bottle or hiking pole to use in these kinds of emergencies?

The drizzle lightens enough so we can cook dinner outside.

Tomorrow we expect to get an earlier start and make it to the Kincora Hiker's Hostel. (How wrong I am.)

Chapter Eighteen

March 30, 2003

During the night I wake to a swishing sound outside the tent—sounds like something moving. It must be a creature, the side of the tent is pushed in by it. I yell to scare the thing away, but the swishing and scraping sound continues. It's cold. The crescent moon is bright enough to create a shadow on the outer surface of the tent. I hit the right side of the tent to chase away the creature, and it slides down to the ground. At the base of the tent there is now a large shadow.

I'm slowly becoming aware of what's happening. I tap the tent's left side and hear the same sliding, scraping sound. The rain has turned to *snow*! What I think is an animal is a white buildup on the side of the tent. The snow's weight bends in the tent and my tapping the sides releases it. As the accumulated snow slides down, it sounds like an animal.

I go back to sleep believing the snowfall would stop. At 5:30 a.m. I'm awake and out of the sleeping bag, still hearing the snow falling. I eat one-third of my usual breakfast, figuring if we get stranded here, we might have to go on one-third rations. We wouldn't really know until it gets lighter, and we can assess the situation.

I turn on my little radio, trying to find information about how much snowfall we're going to have. Through static and fadeouts all I can get is Christian radio, and only briefly enough to hear part of a request for contributions.

The sky is dark turning purple just before the orange of daylight breaks through. Stepping out of my tent my boot sinks into a soft blanket of nearly seven inches of snow. Trees are coated in white; narrow saplings bend under weight of the snow. Rhododendron are engulfed in a light pearl-colored coat. The rising sun suddenly sparkles through falling flakes and lights the scene like the beginning of a Broadway show. Jim's tent—no longer tan—is completely covered. If I didn't already know where it was located, I might not have noticed it at all.

I walk through this Currier and Ives Christmas card, stand in front of Gorilla's tent and announce, "Wake up, Jim. It's snowing."

"What?"

"Snowing. White stuff."

It didn't take more than a few minutes and Jim emerges from his tent, laughing. "Al, you aren't gonna believe this. You know how much liquid I drank yesterday? Well, it all wanted to come out during the night. I had to take a leak so bad. Anyway, you know I usually go outside, insert the catheter, and let the pee flow out the end of the tube. Well, last night it was freezin' cold. I *wasn't* going out of the tent. Instead, I put the catheter in, unzipped the tent door, stuck the end of the tube outside, and pissed. Oh, it felt so good not having to go out."

Jim was reenacting putting the tube outside. "What I forgot was, earlier my boots were wet and muddy, so I left them outside the tent." His index finger gestures the path of the tube outside the tent and an arc downward from it. "When I took a piss, the pee went outside...*into the boots*." Jim laughs at this.

I stand there dumbfounded at the thought of him trying to clean up this mess.

He looks at me. "Don't you get it? I pissed all over my own boots!" and he laughs again.

The absurdity hit me. Last night Gorilla broke his tent pole, performed an actual *Piss in Boots*, and now we're stuck in a frigging snowstorm. What else could I do! The laughter burst out of me.

When I laugh, he laughs harder. Then we both howl so hard that the snow shakes loose from nearby trees.

When silly time was over, we consider whether it would be best to pack up and try to get to the hostel or stay where we are. We look around. As though megatons of flour had been dumped over everything to boot-top height, it is impossible to see the trail. The blazes are hidden by sagging trees and rhododendron branches heavy with a thick white coat. The last thing we wanted to do was to get lost in snowfall. The temperature is in the twenties.

We are anxious to know how much snow is predicted. I tried my cell phone, but can't reach anyone. I could not even get the operator. I remember my brother, Arnie, saying on his cell phone you could always get through to 911, so I give it a try. Surprisingly, I get an operator, but it is difficult for him to hear me. I tell him where we are and get cut off. I call again and get cutoff. On the third call he connects me to Carter County Rescue Squad where I speak to Lisa, and I get cutoff. I call 911, and they patch me through to Lisa again. She says, "As you speak, stand still. *Don't move.*"

I stand perfectly still and tell her our situation.

She says, "It's going to snow all day and into the night. The temperature will drop into the teens."

"Should we hike out or stay here?"

"Where you located? Do you have a GPS?"

"No GPS. We're on the A.T. north of Walnut Mountain Road," I say, repeating what Gorilla and I had figured our position to be.

"Stay put. A rescue squad is coming out to get you."

Those words cut through me like an axe. I didn't think we were in danger until she said *rescue squad is coming out to get you.* I feel sick and gripped with uncertainty. I say shakily, "Can't we hike out and meet them somewhere?"

"Stay where you are. Do you have warm clothes?"

"Sure."

"Dress warm and stay put." Lisa's voice is professional, "*They'll come and get you.*" Her words signal a peril worse than we know. "Leave your cell phone on and we'll contact you periodically." The connection breaks off.

A lonely and desperate feeling I had felt once before, long ago, hits me with a thud.

Just below the surface of our consciousness is a storehouse of emotions whose doors sometimes are flung open. This is such a moment. I believe we won't die here in the snowy mountains, but we need to be rescued, which means we are in danger. Strangers will come to save us—from what? That's what scares me. For a moment I am deeply emotional, shaking, almost frantic—then it passes.

It is cold and Jim has gone back into his tent. Through the nylon wall I tell Jim of my conversation. His only reply is, "Uh huh."

If snowfall continues at the rate it is coming down now, by the end of the day we will be in two feet of snow, and deeper tomorrow. It will be a bad situation because if the rescue squad doesn't find us, we could be stuck here for days.

My tent is caving in because of snow accumulating on the sides. I clear the snow off with gloved hands—amazed at how heavy it gets when packed—and adjust the lines in front and back to make it tauter. The rear stake is coming loose. The last thing I want is for it to come out and the whole tent to collapse. With my boot heel I pound the peg back into frozen ground.

Inside my sleeping bag it's comfortable. A short time passes, I check the radio again and get a weather forecast: snowfall to continue all day, all night, and into tomorrow morning. The announcer goes through a list of churches canceling services due to the weather. The temperature in Boone is twenty-eight degrees, dropping into the teens tonight. It'll be much colder up here at this elevation. It is snowing about an inch an hour.

Four hours go by. Snow is piling up. The temperature inside my tent is now near freezing. Even in the sleeping bag, I'm starting to feel cold. I keep patting the top and sides of the tent to knock snow off so the accumulation won't crush the nylon walls. Also, I want the rescuers to see my lime-yellow tent. Covered with snow, in this white world and only several dozen feet off the trail in the woods, they wouldn't be able to find us.

I first spoke with Lisa around 7:30 a.m. I try calling again a few times from inside my tent, but the reception was terrible. At 11:40 I put on my jacket and go outside to try to get a better signal. I finally reach Lisa and ask, "Why is it taking so long for someone to get here?"

"The snow is deep," was her answer. "The rescue party is on its way. They had lots of snow to get through and it's taking longer than they expected." So we wait.

Around 1:30 p.m., we still haven't seen any rescue people. Jim and I wonder if we should just get moving on our own or stay put.

I go out of my tent to call again. Two people are approaching, a tall man with a day pack loaded with gear and a walky-talky radio and a young woman in a tan parka. "Are you the rescue people?"

They are and introduce themselves as George and Laura-lee. Using their GPS, they determine our exact location. They radio back to Carter County Rescue Squad and decide the closest place to get out is one and two-tenths miles away. They arrange for someone to be at that point with a four-wheel-drive vehicle. Jim and I take down our tents, shake off as much snow as we can, pack up our stuff, and begin hiking out, following George and Laura-lee. By this time, the snow is much deeper, about fourteen inches.

Deep snow makes hiking slow, particularly tough going uphill. I stoop to go beneath a low hanging branch, the top of my backpack hits it showering me with white powder. We stop to check where we are. Where is the trail? Everything looks the same—a ghostly albino landscape. We step into drifts that are thigh deep.

We make it to a backcountry road where Kim and some other rescuers meet us in a large green vehicle with the emblem of the U.S. Forest Service and LAW ENFORCEMENT stenciled on the side. We move in four wheel drive along woods and fields covered with a deep mantle of snow to a road that had been cleared.

They pull up to a brown building with a sign over the entry that reads CARTER COUNTY RESCUE SQUAD, and EMERGENCY 911 on the door. As I sit in the warmth of the cozy interior sipping the best hot chocolate I'd had in years, they tell us how they operated. They sent three rescue teams out. Although, they knew approximately where we were, they wanted to make sure they found us. One group came in from below us, another came in from above, and a third team went farther up to make sure they didn't miss us.

As Jim sips a second cup of coffee and I enjoy a second cup of rich and creamy, dark hot chocolate, we chat and joke occasionally.

One of them says, "You're among the most pleasant people we ever rescued."

"If I'd known the hot chocolate was so good, I would have been here earlier." But as I spoke, deep inside I knew we had avoided a potential disaster.

A man walks through the group around us, stops in front of Jim and me. In slow, deliberate words, he says, "You get lost out there in the snow..." his face is near mine, "...you're a dead man."

Someone else, leaning back in a chair added with a Tennessee accent, "Might not find you till a thaw. You'd be long frozen…board stiff."

That's why every time I spoke to Lisa on the phone, she said, "Stay warm and *stay put!*"

They took us to the Comfort Inn Motel, close to a strip shopping center—and several restaurants. John Burleson is a supervisor known as "Pee Wee." He is about five feet ten inches, weighs in somewhere near two hundred pounds, and is powerfully built—and in case of a fight, I want him on my side. Later that day we get a call from Pee Wee. "The local TV station wants to interview you guys. Do you mind if he comes over?"

"Will the publicity help the rescue squad?" I ask.

"Sure will."

"Okay. Send him over."

A cameraman from WJHL News Channel 11 arrives, sets up a tripod and large TV camera in our room, and interviews us. We don't get to see the broadcast, but the following appeared on WJHL News' website:

Snow Surprises Hikers, Unexpected Weather Causes Hikers To Seek Shelter.

It was a cold night for two hikers on the Appalachian Trail.

Al Dragon and Carl Saxton camped just north of Walnut Mountain last night. Seven people from the Carter County Rescue Squad helped locate the men. Dragon and Saxton say the snow took them by surprise.

"Last night when we pitched our tents it was raining, we didn't think it was going to snow. Surprisingly enough during the night we heard the snow and we got up this morning and it was about seven inches," said Dragon.

"Never believe the weather. The weather might start in the morning where it's sunny and you think all you need is a pair of shorts and a T-shirt," said Saxton.

With the snow, these experienced hikers needed a lot more clothing than that.

> They are safe and warm tonight in a Carter County
> hotel.

Jim doesn't like the idea of being rescued. If anyone is going to rescue anybody, Gorilla is going to do the rescuing. He looks upon our deliverance from the deepening snow with such annoyance, that whenever the subject comes up, he says: "I didn't need any rescue." But then neither did we need to get permanently lost in a deep snowy nightmare.

March 31, 2003

Today I call Pee Wee to ask about the conditions in the mountains. Instead of telling me, he offers to show us. Pee Wee drives us up a tiny one-lane mountain road, just two frozen tracks in the snow. Even in four-wheel drive the SUV skids a bit as we drive alongside shear drop offs. Several times he backs up to show us something or to get back to an intersecting road or jeep trail, each time he comes alarmingly close to the mountain's edge. At the motel the snow is disappearing, but up in the mountains it is still deep. We take Pee Wee's advice and decide to wait a few days, until the temperature rises, before returning to the A.T.

Jim had a groin pull climbing through yesterday's deep snow, so it is just as well that he rests today.

We stroll around the town. Elizabethton prospered in the 1920s when two rayon mills employed thousands of workers. The last rayon manufacturer closed in the 1990s. It is painfully obvious how devastatingly this affected the local residents.

April 1, 2003

Gorilla and I spend the morning cleaning our gear and packing up. We ached to return to the Appalachian Trail, frozen or not.

Late in the afternoon Pee Wee stops by to show us on a map where he will put us back in the woods tomorrow.

Pee Wee has a "rugged guy next door" quality that made us enjoy talking to him. He gladly tells us stories about the area. He mentions that the Ku Klux Klan is still active. This summoned up horrid visions of late 1800s and early 1900s lynchings of people. Perhaps the most bizarre hanging in

Tennessee, though, was not by the KKK, and was not of a human being, but it was in an Appalachian Trail town.

On September 12, 1916, the circus came to Kingsport, Tennessee. A drifter, Red Eldridge, was hired as an elephant handler. He was taking Mary, a five ton Asian elephant, to a pond to drink and splash with the other elephants. Mary reached down to pick up a watermelon rind to nibble on. Eldridge jabbed the elephant behind the ear with a stick. Mary grabbed Eldridge with her trunk, and threw him against the side of a drink stand. She walked to where he lay on the ground, set her foot on his head, crushing it.

There were many onlookers, but Mary calmed down and did not charge them. A crowd began chanting, "Kill the elephant! Kill the elephant!" A local blacksmith, probably revved up by the mob, fired a number of shots at Mary, and so did the Sheriff, without any effect on the enormous creature.

Newspapers spread the claim that *Murderous Mary* had killed other circus workers in the past. The circus moved to Erwin, Tennessee, amidst growing rumors of Mary's attack. The leaders of several nearby cities threatened to cancel the circus show in their towns if Mary kept performing. Public pressure against the animal grew to enormous portions. The show's owner decided to save the circus by killing the elephant in a spectacular public display.

September 13, 1916, was rainy and foggy. On this gloomy day Mary was taken to the railroad yard at Erwin. More than twenty-five hundred people assembled to watch Mary being hung. Children were frightened but wanted to see the lynching. Men placed a chain around Mary's neck, attached it to a one-hundred-ton derrick used to hoist railroad cars. The elephant was lifted off the ground—the chain snapped with the attempt to raise the five ton elephant. Mary fell to the ground, sickeningly breaking her hip. At the sight of the huge loose elephant, the crowd ran in a panic. A heavier chain was attached to Mary's neck. The long and sturdy steel railroad crane strained and slowly hoisted the huge animal, chain links digging into her neck, until she was six feet off the ground—hanged to death.

Chapter Nineteen

April 2, 2003

This morning Pee Wee picks us up at the motel and drives us up the mountain. He's my height with an additional thirty pounds of solid muscle. I suppose they call him *Pee Wee* the same as big guys are sometimes humorously called *Babe*. His real name is John, and he is in charge of rescue operations for the Carter County Rescue Service. He is also in charge of the SWAT team.

On the way to the trail, he talks about this area of Tennessee. I ask him if there are still family feuds like the Hatfields and McCoys. He says that some families burn out the houses of other families with which they're feuding. He then tells us about the time a prison work detail was cleaning a cemetery when one of the prisoners decided to escape. The prisoner took a broom handle and broke a guard's collar bone. The escapee made it up a hill where a farmer held the prisoner at bay with a shotgun. When the sheriff and his men arrived to arrest the man, he would not surrender and shook the broom handle at them. The sheriff said he wanted to handcuff the man, but the prisoner responded, "If you come near me I'm gonna cut you!" The sheriff pulled a gun from his holster, aimed at the man's chest and said, "Either you let me handcuff you, or I'm going to shoot you." When the prisoner refused, the sheriff pulled the trigger and shot the man through the shoulder, then said to his deputies, "Take this man to the hospital, get him fixed up, get me back my bullet, and take him to jail."

We pull to a stop on a dirt road. I put my camera on the vehicle's hood, use the time delay, and take a photo of the three of us, Jim's arm around

Pee Wee's shoulder. Then this burly guy takes hold of my hand, shakes it strongly, looks me in the eyes and says, "Be safe."

Jim and I turn and go into the woods, and we hear John's vehicle driving away.

There is still some snow at these higher elevations. The weather is magnificent, temperature rising close to seventy degrees. Gorilla and I walk without jackets, and the sun melts the remaining snow into little streams

Jim wants to visit Kincora Hiker's Hostel owned by Bob and Pat Peoples. Bob is a delightful man with a mustache and twinkling eyes. Bob and Pat are trail angels who transport hikers, fix them up when they are injured, and spend time repairing the trail. He tells us that the day we were stuck in the snow, one thru-hiker came in wet, cold, *close to being hypothermic*. They put him in a hot shower and gave him food.

Jim and I hike to Laurel Falls. It is the biggest waterfall I've seen, easily taller than a five-story building. These high cascading waterfalls drop from one level to another, kiss the rocks with a splatter, drop to a ledge below, splashing, dropping repeatedly.

We find a campsite nearby and all night listen to the water gushing a hundred feet away.

April 3, 2003

We enjoy the symphony of water with our breakfast. Gorilla and I leave Laurel Falls, walk along the roaring, rushing river—rapids of sharp rocks splashing white foam into blue water.

We hike a few miles to U.S. Rt. 321 and eat lunch at a picnic area. The sun is bright. It's hot, eighty degrees, temperature rising. The Appalachian Trail temperatures are definitely rebounding up. After lunch, on a shaded hillside I go through the provisions to decide if we have enough foodstuff to get us to Rt. 421 a several day's hike; and, if we cut rations, all the way to Damascus, about four days away.

While I'm assessing our food, Jim talks to Charles, an early-twenties local resident who is playing with his dog. Jim and I need additional supplies and Charles offers to drive us to Hampton, Tennessee, two and a half miles away. Charles' car is old and looks beat. Charles sticks a screwdriver through a hole in the trunk lid to open it. We throw our backpacks in.

His dog, Cody, a German Shepherd, formerly a police dog, sits up front. Gorilla and I sit in the back, my feet on jumper cables and other stuff.

Charles takes us to a grocery store. Jim stays outside with Charles and the dog; it is so bloody hot they leave the car doors and windows open, then try standing outside in the shade. I go in, look along the limited shelves of food, and get enough supplies for an extra day's rations for Jim and me. Through the store's open door I yell to Charles, "What would you like?"

"A Mountain Dew and a chocolate bar," he answers in a soft voice. He consumes these items while I check out. Cody, the German Shepherd, watches our every move. On the way back to the picnic area, I tell Charles to stop at a gas station, and we buy some gas in appreciation for him driving us back and forth in this sizzling heat.

We hike, sweating profusely. At the Watauga Lake Shelter, I take off my backpack and lie on the floor. The sweat from my T-shirt leaves a long wet mark on the floor. After resting I say to Jim, "Let's get water at the creek."

"No," he says. "No sense carrying water weight. There'll be water at Watauga Lake near the dam; we'll get it there."

I drink the little water I have, and we trek a sweat-soaking mile or more to the dam. Watauga Lake Dam is about thirty stories high. When completed, it was the highest rock and earth filled dam in the world. Two million cubic yards of rock are steeply piled up its two sides. Nitramon explosives were used to blast the rock from three quarries. One blast alone—over half a million pounds of nitramon—was the largest detonation of its kind in history for the amount of explosives used.

Two mountains drop down to cradle Watauga Lake between them, its placid waters shimmer blue or green, depending on whether you see the blue reflection of the sky or the green mirror image of foliage covered mountainsides. The Appalachian Trail goes across the top of the dam. We stop hiking and look down at this colorful water—it's surface about two hundred feet below!

The dam has sharply steep sides. It holds back a sixteen-mile-long lake far beneath us. The Gorilla man stares over the edge down the precipitous slope. "I'll climb down and get water."

I look almost straight down the sheer wall to rocks far away at the dam's base. No one could safely climb down such steep sides without sliding and falling to a bone-crushing death. "Are you nuts?"

"Well, I said we could get water here, and there are no springs or streams nearby," Gorilla says with disgust. He looks up in the direction of the blazing sun. "We gotta get water."

"There's no way you're going down there!"

"I could climb down carefully."

"A mountain goat couldn't climb down carefully!" I pull the brim of my hat downward to shield my eyes from the glaring sun and search the trail going north—a quarter mile away several construction men are working on a road. "Maybe we can get some water from them."

We hike north, approach a crew working on rock slides and tell them of our water predicament. A man in a sweat soaked T-shirt says, "You just missed the truck with the water container....Left about twenty minutes ago."

"Any water available around here?" I ask.

"Only at Vandeventer Shelter," which we know is over five steamy hot miles upward.

In this brain melting heat there is no way we can hike five miles uphill without water. One of the men says, "There's some kinda public place, mile or so up the road. You could get water there."

Jim and I start to hike up the steep road. I stop to wipe away sweat that's trickling down my face like there's a leak in my hat. My mouth is dry. We are both tongue-hanging-out thirsty. One of the workmen we spoke with, Randy, drives up the road, stops, and leans out the window of the heavy duty pickup truck. "I'll drive you up to the water and bring you back."

We gladly throw our gear into the bed of his construction truck, and he drives us over a mile upward to a visitor's center with a magnificent view that overlooks the lake. Most important, it has a restroom with running water. From the sink faucets Jim and I fill our water bottles, greedily drink, and fill them again. This is a golden opportunity to run water over my overheated head and to wash away the salty mess from my face.

We take our treasure of water and get into the back of the construction pickup, happy to share the cargo area with huge rocks that are its main load.

Randy drives us almost all the way back. We get our stuff and thank Randy for the ride. He's a godsend.

We resume where we left off, climbing a ways, then we drop down into Iron Mountain Gap where we find a place to erect our tents. Our hike today was almost fourteen miles.

After dinner I'm sitting on a rock near a dirt road, micro cassette recorder in hand, dictating my notes for the day. Two guys come by in a pickup truck. The driver asks me, "Seen any turkeys?" He realizes I don't quite get it. "It's turkey season."

"No. Haven't seen any turkeys."

"Ya know," he says, "see that small ridge just to your right." I look at a small rise about two hundred yards away. "Last year at this time I seen two huge bears there. One of 'em must a gone at 650 pounds."

"Really," I say and look up in that direction as if the bears might still be there. Then I tell the men about running out of water, and Jim wanting to climb down the sheer face of the Watauga Dam.

"Whatchu say, man?"

"My buddy, Jim, wanted to climb down the side of the dam to get water."

(Having no contact with the outside world, we aren't thinking much about the war in Iraq. Unknown to us, today the president reported our armed forces are moving toward the outskirts of Baghdad. There is concern for another 911 tragedy in the U.S. by chemical, biological, or nuclear terror.)

"Don'chu know this dam is heavily guarded because a what's goin' on in the world?"

I hadn't thought about this: Guards with rifles might have suspected Jim was going down the face of the dam to place explosives or put chemicals or biological material in the water—and shot him.

"And, know what's in them rocks at the base of that dam? *Copperheads*, that's what."

I envision Jim first being shot—falling to the rocks below—and then deadly copperhead snakes' fangs grabbing his bullet-riddled body and injecting it with poisonous venom.

Later, I told Jim of this conversation. It was the first time I'd seen the Gorilla man speechless.

April 4–5, 2003

We hike twenty-six miles in two days. It rains. The temperature on the Appalachian Trail is like a roller-coaster. It drops into the low forties. We are spurred on by thoughts of being in Damascus on April 6th and getting a shower after five days, washing clothes, and getting a few good meals. Damascus also means we will be leaving Tennessee and entering a new state, Virginia.

Deep in the forest, far from anywhere, we stop our rush and pause. There stands the remnants of a fireplace chimney, alone just like the lonely figure it memorializes. This is the Nick Grindstaff monument, the remainder of his cabin fireplace, a stone plaque imbedded into it with this epitaph to that backwoods hermit:

UNCLE

NICK GRINDSTAFF

Born

Dec. 26, 1851

Died

July 22, 1923

He lived alone, suffered alone,

and died alone.

April 6, 2003

We're so motivated to get to Damascus, Virginia, we move fast and arrive there by 11:00 a.m. I don't want to stay at the hostel, which is popular among the younger folks. We go to the Mt. Rogers Outfitters and a man there tells us about a bed-and-breakfast called the Lazy Fox Inn. "It's an extremely nice place. The breakfast is so extensive, you'll want to take a picture of it."

When Jim and I hear this, we say, "Yeah, let's do that." The man calls the Lazy Fox; they have an opening, which is fortunate for us. They are usually filled up.

On a side street in Damascus is a large, neatly painted white house. It has a big columned porch across the front. The lawn is perfectly mowed and decorated with lily-white wrought-iron furniture perfect for someone to sit on and drink iced tea. The arm of a wooden post in front holds a sign showing a fox curled up at rest and the words *Lazy Fox Inn*. A shorter arm on the post holds a small bird house. Behind the house a broad babbling creek flows by and a hammock is stretched between trees, inviting a tired hiker to join the lazy fox in a warm spring day snooze. Two trees grow from one common origin. Around the base, large crimson flowers hold their faces up to the sun. Turf surrounding the house is emerald green, and the exterior is beyond tidy.

Walking past rocking chairs on the porch and into the house, you'd think you're at your grandmother's home—if your grandma lives in a large five or six bedroom house decorated by *House and Gardens*, and kept immaculate by the staff at the Ritz. The living room has a brick fireplace with replicas of foxes on the mantelpiece. The chairs and sofa have extra throw pillows to make you comfortable.

What makes us most comfy is a lovely middle-aged woman with curly blond hair, a modern grandma, who happens to be a superlative chef. She walks up and introduces herself. "I'm Jenny Adams. My husband, Ben, and I own this place." Jenny wears a smile and a white apron that has a fox on it and the words *Lazy Fox Inn*. She continues to talk as she walks us through the house to the dining room. "You guys hungry?" Jenny asks, knowing this is the most unnecessary question ever asked of constantly ravenous thru-hikers. Several guests are getting up from the morning meal. Jenny continues, "You're welcome to have some of the leftovers from breakfast."

We are overpowered by scents that could only come wafting from a French bakery and five star restaurants. Jim and I look at the long dining room table. "Leftovers" are serving dishes of scrambled eggs, hand-sliced ham, a wonderful combination of baked grits and cheese, biscuits with gravy, yellow and red tomatoes, a sweet apple concoction, peach cobbler, strawberries with whipped cream, apple butter, strawberry jam, and other things that my mind cannot take in because it is busy telling my mouth not to salivate. Jim looks at this flavorful feast, and his eyes can't stop blinking. We have left our backpacks on the porch and hurry to the table like two stray dogs rushing to a heaping bowl offered by a kind stranger.

In the dining room's homey elegance, we try to look like we are dining. We're suppressing a gluttonous need to devour everything on that glorious table. When Gorilla and I finish reaching for platters, spooning food onto plates, repeating the phrase, "Man, this is good," we sit back in our chairs. It is such a fabulous meal that I've decided I'm never leaving.

Jenny comes back to clear the table and chat with us. Jim rises, says, "This is a beautiful thing," gives her a kiss on the cheek, and starts to help take the empty platters from the table.

We had just gone to culinary heaven. Getting up, I say to Jenny, "I didn't know you could get food this good on earth," and join in clearing the table.

After Jenny shows us to our room, Jim takes our filthy clothing to the Laundromat to be washed. I go to the outfitter to pick up the box of supplies Barbara sent us. While there, I buy a few things. When checking out, Dave, the owner of Mt. Rogers Outfitters, tells me there's a place about fifty miles up the trail where we can go into town to get resupplied or to forward some things. (I don't know if it's because he didn't ask me if I needed anything else or I just forgot to respond, but I didn't say anything about twenty-one-year-old legs and lungs.)

Back at the Lazy Fox, we each pack enough meals for a four-day trip, plus some emergency rations in case something happens. (Jim heard there is a forecast of some snow.)

For dinner, Jim and I are craving pizza at the Italian restaurant several blocks away. We stand at the front door looking out at a rain shower. Jim says, "I don't want to walk in the rain."

Jenny's son, Ben, overhears Jim and laughs, "I have two thru-hikers here who are afraid to walk two blocks in the rain. Don't worry, I'll drive you." And he does.

At the restaurant other thru-hikers are sitting in booths, and we all talk to each other across the backs of the cubicles. We previously met some of them at Miss Janet's. A guy in his early twenties, real slender with a long beard and a red bandana around his head says, "I did thirty-two miles today," which is unheard of at this point along the A.T.

"You're gonna burn yourself out or get shin splints or stress fractures," Jim advises, with the experience of seeing other high-mileage hikers break down last year. The bandannaed hiker pauses only for a moment, then continues eating a slice of pizza.

April 7-8, 2003

This morning we come into the dining room to a knockout spread of food on the table. This is one of the most memorable meals I ever had. Our stomachs beg to stay, but our feet want to get back on the trail. I hug and kiss Jenny and we say our goodbyes.

We hike along the Virginia Creeper trail, a former railroad bed, which has had the tracks removed and has been paved over with gravel for bike travel. It's a scenic path along a roaring waterway with rapids and waterfalls. Many steel trestles and wooden bridges cross the pristine trout streams. People rent mountain bikes and are driven to the top of the Virginia Creeper trail, then bike down on this gradually descending and beautiful bike path—seventeen miles to Damascus or thirty-four miles to Abingdon.

We go higher and higher, the roaring water becomes farther behind until it disappears.

We cross one creek, water so high it covers the stepping stones. As I stride from one submerged stone to another, my boot slides on the slick surface and I start to tumble forward. I am falling toward the bank. With a loud splash my lower body lands in the water, and my chin strikes the bank. Fortunately, there is mud there instead of rocks. I am shaken for a moment, but no harm done. Just a muddy face.

We reach the Lost Mountain Shelter where there are a number of young thru-hikers. One of them tells us, "We slack packed from…" (there is a hubbub of noise in the shelter) "…north of here." These alleged thru-hikers do not carry backpacks. Some have only small fanny packs. The slackers carry water and a little food for the day.

They were driven to the highest point and hike downhill—carrying next to no weight. (I read once in *Backpacker* magazine that a synonym for slack packing is "barebacking," and "all-around lame-ass mo-fo.") I say to Gorilla, "How lazy can you get and still say you *backpacked* the Appalachian Trail?"

"It depends, Avalanche." Jim recalls his own injuries on the trail. "Sometimes you can't carry your full load, and you have to depend on others. Everyone has to hike their own hike."

There are healthy and vigorous guys and gals nearby. "These people are better able to carry a backpack than I am," I say remembering the trouble I had the day before climbing, hauling a heavy backpack out of Damascus.

"I admire you, Al. You're determined to carry a full pack all the way."

"I don't think I could honestly say I thru-hiked the Appalachian Trail if I strolled through it just carrying my lunch."

"Everyone's different, my friend. Each person has the right to decide what's their hike."

Yesterday, when I told Jim I was getting worn out, he said, "Shorten your steps climbing up. And, take your time." Jim tells me something else that really changes the way I hike. Looking at the belt of my backpack that goes tightly around my waist, Jim says, "When you're climbing, loosen the hip belt."

"Why?"

"A tight belt around your midsection restricts your deep breathing."

"Okay, Sarge." I follow his recommendation. Damned if he isn't right! Though today is a much tougher course, with greater elevation gains, I hike fourteen miles without being exhausted. *Then it hits me:* Last year's breathing problems may have been partly due to the ill-fitting backpack. Each time the pack had sagged, I tightened the hip belt, restricting my diaphragmatic breathing!

We leave the Lost Mountain Shelter and start the steep trek upward. The weather worsens. Rain gets colder and wind driven. The Gorilla man and I are climbing into clouds and are being pelted by sleet. Each of us wears only a thin shirt over a T-shirt. Rainy and nasty like this, we have to stop and put on just our shells. The insulating layer would be too hot. The exertion of climbing will keep us warm, but when we stop, we'll have to put on a warm mid-layer or risk hypothermia.

Gorilla and I continue to ascend the mountain. As we go higher, conditions deteriorate. Approaching Buzzard Rock at Whitetop Mountain, elevation over fifty-one hundred feet, the winds are seventy miles an hour, blowing me off the trail. Sleet thrusts sideways in a strong howling storm. My glasses are getting covered with slush. We run down into a deep gully and crouch behind rocks. I look behind us at a sharp drop off. The weather is so bad I can't tell how far it drops—and I don't want to find out the hard way.

Jim removes his glasses and takes the lead. We continue hiking, looking for a campsite. Eventually, we find one, way off the Appalachian Trail. The howling has decreased to wailing wind, and we set up our tents in the blowing frozen rain. Jim's tent has a vestibule in front allowing both of us to sit inside his tent while cooking outside under the vestibule.

We talk while eating our fabulous feast after such a hard fourteen-and-a-half-mile ascent.

Back in my tent I am glad to sleep tonight. The sound of rain hitting the tent is a serenade. At least, it isn't snow. Hopefully, tomorrow will be a better day weather-wise.

All things considered, today was fun.

April 9, 2003

It rained heavily last night. Jim estimates about four inches of rainfall. Today the A.T. is covered with water. In many places we get off the trail to step around the pools. Everywhere we walk is either muddy or slippery.

The day is overcast, glove-wearing cold. Something is about to warm our hearts.

One of the A.T.'s treasures is not made of earth or stone. It is snuggly miniature ponies, dozens of them, maybe hundreds. They are small as merry-go-round horses. Full grown their heads only reach up to my chest. Three of them slowly amble over to Jim. One is Palomino-style, white with brown splotches. Two have solid brown coats with snow white tails and manes, forelocks come over their heads like ash blonds. "Stay there," I say, reaching for my camera. Jim stands at the heads of the feral ponies, and while I aim the camera at him, two more try to pick my pocket, looking for food. A pony's muzzle brushes my arm aside so he can get into the compartments of my jacket. They are like family pets, searching me for treats. I am laughing too much to hold the camera steady. "Hey, guys…let me get a picture of the Gorilla man," I say, as they gently bump me. They continue to rummage around my shell and backpack. Gorilla finds it amusing; but now they are frisking him for food.

The area is windswept and bald. Rock outcroppings and clumps of evergreen trees are scattered around the area. A golden brown mare searches through sparse greenery on the ground while she is nuzzled by her similar colored foal. It is a fantastic timeout to glimpse the Wild West herds of yesteryear, miniature style.

We continue our trek and come to a road crossing. I read a sign on a forest service information board. "Oh shit! Look at this Jim." The sign states in part:

*** CAUTION ***
Weather in this area is UNPREDICTABLE.
BE PREPARED for SEVERE conditions
that may change without warning.
The temperature can DROP 20° and
winds increase 20 mph in less than one hour.
FOG can reduce visibility to ZERO.

Gorilla looks at it, raises his eyebrows, thinks back to the unexpected snowfall on Walnut Mountain. "Now they tell us!"

It continues to be misty today. We climb to where the A.T. nears the top of Mt. Rogers, the highest peak in Virginia at 5,729 feet. We hike about eleven miles to a shelter. There are seven or eight other guys here when we arrive. Someone says, "It's going to snow tonight."

That decides it. "Let's stay in the shelter tonight," Gorilla and I say almost in unison. No snow covered tents for us to take down tomorrow. We'd rather be jammed into this small open-front lean-to overnight. By evening, ten or more hikers crowd together on the shelter floor. It's difficult to move about without tripping over hikers' sleeping pads on the floor or backpacks leaning against a wall.

The rain during the night becomes torrential. It sounds as if a hundred high-power fire hoses are shooting at the shelter's roof. To our relief, the rain does not blow into the shelter. The temperature dives during the night. I wear all my clothes and heavy fleece jacket, its thick turtleneck zipped up to my chin. I don't sleep much in the noisy pounding rain and frigid conditions.

April 10, 2003

During the night the rain lessens, turns to sleet, and then snow. We wake up to snow on the ground mixed with about six inches of rainfall. One of the guys says, "It's twenty-eight degrees in here." It's colder outside.

Around me people are burrowed into their sleeping bags, fleece caps covering ears and foreheads, the bags' goose down–filled hoods wrapped around their heads, leaving only a slim slit of space for eyes and noses. My fingers are numb from the cold and are almost useless. It is not only cold, it's damp—very damp. When I speak, I can see by breath. Although I'm dressed in my heaviest clothing, I still eat breakfast while wrapped in my sleeping bag, and with my gloves on.

I get out of the bag, have a shaking chill, and hurry to put on my shell— the only additional layer left to wear. I pull rain pants on over my regular thin hiking pants—not just to ward off wet sleet but as insulation for my chilled legs.

By the time Jim and I start to hike, the snow has turned to blowing sleet. A chilled dampness goes through us. Our blood feels refrigerated. Jim and I decide to give up on this hike. We'll try to get to the closest road and make our way to a motel and then find our way home.

We slog through the sleet storm. There was so much rain lately, the Appalachian Trail has turned into a cold slushy river. Jim and I have to go off to the sides and walk in the woods to avoid the submerged path—we don't want our boots to become waterlogged and freeze. It's bad enough that our gloves are soaked through and our hands are frigid.

Ice coats the trees, wind gusts shower us with frozen crystals.

We trek to the Old Orchard Shelter. Several hikers are here for a break. It is bitterly cold at the shelter. What a raw day! "I can't feel my fingers," Jim blurts out. We want to reach Route 603, another mile and a half away, and try to get a lift into Troutdale to a place called the Fox Hill Inn. We know our hike will soon be finished, so we offer almost all our food to the guys huddled in the shelter, and give them whatever they can use.

Then, we travel fast to keep warm. The mile and a half hike to the road is done in about twenty minutes. The road is completely dead. I look around. No traffic at all. No people. Just accumulating layers of squishy frozen precipitation.

Our cell phones don't work, so we start walking toward Troutdale.

A pickup truck approaches from behind us. We hold up our thumbs. The truck pulls up. A middle-aged gentleman in camouflage clothing drives the pickup. His passenger rolls down the window, and the driver leans over and says, "I'd like to give you guys a lift in this storm, but there's no place for you to sit. The back's got a solid cover over it." The driver and his passenger have a brief discussion among themselves. "Tell you what. We can put the tailgate down, and you guys can ride on it, if that's okay."

It may seem crazy, sitting on the slippery tailgate of a truck in a sleet storm, but we are slowly freezing and haven't seen another vehicle for the twenty-five minutes we've been on this dreary road. "Sure, that would be great," I say with as much enthusiasm as an energy-depleted body can muster.

"You bet," Jim adds, and he is already wearily trudging toward the rear of the truck. The driver joins us and pulls down the tailgate. We shove our backpacks under the cover and hop up onto this narrow rear metal ledge.

"Hang on," he yells from the cab, and takes off, going forty miles an hour on the twisting wintry road. We are riding facing backward, feet dangling over the rear of the tailgate, our backs going through the falling sleet. I pull the hood of my shell up over my hat to block the wind and sleet.

Jim has no hood. The sleet hits the back of his neck, and slips inside his collar, crystals of icy slush sliding down his spine. His shirt becomes soaked and frigid. His body temperature begins to drop. When it falls a few degrees, he begins to shiver. This tough ranger who trained in sixty-five-below wind chills in Alaska, is gradually becoming hypothermic.

I try to turn forward to see where we are going. The hail of tiny ice chips smacks me in the face, and I feel like I'm going to slide off the back of the truck. Troutdale is much farther than we thought. My mind, numbed by the cold, had incorrectly calculated the small town to be much closer. The truck pulls into a general store's parking lot. The driver and passenger come back and ask us, "Exactly where is it you want to go?"

"Fox Hill Inn," I reply.

The driver strokes his chin, looks at us kind of strange. "Hmmm," he says. "Yeah. I think I know where that is," and he hurries back into the truck's cab and out of the storm. There's something weird in the way he spoke and the eerie way he looked at us.

He changes direction and drives several miles more. Through slop-snow he turns onto a secluded narrow lane, only the width of the truck, going up a mountain. There is a steep drop on one side that could have been several hundred feet for all we know. The truck drives in and out of clouds, and, with little light from the dreary sky, we can't see much.

"Al," Jim croaks from his hoarse throat, "I think they're taking us to a Klan meeting."

We climb the mountain into sleety mist—the sliding rear wheels bumping treacherously close to the road's edge—my fingers nearly frozen into a clamp on the rear edge of the tailgate. Jim is shivering uncontrollably, pale as death, and I am getting colder by the windswept mile.

They pull up at an isolated mountaintop. *Deliverance* banjos twang in my mind. We are surrounded by a darkened cloud gradually drifting by. When it passes, we can make out a red brick and Tudor-style building sitting by itself in the mists. Long brick steps lead up to a porch with columns. We wait. It is still sleeting; we are freezing. For a moment nothing happens. The front door opens. A man comes out onto the porch. He looks down on us and says, "I'm Mark, the innkeeper of the Fox Hill Inn.

It is a mystical moment. We are safe and going into a warm place for the first time in many days. I thank the men who drove us to the exact place we had wanted to go. Jim's teeth are chattering so much his words of thanks come out in a low stutter. I offer to pay for their gas and time, but they look at our pitiful condition and say, "We already have our thanks," and smile broadly. Jim and I keep saying our faltering appreciation until they have driven away.

Both of us are soaked. I help shivering Jim as we remove our boots, leave them with our backpacks on the porch, and walk into the inn in our wet stocking feet. Mark shows us to a large bedroom with two queen size beds—and a private bath. Jim is shaking terribly. The Gorilla man is a tough guy. I have never seen him tremble before, and I'm concerned he is suffering hypothermia. I give him a piece of candy to eat and tell him he has to get into a hot shower immediately. His clothes are soggy with water. "Do you have any dry clothes?" I ask. "I'll get them out of your pack."

His body is involuntarily shaking so much, he stammers, "N-n-n-n-o."

While he is in the shower, I get my dry clothes out of a waterproof bag and leave them in the room for him. Mark makes hot coffee with extra sugar and brings it up. While we're waiting for Jim, Mark shows me around. There is a cozy reading room with enough books to satisfy any reader who wants to curl up on a day such as this. Every room is spacious—and warm. Mark shows me the washer and dryer.

In a while, as Mark and I talk near the foyer, Gorilla comes down the wide stairway looking revived, the edges of his mouth lifting ever so faintly, like a person who has cheated the Grim Reaper.

It feels so good to finally be warm.

There is no Greyhound bus nearby and Amtrak trains are 155 miles from here. Jim calls his friend Homer Witcher. Homer and his wife, Therese, and their two children hiked the entire Appalachian Trail as a family in 2002, starting at Springer Mountain, Georgia, and going all the way to Maine. Jim joined them for part of that thru-hike. When the chronicles of earth's kindest people are written, Homer and Therese will be on page one. Their lives are ingrained with doing acts of kindness—particularly to strangers.

Homer agrees to pick us up and take us to his home in Daleville, Virginia. I'd be 115 miles closer to home, and Jim would be near Roanoke, where he could catch a plane. I call my friend Lou Shane, my pal since we were teenagers. We live thirty miles apart and don't see each other often enough, but we would travel into hell to help each other. Fortunately, he doesn't have to go that far, and he is glad to come to Daleville and pick me up.

Homer arrives around 10:45 the next morning and drives us to his house. By the time we reach Daleville, Lou is already there. Jim, still wearing the dry clothes I lent him, changes his clothes, and gives me back my stuff. We give each other a farewell bear hug.

The Appalachian Trail is a sensual, enticing, treacherous lover with whom I have once again danced and consorted. Now it's time to go home.

Lou and I start our drive back to Cherry Hill.

I don't know if I will ever get to hike with the Gorilla man again.

PART FOUR

Chapter Twenty

A person sees a man banging his head against the wall. He asks the man: "Why are you banging your head against the wall?"

The man responds, "I'm banging my head against the wall because *it feels so good when I stop.*"

Do we hike the Appalachian Trail just because it feels so good when we *stop*?

The A.T. is wet and cold at the same time. Mountains are frustratingly difficult to climb with a heavy pack pulling us down. So why do it?

It's a place of perfect peace. It's an escape from worldly problems.

The views are spectacular—at least, sometimes.

The feeling of accomplishment is incomparable.

The people you meet restore your faith in humanity.

The A.T. is not just a physical place. It's a location in your mind that you alone create. A forever ideal outpost of dreamed imaginings. No matter how lousy it is at times, it's still the best…as you see it.

Okay, the A.T. is a sinister disease—an addiction—a craving compulsive enough to be classified a controlled substance subject to federal law. The A.T. is a poison that once it gets into your system you can't get rid of it. The only antidote: *hike it!*

Maybe everyone can't achieve success in love or the working world or life in general. Here, we can master something to be proud of. And do it with others who often help you attain it.

Rarely does a person connect with a stranger the way a hiker does with someone who has this same back woods passion. People who can't speak to a new neighbor in an apartment building elevator gladly reveal innermost thoughts with an unfamiliar person in a small wooden shelter.

This link with the outdoors filled my life with riches. It is a great adventure, a Wild West excitement others only dream of, but don't dare do. When people hear that we've hiked from Georgia, they're in awe.

It's not for folks who want to flop on a couch and spend evenings in front of a TV. It is for those who enjoy bedding down on the forest floor, looking out of their tent at millions of stars in a sky black as a raven's wing. It is for people who love nestling into a fluffy sleeping bag on the floorboards of a wooden shelter when the wind is blowing in, lightning and thunder crashing around them.

It will open you to closeness with nature and a bond with hearty kindred folks.

The knowledgeable Jonathan Dorn, editor-in-chief of *Backpacker* magazine, explained that backpackers climb mountains because "heading into the mountains with your life strapped to your back is the ultimate expression of freedom…and stronger friendships are formed in the mountains—through shared risk, wonder and sometimes tragedy."[15]

The elation you feel in the backcountry is not translatable. Experienced backpacker, Circuit Rider, as he starts his 2009 A.T. thru-hike tries to explain:

> As I listen to the wind move through the yet leafless branches, view the sunset through the window of the tent, visit with friends we have just met and…experience once more a stillness we have yet to replicate in the ever busy and demanding world we walked away from this morning…*if only others could see and feel what we do right at this moment, every campsite along this famous footpath would be crammed full.*[16]

The A.T. is a dog barking in some distant place you can hear, but can't see. It awakens you at night and calls to you. Why do I hike? For the same reason a dog sticks his head out the car window when you're driving... Because it feels good!

Chef Paul, the man who did trail magic for us at Neels Gap was right; I am a section hiker. Gorilla Jim and I planned the 2004 section to be for about fifteen days.

March 30-31, 2004

My buddies Lou and Bob drove Jim and me to Troutdale, Virginia, where we left off last year. We all stayed overnight at the Fox Hill Inn. This morning Jim has nasal stuffiness, so we stop at a general store in Troutdale to buy some Claritin. I walk along the aisle of Band-Aids, aspirins, indigestion remedies, and other things, looking at labels. They don't have Claritin in stock. When I ask the woman at the counter, she says she has some and will get it. She gets into her car and drives away. A little while later, she returns with her own personal Claritin. She had driven home to get it. The woman asks how many I need for Jim, and I say, "Three." She gives me four and doesn't take any money for it. How's that for Southern hospitality!

After we say goodbye to Lou and Bob and start hiking, I'm energized and thinking, "At times the Appalachian Trail seems like an enemy that must be conquered. A foe who's gotten my goat, captured my imagination. I will overcome its appalling weather, and wearying climbs. *I have to be here!*"

April 1, 2004

We hike in cold rain, sometimes in several inches of snow. The wind howls at night. As we go to lower elevations the snowfall gradually decreases.

In a grassy area, trees in the background, we come across a one-room, slate-gray clapboard schoolhouse built in 1894. Three wooden steps lead to a door, opening into a small, now-vacant room with four windows. There is a potbellied stove in the center of a dozen pale wood school desks, each desk formerly shared by two students. Across the front wall is a blackboard and a small oak table where the teacher sat. On it is a bell with long handle that the instructor used to announce the start of class. The solitary room has the mustiness of a century of learning. The Lindamood School had one teacher

for the seven grades in this lone room. If they married, female teachers were
barred from teaching.

For minor infractions a student might have to stand with their nose
pressed against a circle drawn on the blackboard. Punishments included
sharp whacking with a slender tree limb, for such offenses as:

Boys and Girls Playing Together   4   lashes
Playing Cards at School   10   "
Misbehaving to Girls   10   "
Drinking Spiritous Liquors at School 8   "
Wearing long fingernails   2   "

Jim and I took photos of each other at the teacher's desk—I with a book
in hand, pointing to a nonexistent child to recite, and Jim holding the stick
used to whack the kids.

Along the way we meet Glenn, a tall guy close to our age with steel–gray
beard. His trail name is Big Foot. Jim asks Big Foot if he wants to hike with
us, and he is glad to do so.

April 2, 2004

The weather forecast is, "…some snow…cold." The Mount Rogers School
has a two hour delay in opening. In snow, sleet, and rain, we hike fourteen
miles to the Knot Maul Branch Shelter. We didn't see any other people all
day. I did see footprints in the snow and knew someone was hiking ahead
of us.

Sometimes I entertain hikers by looking at footprints in the snow and
describing the long gone strangers who left these footsteps. Once we met
four men who were section hiking.

"See the footprints there," I said, pointing to impressions in several
inches of snow, going up a slight hill, snow clad trees all around. "What
we have here are a man and a woman hiking at a leisurely pace. The man is
carrying a heavy pack." By now, my audience is looking down at the foot
tracks in the snow.

"How do you know by looking at them?" one of them asks.

"People leave clues. Size of the foot, length of stride, depth of the tread, the affect weather has on the imprints. See the bigger footprints?" I point to the, larger, wider footsteps. "That's a man's footprint."

"Yeah, right. You're just saying that because the footprint's bigger."

"Partly." Using both of my hands turned slightly outward, "Notice the toes of the boots point slightly out. That's the way men walk. The smaller footprint has the toes pointing more inward—that's the way women usually walk."

"Yeah, so, how do you know it's a leisurely pace...and he's carrying a heavy pack?"

"Stride, for one thing. Look at her prints. Stride not too long, prints not too deep. If a person moves rapidly, you'd expect long strides, the toe deeper than the heel. Usually when we walk, the heel digs in first and bears the weight. The toe doesn't leave much of an impression." Everyone looks at the woman's clear heel impact in the snow, the snow tire tread design pressed into the soft white stuff, less apparent at the toe.

"He's probably carrying a heavy load because his footprints are deep, the stride is short and slightly wide. Doesn't the print look like he's shuffling his feet? He's a little tired bearing heavy weight."

"Amazing."

Now that I've got their interest, I say, "The man is left-handed, wearing a blue jacket." They are awed and still with me, so I add, "...and he has only one nut." Then they realize I've slid from scientific knowledge to pure bullshit.

April 3, 2004

Yesterday the temperature was about thirty-two degrees and was far below freezing last night. It continues to be cold this morning.

Today we will climb to the Chestnut Knob Shelter atop the highest mountain we'll hit for a long time. We come into an area of snow. As we go up, the snow deepens. I try to step over a fallen tree piled high with snow, my leg punching through the high fluffy mound. It takes extra time and effort to step into and pull our feet out of snow banks. I am leading, but the trail disappears. I turn and yell above the whining wind, "Can anyone see the trail?" The airstream blows snow into my mouth.

Glenn says he can't see the path. It vanished underneath a heavily fallen blanket. We look for white blazes. They're hidden by snow. If we can't find the trail, we can't find the shelter. *Are we going to be stuck out in the open on a mountaintop?* I wonder. We hike higher, the temperature drops. It's cold and fast becoming a dangerous situation.

My worst fear—being lost in the mountains in a storm—is happening. I turn back to Jim, "I can't find the damn trail."

Jim steps up. "I'll take the lead." His Ranger Corps experience kicks in. Jim looks down, walks around in front of us. Like a sniffing hound dog picks up a scent we can't smell, Jim eyes the terrain and visualizes something that is invisible to me. Without turning back, he says, "Follow me!" heads into the biting wind up the mountain, stepping through and around mounds of snow. I strain my eyes to see something that resembles a path. Jim, amazingly, keeps to what he thinks is the trail.

Does the Gorilla man really see a slight, continuous indentation in the snow, which is not perceivable to our eyes?

He continues to plod through the white on white, knee-deep wintery mountainside. I try to wiggle feeling back into freezing fingers that are gripping hiking poles. Our only thoughts are, "Where is the shelter?" and, "Are we going to find it?"

"Hey, Jim," I yell up ahead. "Where the hell's the shelter?"

"It's up there."

We're approaching the top. If the shelter isn't here, it isn't anywhere.

I look up the mountain to where Gorilla Jim stops about seventy-five feet ahead and above me. "Is it up there?" Stepping up to a flatter area at the top, I can tell from the smile on his face…a small stone building sits in a pile of snow, waiting for us.

"Way to do it," I shout.

Glenn is also yelling congratulations.

The shelter is a sturdy, fully enclosed stone building. A great sight to see up here parked in a snowdrift. In front of the shelter the powder is so deep the door piles up snow with its swing and jams to a stop, partially opened. The entryway is so narrowed that we have to remove our backpacks and ease ourselves through sideways. The windows are high up on the walls and rise to the peaked ceiling. The shelter is empty. There are wooden sleeping platforms, one above the other bunk-bed style with ladders at the ends. A large table dominates the center of the room.

The temperature outside has been dropping and later goes down to twenty-three degrees. Inside the temperature is thirty-five degrees and heading toward freezing.

The only water source is a brook two miles back, which we might not find in deep chalk-whitened terrain. Instead, we melt snow in a pan over an alcohol stove. Interestingly, snow has so much air in it, the pan can scorch unless you first put a little water at the bottom and then put the snow on top. Clean as snow may seem, it contains flecks of dirt. No doubt, a tribute to air pollution. We scoop little specks off the melting icy mush.

We cook our dinners inside, Jim wearing his outdoor clothing and a big fleece pullover cap covering his cold ears. Eating a hot dinner on the table inside the shelter—away from cold wind and snow—is an enormous treat.

Mouse hangers hang from the ceiling These are strings hanging down from an overhead beam. The string goes through the center of a can or lid suspended in the middle of the string. We attach our food bags to the bottom of the string. The purpose of the can or lid is to prevent mice—which creep along a ceiling beam—from crawling down the string and getting to our food. Usually, this works. When it doesn't work, the contraption is known as a "mouse trapeze."

We believe it is so cold tonight that the mice will not be active.

Later, we go outside, bundled up against the gusts. The sun is low in the sky, and there is a beautiful view of the green valley below. Amazing! Fifteen inches of snow on the mountaintop and no snow faraway down in the valley.

At night, beyond thick stone walls, the wind roars.

April 5, 2004

Today is beautiful—sunny all day, high in the upper thirties.

The Appalachian Trail crosses Little Wolf Creek *twelve times*—no bridges. Rain, sleet, and snow swelled the creek's water to a dangerous level. While telling Glenn a story, I'm interrupted three times in order to navigate the rocks across the rushing water. We have to be careful going back and forth across the creek or we'll get soaked. In many places the water comes over our boots. At one point we have to walk down the center of the creek, stepping from one stone to another and onto a small island before we leave the cascades and get to the other side. It takes awhile to cautiously negotiate all the crossings and gushing water.

"What a mess," I say, when it's over.

Gorilla adds, "I could do without this."

"You could have done without any creek crossings," Glenn replies.

"What do you mean?"

"The guidebook says when the creek is not passable, we should take the high water route. Glenn points to a higher area away from the water. "There's a route up there that avoids walking across—and through the creek."

My eyes go to where he is pointing. "High water route!" We are all walking with cold water in our boots. "Why didn't you say so before?"

"I thought you guys knew of the high water trail, but just wanted to go through the high water."

We hike eleven and a half miles to U.S. Route 52 and U.S. 21. We need a ride to Bland, Virginia, two and a half miles away. Big Foot and I wait by the trailhead with the backpacks while Jim walks to a small church nearby to see if anyone is available to take us to a motel in Bland. No one is at the church. Jim continues down the road to a house where an elderly gentleman sits on his porch trying to fix a broken toilet. Jim returns and tells us the man's name is Leonard Norris and he's agreed to take us to the Big Walker Motel.

Leonard drives us to the motel. There is a Dairy Queen, gas station and mini-market nearby where we get the supplies we need. While there, Jim speaks to a woman who says tomorrow she or someone else will drive us back to the trailhead.

No laundry facility at the motel. I wash my rancid socks and hang them out to dry on a fence across the parking lot from our motel room.

April 6-7, 2004

Jane Green shows up in a large Yukon SUV. She is a pleasant woman who likes to help hikers. When we get to the trailhead, we offer to pay for her gas and time. She wouldn't take money but said, "Just send a card addressed to

Jane Green, Bland, Virginia, and put the zip code in, and it will get to me. I just want to know where you end your hike." We don't have a pen and paper handy, so to remember her name, we periodically yelled out in the woods: "Jane Green, Bland, Virginia."

In the past two days, as we crossed roads, we came across trail magic where people left insulated containers of soda, water, juice—all cold. The third time, the trail angel had also left a bottle of Captain Morgan Spiced Rum (which we left alone).

We passed by a shelter and did not find a good campsite for a long time after that. So we trekked seventeen and a half miles today. This is a record for us.

With a burst of energy and a desire to do high mileage, on April 7, we hiked eighteen miles to the Doc's, Knob Shelter, exceeding yesterday's mileage record.

April 8, 2004

It's a very steep downhill drop into Pearisburg, Virginia—two thousand feet in about one horizontal mile. Our feet burn, and our knees are sore. After hiking thirty-five and a half miles in the last two days, we're tired. We decide to take a zero day here tomorrow and revise our plans.

The Rendezvous Motel is on the outskirts of Pearisburg, across from where the Appalachian trail comes down to the road. A woman in her thirties, somewhere north of five feet tall greets us with, "My name is Brenda, today, but it may be different tomorrow," and she give me a quizzical smile. She is one of the motel's owners and has a wild sense of humor.

Big Foot wants steak and beer for dinner. We couldn't locate a steak restaurant, but Jim and I stop at a gas station and buy a twelve pack of beer, which we keep cold with ice and a cooler provided by Brenda. She is kind enough to drive us up a steep hill to a restaurant in town where we stuff ourselves.

April 9, 2004

The forecast is for no lower than forty degrees in town. I'm sending home my long underwear bottoms, outer gloves, and some other winter clothes.

We need to go into town. Brenda is busy and can't drive us. She hands Jim the keys to her Isuzu Rodeo. It's unbelievable that she'd loan her vehicle to total strangers. The gas gauge reads empty, so we pull into a gas station and fill up. The gas gauge still reads empty.

When we return the SUV to Brenda, she tells us she likes helping hikers. She tells us that one time her husband, Buck, came into the motel office to find her washing the feet of a hiker whose feet were bloodied from hiking.

The afternoon is sunny, warm, and lazy. We take beers outside and lean on an old SUV in the parking lot. Brenda lugs a chair out of the motel, sits in it smoking a cigarette, and entertains us with stories of her and Buck. One time they went to Ohio and were at a bar that had a pool table. Although Buck is a shrewd businessman—he owns a fifteen-hundred-acre farm and has a business laying epoxy floors in factories—he and Brenda played the part of dumb hillbillies. Using their Appalachian accent, Buck told people at the bar he just got his "disability check" and played pool for quarters, acting awkward. Brenda showed us how she played her part by shyly lowering her head and eyes and told the bar patrons she was accustomed to dancing in places that had sawdust on the floor. Buck lost a little, hustled the players, and eventually walked away with four thousand dollars. The owner of the bar told Buck he was lucky to get out of there alive.

Brenda flicks cigarette ashes and says she and Buck once stopped at a hotel whose employees were rigid. Brenda says, "They had tighter asses than an Atlantic City pit boss."

Brenda is tough talking, but she hides a heart softer than the down in a sleeping bag. At Christmas time, Brenda gets the letters local children address to Santa Claus and answers each of them. She writes to about two hundred thrilled Giles County kids, telling them that they are on Santa's list of good boys and girls and encourages them: "Tell all your friends not to be naughty and always be nice."

She tells of the time an eighty–year-old motel guest, Chicken John, went on a slack pack and Brenda was to pick him up later that day. When the elderly man did not show up to meet Brenda, two hikers told her the aged gentleman was a mile or two back on the trail, unable to move further. Brenda returned to the motel, gathered a search party of motel guests. They found the man lying on the ground without food or water and helped carry him back to the motel.

April 10, 2004

Sending home warm clothes and carrying less water lowered my backpack's weight. It's a steep hike out; still, it feels great to have my pack weigh much less.

We hike seven miles to the Rice Field Shelter, a small log shelter, but plenty of room for three of us to spread out. After dinner we settle around a fire pit and sit on thick logs surrounding the fire. In the light of dancing flames, we talk and reminisce about other hikes and plan the next day's trek.

April 11, 2004

Jim, Big Foot, and I hike over thirteen miles to the Pine Swamp Branch Shelter. Someone wrote in the shelter register that they saw a bear cub a mile from this shelter.

This is an older stone shelter and we expect to find mice here. You know there are mice around when you see their feces, looking like small black grains of rice. The first thing I do when I get to a shelter is to use the shelter's broom to sweep up. I sweep plenty of droppings here.

During the night, mice make scratching sounds as they scurry across beams, and sometimes across the floor where we're sleeping. I don't hear them because of plugs in my ears to deaden noise of others (snoring). It's unnerving to have mice run across my sleeping bag. Worse, some people have had mice run across their faces.

Most shelters have a picnic-type table out front. Sometimes hikers leave cooking utensils on the table overnight. In the morning they find mouse crap in their cooking pots. One morning, Just Do It got up and found his pack towel had been chewed up overnight. It looked like a large slice of blue Swiss cheese. Morris told me that one morning he found acorns in his boot. I got in the morning habit of turning my boots upside down and shaking them our before putting them on. This jiggles out any spiders that crawled in during the night, and shakes out any mouse "presents." Mostly, a tiny pebble or small twig falls out along with any of the night crawling bugs or small animal residue that may have settled there in the darkness.

Whether our backpacks sit on the shelter floor or hang on a nail in the wall, we always remove all food and leave the pockets unzipped. The reason? Mice are curious. If they can't get inside, they will chew through the side of the backpack.

There are many mouse hangers here. In the middle of the night Big Foot shines his headlight into the shelter's rafters. I whisper, "What's happening, Glenn?"

"I heard mice above us." He shines his light on the mouse hangers. "Nothing," Glenn says. "Earlier, mice were pawing the tin cans, trying to get down to our food bags."

We go back to sleep.

April 12, 2004

Glenn and I had removed all food from our backpacks the night before, but Jim forgot to remove a block of cheddar cheese from his backpack. During the night, a mouse chewed a hole through the top of his backpack and ate part of the cheese. "Damn!" Jim shouted, when he saw the hole. The opening was so big he stuck his index finger through the hole.

Some privies provide toilet paper in a mouse-proof holder. This is a rural mailbox (with the red flag) inside the privy. Open its front, put in a roll of TP, and when you slam it shut, it is waterproof and rodent proof. I once entered an outhouse where someone had left open the door of the mailbox/ toilet paper holder. Mice had taken out the toilet paper, torn it up, and made a nest on top of the mailbox. One mouse, still perched on the mailbox, stared at me with its dark eyes, little gray and pink nose and twitching whiskers. I looked him straight in the eyes and boomed, "This privy isn't big enough for the two of us." He scurried away.

Hikers typically carry their own toilet paper because most privies don't have any. Returning from the privy, plastic bag of toilet paper in hand, Jim announces he's seen a dangerous spider. "There's a Black Widow in the privy, on the toilet seat."

"Do you think the widow will be using the privy long, others may want to use it soon?"

The humor is lost on Jim, who replies, "Avalanche, if you get bitten in the ass by one of those things, it may be the last time you ever take a shit.

Their venom is deadly." He looks at me, "Do you even know what they look like?" The Gorilla man doesn't wait for an answer. "The Black Widow is dark, well, almost black with a red hourglass shaped mark on its back...or is it its stomach? Anyway, the female is much bigger than the male."

"Really?"

"Now, here's the interesting part. After she has sex, the female eats the male."

Jim has aroused my interest. "Do you mean 'eats' in a *sexual* sense?"

"No. The female actually eats up the male."

"Not much gratitude for showing her a good time."

"Maybe she didn't have such a good time. And that's why she eats up the male."

I ponder this sexual cannibalism. Last try at humor: "That's why you should never have sex with a Black Widow spider."

Jim laughs. "Don't worry, I killed it. Did I tell you I have a tarantula at home?"

A big, ugly, hairy, spider comes to mind. "Ech! Do tarantulas make good pets?"

"Very good."

Envisioning the large scary spider I ask mockingly, "Do you take it for walks?"

Jim ignores my question.

"Can you snuggle up with it?"

Jim examines my face to see if I'm serious, or putting him on. He ventures a reply, "I put it on my arm...it walks up and down."

"What do they eat?"

"Crickets and grasshoppers, small frogs. Now you take Rosie—"

"—Rosie?"

"Yeah, that's her name."

"You named a tarantula *Rosie?*"

"Rosie likes crickets, but she loves spiders. She ate three large spiders I found in Oklahoma and put in her cage." Jim cups his hands to show their size.

I'm wrinkling my face and eyes and say sarcastically, "Sounds like a *great* pet!"

"This is interesting. After sex the male tarantula must get away quickly before the female eats him."

Gorilla continues, "If the female doesn't care for the male tarantula's advances, she might kill him just for *trying* to have sex."

"I've heard of pickup bars like that."

"**Hypothermia.** A cold rain can be the most dangerous weather of all, because it can cause hypothermia (or 'exposure') even when conditions are well above freezing. Hypothermia occurs when wind and rain chill the body so that its core temperature drops; death occurs if the condition is not treated in time."[17]

We leave the shelter and today we're trudging in wretched waves of stinging sleet. The windy rain-snow comes through our rain gear. A bitter dampness cuts through to our bones.

We pass Dismal Branch and climb steeply to a gusty ridge where we slog hour after hour along the high ground to appropriately named Wind Rock. Our gloves are soaked. There are no signs of animal life. In gray silence we hike fast—almost recklessly—for miles just to keep warm, and to reach a shelter to get out of the sleet and misery.

On the edge of hypothermia we stop only for a moment under a spreading evergreen tree to grab a handful of gorp and a swig of water, shiver and hurry on. We couldn't stop for lunch for fear of freezing. With muddled minds the three of us move as quickly as we can, trying not to skid on the wet, slippery rocks. At Lone Pine Peak the trail sharply dips down almost two thousand feet to the War Spur Shelter.

At this refuge, I try to take off near icy clothes. My hands are like rubber gloves filled with freezing slush. My fingers are so iced, they refuse to respond to anything I want them to do. It's an unwritten rule to always have dry clothes, but to lighten my load I sent my extra clothes home. The only dry things I have are a long underwear top and my fleece jacket.

Glenn's fingers are so frozen stiff he can't unwrap an energy bar.

A line is strung across the shelter for hanging wet clothes. I hang my pants, shirt, jacket, gloves, everything. I'm standing in an open shelter in frigid wind, wearing nothing from the waist down but wet underpants. I'm shivering uncontrollably. I clench my teeth to halt them from clattering against each other. Now, instead of my teeth chattering, my entire head shakes.

With numb and shaking fingers I inflate my sleeping pad and get into the down bag—my only refuge. The trembling continues. Jim has made hot soup on his little stove. He looks at me shaking, and passes me some of the soup in the lid of his pot. It's good to get something hot inside of me. Jim makes a pot of mashed potatoes and hands it across the shelter to me. My fingers wrap around the cook pot to get warm. I have never tasted such vital food. I stop shivering. It's too cold outside of my sleeping bag for me to cook; I just eat what Jim made, nibble my block of cheese, crackers, and anything else easy to eat.

My sleeping bag is on the floor next to the wall. In an effort to dry my drenched pants, I drape them on a wooden shelf above me. During the night I reach up and feel the pants; they are not drying. I take down the pants and put them in my sleeping bag, intending to dry them with my body heat.

April 13, 2004

We stay in our sleeping bags until 8:30 this morning trying to keep warm, and hoping the sleet and rain would stop.

It didn't.

Jim, Glenn, and I have had enough of near hypothermic conditions. We're cold and concerned about continuing to hike in steady shivering precipitation. Today is the last day of our planned hike. The three of us decide to walk out to the road, a little over a mile from here, and try to find a paved highway where we could hitch a ride to where Homer is to meet us, or use someone's phone. My cell phone doesn't work here.

On go the wet, frigid clothes. Our gloves are soaked and useless, so Jim and I use socks to cover our hands. The sock mittens get soaked through and cold. We trek to the road. After fifteen minutes of walking, a red automobile stops. The driver rolls down the passenger side window and looks at our scruffy appearance. A shotgun leans on the front seat. He says he is going turkey hunting and suggests we stop by a brick house somewhere behind him. We don't find the brick house. In fact, there are hardly any houses along this long remote road, and the sparse residences we do see look like no one is home. We trek in sleety conditions and come to a house that has a pickup truck parked outside. "I'll go to the door and ask to use the phone," I say. "To sound like I belong down here, I'll use my best Southern accent."

Gorilla and Big Foot ask me for a sample. I say a few words, and they both laugh. "That's no Southern accent."

"Okay, I'll just be gracious."

More snickering.

This is such a remote area, having three grubby strangers come to their door might be intimidating, so Jim and Glenn stay under a carport out of the rain while I go up on the porch and knock on the door.

A late middle-age woman opens the door.

"I'm sorry to bother you, ma'am. We are wet and cold and need to make a phone call."

Eying my bedraggled and weary condition, she answers, "Have you had breakfast?…Are you hungry? Come on in."

"I'm wet, ma'am and don't want to drip on your floor."

Her husband comes to the door and stands behind her. "Where you from?"

"New Jersey, but there are two good old Southern boys with me. One's from Tennessee, and the other's from North Carolina." I point to Jim and Glenn and motion for them to come up to the porch.

"You boys have to come in out of the rain." The three of us take off our dripping backpacks and rain jackets, leaving them on the porch. We start to unlace our boots, but she says, "You don't have to take off your boots. I'll mop up any water. How would y'all like some breakfast?"

We politely decline, but she ushers us into the kitchen where she makes us coffee. Even though we told her it wasn't necessary, she scrambles eggs and heats up some ham. She tells us her name is Claire. Her husband says his name is Rune Field. She calls him by his middle name, Philip. Claire puts the scrambled egg and ham sandwiches on the kitchen table—excellent eating. It feels good to be in a warm home.

Jim calls Homer, who is just leaving his house and we caught him at the last moment. Philip and Claire said they would drive us to Newport, Virginia, a town about fifteen miles away, and we plan to meet Homer there at a large general store.

We put our backpacks in the back of Philip's pickup. Jim rides with Philip. Claire drives Glenn and me in their family automobile. The roads are wet, but Claire races around hairpin turns through the mountains. "I could never drive so fast in these conditions," I say, trying to suggest she slow down a little.

"I've been doing this all my life," Claire says. "I know every inch of this highway." At a crossroads, in the middle of what appeared to be nowhere in particular, there is a general store. Philip and Claire drop us off. We offer compensation, they won't take anything, not even for gas. "We're glad to help," they say.

We leave our wet backpacks outside, go in, and get something hot to drink. A while later Home shows up. Homer drives toward his home over mountain roads, some covered with water from falling, rushing streams and creeks. In places, flooding is up to the roadside. Driving into the mountains, below us creeks and streams far overflow their banks. The Appalachian Trail has turned into a frigid river as it did last year.

At Homer's house we rejoin civilization, welcome taking a hot shower, and enjoy the warmth of this family with their two children, Taylor and Bennett.

Once again, we have been delivered from a cold hell.

Okay, we're slow learners. March and early April are lousy months to be hiking the Appalachian Trail this far north. Gorilla Jim, Big Foot and I agree to resume our trek next month when the weather turns warmer.

Chapter Twenty-one

May 8, 2004

Bob, Lou, and I drive to the bus terminal in Roanoke, Virginia, where we pick up Jim and Glenn. Then it's off to the trailhead at Johns Creek where we continue our hike.

A month off from hiking dulled recollections of frigid conditions, particularly since the weather now is the opposite of last month. Topsy-turvy A.T. temperature is at it again: a searing hot, steamy, and buggy spell so early in the season. We meet other hikers, their clothes sticking to them.

Whatever insects make merry little sounds, are doing their thing providing a peaceful background. On the other hand, mosquitoes are out in force. We put on insect repellent which Jim brought with him. The buzzing little bastards start their campaign to ravage our skin.

May 9, 2004

Moving through lofty old growth trees, oaks, tall pines, today we have a unique experience. We hear the sound of something large falling ahead. A bare tree comes down gracefully. As in slow motion its tree top floats to the ground, strikes dirt with a heavy smack, bounces up slightly, and then settles in a pool of dust. From somewhere above, broken from an adjacent pine, several branches tumble into the dusty heap. It's unusual to witness a huge senior expire.

Often we come across the aftermath, but to see it happen is quite something. Later that day I hear the sound of creaking, a sort of wailing in the light wind. An aged tree that has long ago fallen sideways and is being supported by a young tree, is rubbing against the strong branches that support the slumped elder. In woods all over, old trees drop into the arms of youth— the mournful sound of death repeated.

Today we hike sixteen miles, a more difficult climb than we expected. The weather is up into the nineties. It's another very humid day. We carry more water than usual because it's nine miles before we can fill up. Jim refuses to drink enough water because the more he drinks the more he has to catheterize—which is painful and inconvenient. Jim says, "My mouth feels dry. I've got this bad headache like I'm getting over a hangover from cheap booze."

Jim wears an electric-blue T-shirt made of material that whisks away sweat. It is stained dark with perspiration. His pant legs are rolled up, almost to his knees. He is walking in a lethargic and sometimes aimless way. It's not like Gorilla Jim.

"You've got to drink, buddy," I tell him.

A seventeen-ounce water bottle hangs from Jim's backpack strap. He removes the cap and takes a light swig. In this heat he should guzzle the entire bottle and a heck of a lot more. I give him a Gu pack, a gel of carbohydrates that provides instant energy. Jim revives temporarily, but then he lags farther and farther behind. We stop often so Gorilla can rest.

On Brush Mountain we come across a four-foot-high, light-colored stone monument, recognizing Audie Murphy, the most decorated American soldier in World War II. It says that Murphy "earned 24 decorations, including the Medal of Honor, Legion of Merit, Distinguished Service Cross, and Three Purple Hearts."

At Pickle Branch Shelter we go down to the stream to filter water. I scoop a handful of cool water and throw it onto my face, splashing some onto my shirt. Off with the shirt, toss it on top of a bush. Sitting on a rock, my pack towel soaks in the stream, until I yank it out and use it to wash myself with cool water. It feels good to be refreshed and clean.

During the night an owl hoots in the distance. I am really tired…sleep well …until awakened by my extremely itchy bug bites. My arms and legs are becoming a mess of white bubbles splotched red from rubbing and scratching.

May 10, 2004

We hike to Catawba, Virginia, pick up supplies, eat lunch, and talk with a half dozen other hikers sprawled on the sidewalk in front of the store.

Gorilla Jim doesn't look well and we suggest staying in Catawba; the Gorilla man doesn't like that and wants to cover more miles, so we continue our hike in the hot, humid weather. At one point it seems to be drizzling because the sweat from my head is dripping off the brim of my hat. Glenn and I drink gallons of water that runs through our systems and out porous skin, the sweat is soaking clothes in wet blotches, but Jim still isn't drinking enough water because he doesn't want to use his catheter.

Gorilla falls behind, asks for breaks. He takes off his hat, rubs his head, and says "I've got a headache." Later he adds, "I can't swallow and the roof of my mouth feels dry."

I ask Jim, "What's the color of your urine?"

"Dark orange."

Dark urine is not good. Jim knows what I'm about to tell him and weakly follows up with, "I've been drinking more today, and it's not as dark."

I give him a look of skepticism. "You better start drinking more—now!"

He halfheartedly reaches for his water bottle and takes a swig. As we hike, Gorilla's steps are slow and uneven. He barely lifts his feet, scraping them along dirt and dry leaves. Jim is falling way behind. He is a piece of machinery breaking down.

Jim is not sweating as much, his eyes are sunken. I keep urging him to drink. "You don't look well," I say, stating the obvious.

Jim lurches off the trail. I ask him if he's okay, and he seems punch drunk, mumbles half thoughts, incoherent sounds: "...grnd...on trail...dry mou..."

I yell to Glenn, who is farther up the trail, "Jim's getting sick."

Glenn comes back, and we sit Jim on a log in the shade by the side of the trail. Glenn takes Jim's water bottle from the strap on his backpack, opens the bottle, and hands it to Jim. As Jim previously faltered, several times I tried to reach Homer on my cell phone, but no one answered. This time he picks up. I start to tell Homer about Jim's condition when Jim says the first clear thing: "Avalanche...I got...a medical emergency!"

Homer responds, "I have a commitment and can't take care of the situation personally. Don't worry. I'll arrange for someone to meet you at route 311. How long will it take you to get there? "

Jim has cooled a bit in the shade, and feels a little better after getting some fluid in him. He insists he can make it in about an hour and a half. Once we get up and hiking, Jim starts to feel bad again.

It turns out, we walk much slower, stopping periodically for Jim to rest. It takes us over two hours. At one point, Glenn and I decide that Glenn should hike on ahead and meet the person who is going to pick us up.

Jim and I slowly come down the mountain at route 311. In the small parking area, a chunky man, pleasant but professional, introduces himself, "Homer called and told me to meet you guys here. My name is Del." Delwood Schecterly is a nurse known as the Trail Angel. He looks Jim over, shakes his head, and says, "He needs to get to the hospital and get intravenous fluids."

Jim hears that and refuses. I'm trying to get Jim to drink from his water bottle. Del says, "That won't be enough fluid now." Del walks me to the rear of his vehicle, his brow wrinkled with concern. "I contacted the rescue squad in two counties. If necessary, I'll call them and they'll come and get him."

Jim sits on the ground in the shadow of Del's vehicle. I kneel down to the Gorilla man, look at his weary ashy-red face. "The rescue squad is prepared to come and take you to a hospital."

"I don't want any... rescue squad...and don't want...hospital."

"You've got to go Jim. You're sick and you need the hospital."

"I'll be okay." The worn out Gorilla's voice is soft, "...not goin' to a hospital."

Del and I try again. Jim won't hear of it. He starts to get up, wobbles a bit, and shakes his head to ward off dizziness. Gingerly, we sit him back down.

"Del, you heard him. Believe me, this guy's tough and stubborn. If he says he won't go, he isn't going."

Del shakes his head again, kneels down to Jim. "We've had many cases of people who were dehydrated and went into heat stroke."

"...not going to hospital...no matter how bad my condition is!"

"Okay," I say to Del. "What's the next best thing?"

"Drink Gatorade." Del is resolved to taking us to Homer's house.

We stop at a supermarket on the way, and I pick up several gallons of Gatorade. At Homer and Therese's house, I pour a glass of the cherry-colored drink over some ice and give it to Jim. For the rest of the afternoon and evening, I make sure Jim's glass is never empty. As Jim takes in the fluid, he rallies slightly. However, he is still very much out of it.

Del recommended that "Jim should not go back on the trail for several days." When Glenn and I tell him he's not going back on the trail, Jim says weakly, "I'll be back on the trail tomorrow."

I'm emphatic: "You're not hiking with me!"

May 11, 2004

Glenn tells us the meteorologist on TV reported that yesterday it reached within two or three degrees of the record high temperature for this time of the year. We take today off and make plans to resume hiking.

"Look, Glenn," I say, "you and I can hike for two days and then we'll be back at Daleville, where Jim can continue hiking with us."

"No, I want to start hiking tomorrow," Jim interjects, sounding hurt to be left out.

I have the greatest admiration for Homer's years of backpacking experience. He offers a compromise. Glenn and I will hike to the Lamberts Meadow Shelter. During the afternoon Homer will drive Jim to a trail where he'll only have to walk two miles to the shelter. That way, Jim gets more rest time and can ease himself back into hiking.

May 12, 2004

It's going to be a hot day. I camel up, drink as much water as I can, before starting the steep climb to McAfee Knob, passing wildflowers and ever present Rhododendron. Although it is a steep climb, Glenn and I feel good. Our packs are light due to carrying only food for a few meals and no heavyweight clothes.

McAfee Knob is a triangle-shaped mountaintop ledge that sticks out about twenty-five feet over a two-thousand-foot drop-off. From the side, the Knob looks like a gigantic eagle's beak with a pock mark in the stone for an eye. This is possibly the most photographed spot on the A.T. and appears in most illustrations of the rugged beauty of Appalachian Mountains along the trail. It has a killer view of the surrounding mountains. When you look out and down at nature's handiwork, you can only say, "Wow!"

Standing on the narrow tip of the Eagle's beak looking down far more than a quarter of a mile, the view to the floor of the Roanoke Valley is dizzying. Death is only one slight misstep away. I have the unnerving sensation that the fragile point may give way, and without railings to keep you from falling, I have a strong desire to back up. Instead I stand on this precarious perch, hands-on-hips, while my photo is taken. Homer and Therese got married at this spot. I now understand why.

Supposedly, over a million years ago, the continent of Africa crashed into our continent, causing an uplifting that resulted in the crazy rock formations in this area. Big Foot and I continue our hike to Rock Haven, a large overhang of rock, and eat lunch in the shade of a huge stone ledge sticking out above us. We continue on our way up to Tinker Cliffs and meet several guys. One of them is finishing college. He says the climb was more strenuous than he expected. A friend tries to say something to him. He replies, "Don't bother me, dude. All I want now is to take a nap."

About a third of a mile from the Lamberts Meadow Shelter is a camping area where we meet up with Gorilla Jim. While Glenn and I pitch our tents, Jim filters water in a stream running within yards of the tenting area. There are loads of mosquitoes and other biting insects here, mainly because it is near the brook. I had tied Bounce dryer sheets to my backpack; they are supposed to keep away bugs. They didn't. (But they did make the mosquitoes fresh smelling and fluffy soft when I squashed them.)

May 13–14, 2004

We hike the days away. It's hot and humid. Every afternoon there is distant thunder.

The insects love this weather and are relentless, leaving behind injections of nasty fluids that create hives—red, itching, maddening bumps that only fingernails can alleviate, often leaving their own marks down tender arms and legs.

May 15, 2004

Today, we plan to hike fourteen miles to the Cove Mountain Shelter. It's another humid day. We consume large quantities of water mixed with Gatorade powder to provide nutrients. We are sweating profusely. Two scruffy men are piling gear into an SUV. "Your literature might have said the Cove Mountain Shelter has water," one of them says. "There is no such thing."

"No water?"

"That's right. You got to move on to Jennings Creek and camp area."

Jim checks the map. "That's another three miles."

Instead of going fourteen miles today, we trek seventeen miles to a small rocky beach next to a clear, slow-moving creek. Two hikers we met earlier are barefooted and shirtless, stretched out on the beach's sand and smooth river stones, trying to cool off near the water. I peal off my soggy shirt, boots, and socks and wade into refreshing water to wash away the sticky, salty residue of hot Virginia humidity.

Jennings Creek is accessible by road and is a popular spot with locals. It's Saturday night. After dinner other people start coming into the camping area. Jim walks over to them to find out if they have beer or anything else they want to share with us. The Gorilla man returns, reporting these people have all kinds of food, beer and liquor.

The bugs continue to be extremely numerous—and the little bastards are hungry. I have a huge collection of insect bites all over my arms, legs, and head, and figure alcohol therapy is called for.

I walk to their campsite. They have two fires blazing. Jim got in their good graces by helping gather wood for the fires. There are two couples enjoying a night in the woods. John and Shane offer four kinds of beer in their cooler. I take a refreshingly cold Rolling Rock. Their two women companions have gone for a walk. The men say they're going to barbecue ribs and corn and ask us to stay. It's already nine o'clock. After half an hour of talk and brews, we go back to our tents.

Around 11:00 p.m. there is a series of four gunshots followed by a couple more. I hear voices and laughter about a hundred yards away. I hear Jim's annoyed groan.

"What the hell is that?" I ask.

Jim answers, "It's coming from some people who passed us to get water."

I'm not sure what he means by that. It doesn't seem to be a problem; there are no further shots. I assume everything is okay and try to go back to sleep. It's hot and humid in my tent. Even though I'm wearing next to nothing and both side flaps of my tent are up, it's still too hot to sleep.

During the night there was another distant gunshot.

May 16, 2004

Humidity and bugs persist. They are worse in the early part of the day and late in the day. I had been wearing a long-sleeved shirt and long pants with zip-off legs in the morning. This morning, for the first time, I start off with shorts and short sleeves, figuring it is better to get bitten than to pass out from the heat.

We reach the Bryant Ridge Shelter, located on a stream and overloaded with gnats, which are biting the hell out of all of us. A swarm of the minute dark, flying bloodsuckers gathers around my head. I inhale one of the tiny flying vampires and try to cough it out of my throat. That effort to dislodge the little beast fails. I take a deep gulp from my water bottle and swallow the critter. Instead of staying to eat, we get out rapidly—not even stopping to filter water.

The climb to the Cornelius Creek shelter is a five-mile-long, steep rise. It's an exhausting ascent on this stifling, muggy day. The more I walked and scratched my red swollen arms, the more I thought I had done as much as I wanted to do. The humidity and maddeningly itching arms would only get worse as the weather got hotter. By the time we dragged ourselves up to the Cornelius Creek Shelter, we knew it was time to leave. As I often said before, "When it stops being fun, it's time to go home."

I dropped my backpack heavily, lay down on the shelter floor, used the pack as a pillow, closed my eyes, and rested for a long while.

Since I first began in 2002, I have traveled 750 miles of the Appalachian Trail, from Springer Mountain Georgia to the Cornelius Creek Shelter.

Homer, our own Trail Angel, came through for us again, meeting us about three miles up the trail and off on a dirt road. I call my buddy Lou who says he can pick me up. The next day Homer drives Glenn and Jim to the bus station, and they go on to Knoxville and Oklahoma. Lou arrives in the morning. We start on our way home for what I believe will be the last time.

Back in Cherry Hill, I count *eighty-seven* bug bites on my puffed up arms and legs. They didn't include multiple itchy bites on my head and back, which I couldn't see.

While we were on the trail this May, the wicked heat broke through temperature highs. Atlantic City reported the warmest May on record. Little Rock, Arkansas, had the warmest spring ever recorded. A report from Roanoke, Virginia, close to the Appalachian Trail, stated it was the *"Warmest May on record."*[18]

They all mean hottest May on record!

It didn't surprise me. Somehow we had again picked a time to hike in the most extreme weather.

I didn't know it then, but my next hike on the Appalachian Trail would not be with Jim, but would be with a most unexpected person.

Chapter Twenty-two

2005

Despite all my bitching at the end of our last hike, in 2005 Jim and I planned on picking up where we left off in Virginia. Jim took sick. He was not able to go and the trip was canceled. Something happened equally good—maybe better.

Barbara and I have nieces and nephews, any one of whom would make a parent proud. Laura, adorable as a child, delightful as a young adult, worked hard to get good grades in high school. She is like our own daughter.

It was a weekday evening. The phone rang. "Hi, Uncle Al."

"Hi, Laura. What's up?"

"I want to hike the Appalachian Trail with you."

"Huh!"

"Yeah, as my high school senior project I want to hike part of the Appalachian Trail with you and report on it."

I felt warm and fuzzy as anyone would, if, out of the blue, one of your kids suddenly showed an interest in something you held sacred.

Part of the A.T. closest to where we live is in the Kittatinny Mountains in northwestern New Jersey. The Kittatinnies rise from Pennsylvania, through New Jersey and into New York State. To the Lenape Native Americans, Kittatinny means "great mountain," although they are not very high. Some of Pennsylvania's rockiness carries through. It's not tough like in Georgia and parts of North Carolina, but is challenging enough to make backpacking interesting. That's where lifelong trail angels Lou and Bob dropped us off on a sunny May morning.

Laura is between five feet two and five feet three, slender, with an almost perpetual smile and a Mother Teresa kindness. She may be petite and gentle, but she has a strong determination. Shortly after we started our hike her new and relatively stiff boots were giving her blisters at the back of her heels. I put whatever blister remedies I had onto her raw, weeping heels and told her it would be perfectly fine if she wanted to terminate the hike.

The next morning, she looked up at me, the warm smile temporally replaced with tough resolve. "I want to continue hiking because I don't want to feel like a failure."

We changed our plan, making each day's hikes shorter. There was a Boy Scout camp not too far away that had a cabin for hikers. When we arrived early in the afternoon, there were people getting the campground ready for the season. One of the women in the office informed us, "The camp is not yet open." She hastened to add, "The cabin hasn't been cleaned up. You're welcome to use it, though, if you want." Laura and I took a broom to the place, and by the time we finished and returned to the main office we were surprised to find the place deserted. Everyone had gone for the day. The camp is on a beautiful lake of blue water, gentle hills of greenery behind it, powder blue sky with fluff clouds here and there. We cooked dinner on a picnic table in temperatures comfortable enough to sit around in hiking shorts.

Laura and I spent the days hiking, talking, and enjoying late spring weather. On the final day, we were descending into a gap where our hike would come to an end. Laura was in the lead when she suddenly started backing up toward me. She quickly turned around and was about to run past me. "There's a bear up there!" I looked ahead on the dirt road and saw a huge dark furry figure walking down the hill, across the road, and toward the woods. I started moving toward the animal. "Where are you going?" Laura shouted.

"I never saw a bear before," I said breathlessly, hurrying toward the disappearing creature.

So it was that I did have my 2005 hike on the Appalachian Trail. It wasn't with Jim, but it was with someone I adore. And I saw my first bear.

What's in store for me next year?

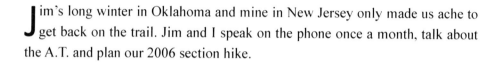

Chapter Twenty-three

Jim's long winter in Oklahoma and mine in New Jersey only made us ache to get back on the trail. Jim and I speak on the phone once a month, talk about the A.T. and plan our 2006 section hike.

May 23, 2006

The Virginia weather is fantastic. Today, early in the morning it's around forty-six degrees and in the afternoon it's supposed to get to the high sixties. Not a cloud in the sky. Jim and I are hiking together for the first time in two years. We get off on the wrong trail and realize that there was no white blaze for over a half mile. We turn around, walk back to the place where we had strayed from the trail, get on the A.T., and continue on our way to Marble Spring, Virginia.

May 24, 2006

Sunny and mild all day. We pass through mountain laurel with its perfumed aroma. We cross the James River on a long footbridge. On the other side, a seventy-one-year-old gentleman trail named Peanut Butter Kid waits with trail magic: cold sodas.

Jim tells Peanut Butter Kid that when he started the A.T. he had a seventy-eight pound pack. At the Foote Lodge where Jim spent the first night, someone asked what he was doing with so much weight. Jim said he had been a U.S. Army Ranger. The guy said: "You ain't no Ranger. You're just a dumb ass!" He then helped Jim remove over thirty pounds of gear from his backpack, including a hatchet, machete, and spice rack, among other things.

We're at the Johns Hollow Shelter tonight. Jim and I have the place to ourselves. I make a makeshift washing machine—actually, a gallon Ziploc bag into which I put a few items, such as socks and underwear, add in a little liquid soap, pour in water from a nearby stream, zip the bag, mash it until soapy water gets into the clothes, and pour out dirty sudsy water, pour in fresh water, shake it around, pour out dirty sudsy water, and repeat several times to rinse them out. I hang up the items on a clothesline made of my bear bag cord.

In the evening we hear a loud piercing sound like whippoorwill ... whippoorwill...whippoorwill. This goes on most of the night. Off in the distance these treetop troubadours sound like song birds. In a tree above you, when you're trying to sleep, they are a piercing nuisance! Gorilla and I get out of our tents and throw rocks up into the tree. The thud of stone against wood silences the boisterous night intruder. We stumble back to our tents and return to sleep.

A short time later, the same loud, offensive bird sound wakes us. It's dark. I go outside and throw some more rocks, but they miss the branches. I decide to throw a rock underhanded, expecting it to go upward and out. I'm still sleepy, when I release the rock it goes *straight up*. It is now rapidly dropping toward my skull! Furiously I backpedal, turn and run in time to avoid a backwoods craniotomy. The rock lands in the exact spot where I had been standing.

The bird laughs its last whippoorwill...whippoorwill...and leaves.

May 25, 2006

We feel good.

In the woods we meet a middle-aged husband and wife who are Appalachian Trail volunteers. Their trail names: Flash and Hot Flash.

A section hiker tells us about the abominable rocks in Pennsylvania. "In Pennsylvania, if a stone is kicked free and goes off to the side of the trail, at night someone comes along, picks up the rock, sharpens it and puts it back on the footpath!"

This evening we are at the Punchbowl Shelter, located on a large pond. Late in the afternoon a group of fathers and sons arrive. They go around the miniature lake, cross the stream that feeds the pond, and set up tents in a meadow. There are fourteen children about six to twelve years old. After dinner we hear the kids yelling and laughing. Jim and I join them to see what all the fun is about. The boys are running around. One of them is playfully waving a machete. A large fire blazes in the fire pit. Dads sit in a large circle around the flames and the tired boys flop down in front of them. In fire glow we chat. They ask us about hiking the Appalachian Trail. One man brings out a guitar and starts to sing. We listen as fathers and youngsters join in. After an hour, we say good night and return to our tents. The croaking frogs at the pond are in full force. Somewhere above them, in the background as we drift toward slumber, we are serenaded by the distant singing of fathers and sons.

May 26, 2006

Jim and I stop for lunch at a wide creek with boulders as stepping stones going across. We sit on the rocks. Gorilla takes his boots off and puts his feet in the water. When we are finishing lunch, along come two young women, She Bear and Jodie Foster. They sit on the boulders, eat lunch, and put their feet in the water. While they eat, I take off my shirt, and with cupped hands splash water on my head and face. It feels fantastic to get cleaned up after not having a shower for four days. Refreshing creek water washes away sweat and salt. Even though I have to put back on my same crummy T-shirt, it feels phenomenal. She Bear, who has a crew cut, says that two days earlier she came across a camper who had a five gallon bucket. He filled it with hot water, which she carried into the woods and took what she calls a "bitch bath." Somehow the young women always look cleaner than the guys.

At the North Forks of the Piney River we set up our tents next to the water. There is a fireplace here. Gorilla makes a fire, which helps keep away mosquitoes. Jim washed clothes the day before and they have not dried, so he is trying to dry them by hanging his pants and other items over the fire.

May 28, 2006

Our goal today is to reach the Dutch Haus Bed-and-Breakfast early enough to enjoy their renowned lunch. We are hiking by 6:15 a.m., hike four miles to Fish Hatchery Road where we meet a young couple who drives us to the Dutch Haus in Montebello, Virginia. This B&B is a beautiful place. The bunkhouse is the nicest I've seen. Everything is spotless. There are four bunks on the first level and an upper level of three more neat bunks.

The Dutch Haus gives free lunch to everyone who shows up—even if they are not staying there. Cell phone coverage is terrible. Lois and Earl who own the Dutch Haus let me use their telephone. After trying several times, I finally reach Barbara.

Today is the Sunday before Memorial Day and guests at the Dutch Haus are invited to attend a community dinner at the fire house in Montebello. We are driven down a rural road with a few houses nestled here and there, and a general store, into Montebello—one of the best places to celebrate a national holiday in the heart of small-town America. Montebello has only seventy voters who all vote at the small firehouse on Fork Mountain Lane. We are greeted there by women and men preparing and setting out food on long tables. We join other townsfolk and their children for a jolly commemoration of this country's spring holiday.

I walk around the firehouse and look at a wall display of 9-11 photographs. First are photos of New York's majestic twin towers. Then, horrifying scenes of destruction, firefighters, anguished people. There is the photograph of three firefighters raising an American flag in the World Trade Center rubble similar to the flag-raising at Iwo Jima—symbolizing strength and courage of all Americans who joined in lifesaving efforts in that horrendous tragedy.

She Bear joins us at our table. She has a knee problem and sits with her leg up on a chair, a pack of ice on her knee. She sees me looking at the photos of destruction, turns slightly to view them better. I tell her about ironworkers from Philadelphia who immediately went up to New York to help. She Bear is a massage therapist. She says after 9-11 massage therapists went there too. When the firemen returned from their day facing the removal of bodies, death, and destruction, the massage therapists would try to ease their pain by massaging them, but as soon as the massagers put their hands on the fire fighters, the men broke down and cried.

May 29-31, 2006
Back on the trail a thru-hiker said he saw two rattlesnakes. I would love to have seen them.

On May 31 we hike to the Paul Wolfe Shelter built into the side of a hill.

We're hanging out on the porch before dusk, leaning on the railing, when a guy in his mid-twenties with red hair and red beard comes hiking furiously toward us. When he reaches the shelter, he tries to catch his breath and says, "I just saw a *mountain lion!*" The hiker, Rematch, says he was at an overlook. He saw two deer running and looking behind them. A mountain lion was following them.

The powerful mountain lion, or cougar as it is also known, was thought to be extinct, but they are just hardly ever seen. Cougars are gray to brown in color, have a broad face, and are about seven feet from nose to tail. The cougar ambushes its prey, and sinks its huge pointed teeth into the back of a victim's neck to sever the spinal cord.

Fortunately, it prefers to eat deer.

June 1, 2006

We're at the outskirts of Waynesboro, Virginia, reputed to be the most hiker friendly town on the Appalachian Trail. Even the bikers are friendly. A group of them who just mounted their motorcycles, and are pulling out of a motel parking lot, stop the roaring of their engines long enough to surround Jim and me. One of them looks us over and says in a slow, deep voice, "You been hikin' long?" He sees us sweating in the bright Virginia sunshine. "Ya know what? We just left our rooms at this place," he says, glancing sideways toward the motel. "Left the doors open to the rooms. If'n you guys want to use them to take showers, yer welcome to do that."

I picture a room with traces of shiny blue-white shards of crystal meth and other controlled substances lingering in the debris of these premises. I try to sound friendly as I say, "No...thanks...We're going to a motel in, uh, Waynesboro."

Waynesboro is full of trail angels who regularly drive people between the A.T. and the town, a distance of four and a half miles. One trail angel is dropping off several hikers and picks us up. He takes us to our first request, the outfitter, which is part way into Waynesboro, and then the rest of the way to the Quality Inn. The trail angels won't accept any money, not even for gas.

June 2, 2006

Jim and I go to Weasie's Kitchen, a favorite with thru-hikers because of its all-you-can-eat pancake special. We're told the record for the most pancakes eaten at one sitting is twenty-four. I have bacon and eggs with mine and can't even finish three large Frisbee-size griddlecakes. While we're eating at Weasie's, we talk to a man seated at the next table. He tells us he used to be captain of the Waynesboro fire department and now owns a furniture store in town. After this friendly gentleman leaves, the waitress comes to our table and says the man paid for our breakfast. We ask his name and the waitress tells us it's Sam McVey.

A younger gentleman takes Sam's place across from Gorilla and me and starts talking to us. He grew up in the mountains and tells us, "When I was younger, my father, brother and me cut wood in the mountains. Sometimes, when we went to a new tract of land and were cutting trees, dad would suddenly say, 'Lets get out of here!' After we left, my father would tell us he'd found someone making moonshine with a still."

"Moonshine!" I'm only slightly surprised. "They still make illegal booze out there?"

"Yeah. It's not unusual to make moonshine. My own family had made and sold moonshine up in the mountains. They made it from corn … it took a lot of sugar and sometimes they would make it from grain. I still buy and use moonshine. Good stuff!"

On our way to the supermarket to buy some supplies, we see Sam's furniture store, Second Time Around. We stop in to see Sam and thank him for buying our breakfast. I tell him it was a special treat because today is my birthday. The store is loaded with all kinds of used furniture, antiques, collectibles, and other items. Sam shows us a pre-baby grand piano from the mid-1800s. It's shaped like a pool table, oblong with rounded corners, but only about three feet deep. He bought it at an auction for twenty-five dollars and it's worth about twenty-five hundred dollars. Sam got it so cheap because no one else at the auction had a truck large enough to haul it away. Sometimes the Salvation Army comes to him when a poor family moves into town and doesn't have anything. Sam furnishes their house with merchandise from his store, without any payment.

Gorilla wants to go to the Rock Fish Gap outfitter, about a mile and a half from our motel. We start walking down the long steep hill. A short woman with glasses calls to us from a small shopping area, "Do you need directions?"

"No," I yell back from across the street. "We're going to the outfitters."

"Wait a few minutes and I'll drive you down." And she does.

Back at the motel another thru-hiker invites us in for a beer. We spend the rest of the afternoon drinking beer and talking. We all go to dinner at the Italian restaurant in Waynesboro where the waitress brings out cheesecake with a lit candle on it for my birthday. Everybody in the restaurant sings *Happy Birthday*.

Waynesboro is a *very* hiker-friendly place.

June 3-5, 2006

We hike through central Virginia with its marvelous wilderness and gentler trekking than Georgia and North Carolina; ending at a road in a remote spot near the Pinefield Hut. It never ceases to amaze me how our friends can find us in the middle of nowhere. Circuit Rider and Sherlock find their way here to pick up Gorilla Jim. Lou and Bob locate our exact position to pick me up. This leg of our Appalachian Trail odyssey comes to a close until autumn.

Chapter Twenty-four

September 1, 2006

Hurricane Ernesto is coming up the coast. The U.S. Weather Bureau forecast for Shenandoah is extremely heavy rain—up to eight inches—and flash flooding with this warning:

> "FLASH FLOODING IS A VERY DANGEROUS
> SITUATION. IT IS THE NUMBER ONE WEATHER
> RELATED KILLER IN OUR REGION."[19]

In the face of this ominous forecast, Gorilla Jim, and I head to Virginia. Lou, accompanied by his friend Helen, drive us toward the wooded area where we had left off in June. Windshield wipers on the highest setting cannot clear the fast falling rain. We decide to wait until tomorrow to begin our hike.

September 2, 2006

The hike is moderately easy. Yet, Jim has difficulty and looks as if he is struggling. He is wearing a back brace because of a strained back he got lifting a large rock in his garden at home. The corset type back brace restricts his breathing. He is having the same problem I had several years ago. When Jim removed the corset and could breathe freely, he was okay to hike.

September 3, 2006

While hiking we meet a trail maintainer who says we will go down a stone face into a place where a tree is lying across the trail. "The tree is loaded

with nasty yellow jackets. Go off the trail and around the infested tree."
We get to the tree, go off the trail, almost get lost in the backwoods, and
when Jim and I come back out, we are exactly where the yellow jackets have
congregated. Back into the woods, walk about thirty feet, and come out past
the tree loaded with yellow flying stingers.

Jim wants to write a warning to other hikers. He hunts in his pocket for
something to write on, brings out a roll of toilet paper, tears off a few sheets,
writes a note, and hangs it on a bush. After walking about a hundred yards,
we meet a young couple who are day hiking. Jim strenuously cautions them
as if they are about to run into machine gun fire. They have an awkward look
on their faces as they head to the fictitious war zone identified by a toilet
paper warning.

No one is at Bearfence Mountain Hut until we finished dinner, when
two guys showed up. One of these hikers, Noah, saw a bear during his
hike today.

September 4, 2006

This morning Noah says a bat was flying around the upper level of the shelter
where he had been sleeping. He reads in the shelter register that another hiker
said during the night a bat had *pooped in his ear*. We hear the bat chirping as
it flies around beneath the shelter's roof. All of us look up to make sure we
are not targets.

Everybody says they see bears in the Shenandoas. We have not seen a
bear. On the way to Big Meadows we meet hikers who just saw several bear
cubs. A woman says, we had passed through an area that was notorious for
bears, but we didn't see any.

September 5, 2006

It rains through the night. This morning it's still raining heavily. We'll make
it a short day and hike five miles to Skyland Resort, an outstanding place to
stay in the Shenandoah National Park

At thirty-seven hundred feet, Skyland is the highest point on Skyline
Drive. Its contrasting rustic cabins and luxurious suites are spread out in the
mountains of the national park, isolated from civilization. Skyland began
in the late 1800s as a place where affluent folks from cities could enjoy

spectacular views in a dude ranch type setting. In those early days guests arrived by horseback or in a wagon. Today, most guests drive up by car; very few hike in, as we did.

The main buildings are in a stone, National Park motif with chalet sloping roofs. After registering, the clerk hands me a map of the resort. You need a map because spread out across the mountainside is an amphitheater, conference hall, dining room/craft shop/lounge, cabins, lodges, and many other things most people drive to. Unfortunately, we walk, carrying backpacks in the thickening fog.

Our countrified cabin room is clean and comfortable with a small bathroom. It's fifty-six degrees outside and as cold in our room. The heater is not working. There are no telephones in the rooms, so we use a cell phone to call the office. The maintenance men arrive, take apart the heater, and say the dreaded words, "We have to take it to the shop." The men remove the heating apparatus and leave.

Skyland's spacious and well-appointed restaurant has windows that rise to the ceiling. This transparent wall usually provides a spectacular panoramic view, but I can't see anything in today's dense clouds smothering the other side of the glass.

Sitting at a nearby table are two personable women from Germany and the tall, pretty daughter of one of them. I speak a little German, and Jim is fluent in the language from his extensive military duty in that country—and his former marriages to three German wives. We strike up a conversation. "*Guten tag.*"

They mercifully respond in English that they are making a tour of the United States. Jim entertains them with his memories of Germany and the three previous wives.

Surprisingly, the maintenance men had fixed the heater while we were at lunch, the room is sauna-hot and all of our wet things are drying.

The lounge has an evening attraction advertised as "live family-friendly nightly entertainment." Tonight's entertainment is a group of women clog dancers.

By the time Jim and I finish dinner the lounge is alive with laughter and sounds of people who just enjoyed a good meal and are sipping the cheerful drink of their choice. The room is filled; we stand and watch.

Clogging is hillbilly tap dancing that looks like Irish step dancing with metal taps on their shoes, enthusiastic high knee-lifting footwork to lively Bluegrass fiddling. The women, mostly slender, in their twenties and thirties, bound around energetically doing their movements simultaneously as in line dancing, but then break into a bouncy square dance. They all wear short blue fluffy skirts with crinoline undergarments beneath that make the skirts billow out at the knees and fly about. Almost every woman dancer has long hair tied up with a ribbon to keep it from bouncing on her face. With the aid of vodka on the rocks, I'm loose, wildly tapping my foot to the beat and looking around the room at people robustly clapping hands to the music.

September 6, 2006

Terrain in the Shenandoas is much easier than anywhere else on the trail so far. There is *no* such thing as an *effortless* part of the Appalachian Trail. It's all difficult to some degree. However, the trail here has been smoother; most rocky places are filled in with crushed stone. The rises and drops in the trail are gradual, and there are areas you can hike for a mile or so on a relatively level path.

We hiked approximately eleven miles to the Pass Mountain Hut. After dinner the two of us try to make a fire in the fire pit outside the shelter. We pour capfuls of alcohol on damp wood. It would not light. I search out dry branches, put them in the fireplace, put paper under them. They wouldn't ignite. All we produce is smoke and paper ash. Later, I read on page twenty-nine in the shelter register that the fire wood piled next to the Pass Mountain Hut is pressure treated with toxic chemicals and should not be burned, should not even be touched, and the ashes of such wood should not be touched. This is the first time Jim and I tried to make a fire and neither of us could get one started.

A south bounder we met earlier in the day, Cowsie, wrote in the shelter register:

"I slept in the hayloft with the mice, they sure can put on a show, swinging from the food bags, flipping through the air from bag to bag…it was better than Cirque Die Soleil!"

September 7, 2006

We are hiking in a lightly wooded area south of the Elk Wallow Picnic Area. Ahead of me and to my left something huge and black is moving. All senses spring alive. I'm seeing a bear—actually, two bears, a large bear and a small one—for a few seconds. Then, with their bearish swagger they are gone into denser woods. We come up to where the bears had been and look around. It is the first time I saw a bear in the 936 miles from Springer Mountain, and I saw two here in the Shenandoas.

At the picnic area I look for water. A man driving by in an SUV stops to talk. His name is Matt; his dog is Rocky. They were out hiking and camping with friends who had already left. Matt says if we need any food he has plenty left and would give it to us. He parks and welcomes us to join him in a meal of eggs and bacon. The back of his SUV is loaded with coolers of all kinds. Matt produces a carton of eggs, bacon, bread, milk, butter and a large (by hikers' standards) stove which he bought at a yard sale. Gorilla Jim volunteers to be the chef. He cooks up the eggs and bacon in a large skillet that we also use to toast bread.

You have to hike for a few days eating only camp food to appreciate the utter delight of a meal like this out in the open on a picnic table!

September 9, 2006

The Manassas Gap Shelter is known for harboring poisonous snakes. On a wall inside the shelter is a paper with pictures of two venomous copperhead snakes, information about the vipers, and a request to write in the shelter register information about sightings of these deadly reptiles. Copperheads are the most common venomous snake in the eastern United States. The stout-bodied snakes with copper-colored heads have heat sensitive sensory organs enabling them to find warm-blooded prey. Because copperheads don't have to see their target, they can strike accurately in the dark. Their poison causes a breakdown of its victim's red blood cells; hemorrhaging destroys its victim.

The Manassas Gap shelter register indicates that visitors found life-threatening Copperheads in the back of the shelter—a reason why many hikers don't want to stay here. Some people wrote that they didn't see any.

Jim and I talk about the legendary snake-bite remedy of cutting an X cut over the snake bite and sucking out the poisonous venom to save the snake bite victim's life. Both of us know the remedy of cutting the wounded area and sucking out poison is no longer medically accepted. Mainly, because cutting can damage underlying organs and increases the risk of infection.

We look around and do not see any signs of copperheads. Jim and I take the matter philosophically: If there were snakes, there would be no mice (the snakes would eat the mice). If there were mice, there would be no snakes. Either way there was something to be gained—so we slept here.

September 10, 2006

We meet day hikers and people section hiking. The only thru-hikers we meet on this trip are mainly south bounders, so called SOBOs. A north bounder is a NOBO.

A couple approaches us from a distance. All focus is on the young woman who, even bent forward under the load of a heavy backpack, shows the most enormous bosom I had ever seen. Her T-shirt is stretched to its limit. We stop to talk.

Her animated movements bring rippling to the monumental breasts. She says, "We're out hiking the trail for a few days. I've never backpacked before." This is obvious because her sternum strap, the strap going horizontally across the upper part of a person's chest, is positioned too low. It goes across her bust, squeezing her huge breasts out like balloons below and above it.

Gorilla Jim notices this and says: "Your sternum strap's too low—it should be higher." The strap has slide fasteners at each end that can easily be adjusted by pulling upward.

It is obvious how brawny her boyfriend is as he easily flicks off his heavy backpack. He stands to the side, gazing at his overdeveloped female companion as a farmer admires a prize heifer.

Jim likes to gesture with his hands, and he now waves them wildly as he moves closer and reaches for her chest. The boyfriend's eyes open wide in surprise and suddenly narrow. A sneer develops on the guy's face. Muscular arms, which had hung at his sides, start to move. His denim shirt, sleeves torn off, is open to the navel, upper body showing a tattoo of a pit bull ripping out the throat of another dog, the attack dog's mouth dripping red drops.

Boyfriend straightens to full six foot three height, a twitch in the powerful bicep of his right arm where a drawing depicts a skull. I know somewhere on this muscleman's body is a tattoo that reads: *Die Mother Fucker*. With one slip of Jim's fingers we are going to be in deep shit.

She looks at Jim and smiles invitingly.

Now the enraged boyfriend takes a step toward Jim.

Uh oh, I think. Here's trouble.

Jim is oblivious to the danger. Gorilla's fingers move near to the boyfriend's two pride and joys. Muscular boyfriend moves forward. Gorilla comes perilously close to causing a disaster. Instead, he just shows the place to which the strap should be raised.

I start breathing again.

After they are way out of sight, I wipe my brow and say, "Gorilla's got a new job: Sternum Strap Adjuster. Only for girls with big tits."

"I was just trying to be helpful."

"Yeah, you almost helped yourself to getting your face remodeled."

We meet hikers on the way to the Rod Hollow Shelter. They talk about the ominous upcoming Roller Coaster, a series of steep mountains, one peak after another without a break. One person wrote in the Rod Hollow Shelter register:

"Made it through the Roller Coaster. Sadistic Bastards."

Earlier today we met two marine corps colonels who were section hiking. They were around sixty years of age. The marines jokingly told us the Roller Coaster wasn't too bad, but they wrote in the shelter register: "Roller coaster—tough on two 60+ hikers."

A couple wrote in the register: "in for the night, food was good, sex was great." Gorilla and I are thinking, *A few evenings ago they were having sex in the same place where we're sleeping tonight.* Jim says, "I'll bet it was the girl with the big boobs, having sex right here."

I picture their sweaty bodies entangled, screaming enough to scare the bears. My brow reddens momentarily. I shake my head in a shudder to erase the scene from my mind.

Instead, I concentrate on a good joke in the shelter register. Think of someone in politics you really dislike and insert their name:

> "A nuclear physicist, the Pope, a boy scout, and [political figure omitted to avoid offending anyone] were the last four left on a falling airplane with only three parachutes left. The physicist declares his knowledge vital to the advancement of mankind, grabs a parachute, and jumps out of the plane. The political figure declares himself necessary to prevent chaos in the world sphere, grabs a parachute, and jumps. The Pope turns to the boy scout and tells him that he is old and has lived a full life and will stay on the plane so that one so young may live. 'That is not necessary, Father,' said the boy. '[political figure] jumped with my backpack."

September 11, 2006

Raining. At 9:25 a.m. we start climbing the much ballyhooed Roller Coaster. It's a rough climb, particularly doing it in a constant rain storm. As soon as we descend one mountain, we are faced with the next. So it goes all day. The terrain is rocky, and the rocks are wet and slick. Jim and I try quickening our pace to get out of the rain, but the slippery trail keeps slowing us down.

From the outside, Bears Den Hostel is reminiscent of a castle in the woods. The stone mansion is managed by Queen Diva, a very outgoing woman. The bunk room has a number of bunks and is clean.

At night Queen Diva makes a lovely dinner and baked mountain-size chocolate chip cookies. Sitting around the large table are Queen Diva, a middle-aged woman, Della, whose trail name is No Agenda, Smasher, a woman who operates backpacking trips and her clients, two women from Austin, Texas: Spirit and a younger woman who has extensively traveled and hiked. The subject is *hitchhiking*. We all agree it is as important *who* you get a ride with as getting the ride. This story was told by one of our dinner mates who got into a vehicle driven by a man who looked a little strange. As they went down the highway, the driver volunteered that he probably shouldn't be driving because he no longer had a license. He said he caused a bad accident, severely injured his head, was seeing double, and had trouble concentrating. The backpacker said, "I think I have to make a telephone call. Just drop me off over there," and hurriedly got out of the car.

I told of the famous hitchhiking scene in the renowned movie *It Happened One Night* with Clark Gable and Claudette Colbert. Stuck on a back road, the dapper Gable tells of his prowess in getting cars to stop to give him a lift. After several failed thumbing attempts, Claudette Colbert gets a car to jam its brakes to a stop by pulling up her skirt and showing a shapely leg.

Della says no one likes to pick up a gray-haired woman such as her. The women at the table all nodded their heads in agreement that the most likely person to be picked up is a younger woman, especially good looking girls. The next most likely to get a ride are men. The least likely to be picked up are *older women*.

"Why is that?" I ask.

"A man driving down a highway who sees a gray-haired woman hitchhiking assumes the woman is a weirdo; otherwise, what would she be doing out on the highway trying to get a ride with a stranger."

Jim then gives his imitation of how odd such a woman would appear to someone driving down a highway by making goofy faces and exaggerated gestures. The women laugh at the sight of Jim with his contorted face.

I thought back on what Jim and I learned from our experiences and what others have said about trying to get a hitch.

- Try to look as neat and clean as possible. Comb your hair.
- Fold up your hiking poles to make them less imposing and less like a weapon.
- Smile pleasantly so drivers know you are not dangerous.
- When the vehicle stops, talk to the driver before getting in. Look into his or her eyes and assess whether you feel safe being with this person. Ask, "Where are you going?" Do they look malicious, alcohol or drug impaired, whacky? If you feel unsafe or uncomfortable, just say, "No thanks." Just because a person stops, puts you under *no obligation to get into their vehicle.*

- Some hitchhikers use their cell phones to call or text message a friend to tell them where they were picked up, and might give enough description to ward off any problems by telling the listener something like: "A man picked me up in green Chevy SUV, probably 2008 model, and we're heading for, etc."
- Women should be extra cautious, among other things: dress modestly so a male driver does not mistake you for a hooker looking for business. If you feel sleepy, stay awake, engaging the driver in conversation.

Is hitchhiking dangerous? Yes! Avoid it or reduce the risk by choosing whose vehicle you enter.

The Appalachian Trail Conservancy states:

> **Avoid hitchhiking or accepting rides.** * * * * * * If you must hitchhike, be sure to have a partner. Make a careful evaluation before entering a vehicle. Size up the driver, occupants, and condition of the vehicle. If anything just "doesn't add up," decline the offer. Maintain enough distance between you and the vehicle so as not to be in a position to be pulled into the vehicle. If you do accept a ride, don't let your gear get separated from you. Keep your wallet and ID on your person. Memorize the license plate and note the make, model, and color of the vehicle. [20]

September 12, 2006

Hurray! Today, we pass the *one-thousand-mile mark* from Springer Mountain. Finally, we leave Virginia and enter West Virginia. We hike about eleven and a half miles to the David Lesser Shelter. Other guys show up. One brings his dog, a black lab mix. We're a bit crammed in. Three of the men are from Kansas City: D. B., Boulders, and Road Runner. They hike a section of the A.T. every year.

September 13, 2006

We leave the shelter in the early morning darkness. Jim insists he's on the right path. He finds it's the pathway to the privy. Jim says he has absolutely no recollection of how we arrived. He is concerned about his mind. It starts to rain. Jim looks glum. We walk in rain for hours in silence.

The Appalachian Trail Conservancy office is in Harpers Ferry. (The A.T.C. recently changed its name from *Conference* to *Conservancy*.) They take a Polaroid photo of me. I write my name and date on the photo, which is put in an album of people who hiked the A.T. and came through Harpers Ferry this year. Jim looks through the albums on a shelf, finds the 2002 book, the year he thru-hiked, and shows me a photo of Homer Witcher's family, whose children looked very young at the time.

At the motel I call Bob who says he will come to Waynesboro, Pennsylvania, with his wife, Aileen, to pick us up in a few days.

September 14, 2006

Today we come across what appeared to be the first homeless person I'd seen on the A.T. Looking like he fell from a freight train passing through an ugly part of town, this gaunt man who needs a shave sits on the trail surrounded by his dirt encrusted backpack, several ancient suitcases, and several black trash bags full of things.

They say eyes are windows to the soul. His lifeless eyes are murky portholes to an empty drab chamber. His voice is that of a mummy, muffled, without expression, and we strain to hear his emotionless words. He speaks low, haltingly, almost impossible to understand. "I had...bad ride (A.T. jargon for a bad hitchhike)...car door hit me in the head." There's a slash across his forehead.

Privies usually have a hook-and-eye closure so you can close the door and keep it from blowing open or keep someone from opening it while you're inside. The outhouse at the Ed Garvey Shelter is nicer than most; it has a door knob like a bedroom door. I close the privy door, the latch engages, latching the door and me inside. A sound of metal clanging against wood, an object lies on the floor—metallic—the knob that opens the door!

The doorknob was attached to a metal rod that goes through the door and releases the latch when turned. Unfortunately, the knob fell off inside so I cannot open the latch to get out. I try putting the knob back on but it is broken; try sticking my finger into the hole where the knob had been, and only succeed in pushing the rod toward the outside where it and the outside doorknob fall to the ground with a thud. I think about it and decide I don't want to spend forever in this vertical coffin-like potty. There are two options: kick the door out or call to Jim.

I yell. Jim comes and opens the door. I'm annoyed. "Why does this privy have a complex latch instead of the usual hook-and-eye closure that couldn't fail and trap someone in the outhouse!"

Jim is not sympathetic. "Why don't you just leave the door slightly open like most other people do?"

"I don't think that's what other people do," I reply. "And what if some young kid or slightly built hiker got locked in the privy with no one around to get them out?"

Gorilla wasn't concerned. "They should just leave the door ajar!"

On the shelter wall is the name of a person who maintains it. I call him. He isn't in, so I leave a message, explaining that someone could get locked in this privy. This is no criticism of folks who maintain the shelters. They do a great job building the shelters, repairing them—even leaving brooms for us to make the shelters livable as possible. I have the greatest praise for all who give generously of their time to shelter and trail work. Just, *please*, no door contraptions that can entomb a hiker.

We're trekking. A recent college grad, muscular as a triathlete, rushes by, leaps over a downed tree and almost knocks me over. He ignores us and bounds up a steep elevation. As he goes out of sound range, I shake my fist at his back. "Bring your father around, and I'll kick his ass."

Jim watches the speed-hiker effortlessly dash up a pile of high rocks. "Avalanche, better make it his grandfather." Mumbling even lower, "Maybe his great-grandfather."

During the day we cross the state line into Maryland, hiking twelve and a half miles from Harpers Ferry to the Crampton Gap Shelter. The three guys from Kansas are already at the shelter when we arrive around 1:30 in the afternoon. There's plenty of time with nothing to do, so Boulders and I try to make a fire using wood that is available. The wood is wet. With a large knife, Boulders shaves down fire-starting sticks so they look like miniature palm trees. Others join in the effort, and I photograph the guys trying to start a fire. Three of them work for a power company in Kansas; that didn't help much and it still takes us twenty-five minutes to get a decent blaze going in the fire pit.

September 15, 2006

Autumn is approaching. The ground is covered with leaf castoffs the shades of pumpkin and wheat bread; trees stand erect with leaves flame colored, straight like large candles on a birthday cake. We're hiking through Civil War history. Battles occurred right where we are passing. Many times we see rocks heaped into stone walls and imagine soldiers long-ago hiding behind them—firing on the enemy. We talk about young troops in heavy wool uniforms in this hot humid climate piling up these hefty stones.

Jim and I hike to Fox's Gap. A gentleman, who has been riding his bike, gets off, leans the bike against his leg, and tells about a battle that took place here. The Confederate forces defended the gaps so the Union forces could not get through. General Jesse Reno's forces were attacked. Confederate General Garland died and the Confederates scattered into the gap. He tells us that Robert E. Lee had his orders wrapped around cigars and delivered to his generals by runners. One of these cigars fell into Union General McClellan's hands.

Back in the woods, there are a group of kids from a middle school in Baltimore. They have an outdoor course, students hiking and exploring nature. As we come upon the kids, Jim lets out an earsplitting gorilla sound, which compels their attention to us. We take photos and josh with them. They ask about my pack and how much it weighs.

I remove it and place it on the ground, "How would one of you kids like to carry it?"

One slender boy who looks as if he can't even lift it asks, "How much will you pay to have it carried?"

"I won't pay you anything, but I'll give you a real nice thanks when you're finished!" I explain that my pack weighs around thirty pounds. "How much do you weigh?"

"Seventy pounds."

"This may be too heavy for you."

A husky boy behind him responds: "I weigh 120 pounds." He looks like he could carry the backpack and me.

They ask questions about where we slept, the food we ate, where we came from, and where we're going. The youngsters ask about my clothes, and I tell them I was wearing the same shirt for the second or third day. One girl says she once wore the same T-shirt for three weeks. A boy adds, "I wore underwear for over three weeks." The other kids go: "Eeew!"

Pine Knob Shelter is surrounded by large trees whose branches extend out over its metal roof. Squirrels drop nuts onto the roof and every time one crashes against the shelter's metal covering, it sounds like a gunshot.

At day's end we sit around and trade stories with shelter mates about hikes we've been on, equipment, tell jokes, kid each other. Conversations go from talking about tractor pulls to trips these folks want to take in the future. It's the warmest camaraderie. A kinship of souls bound together by a common effort. We talk about getting tired, both physically and emotionally. I see hikers taking Motrin or rubbing ointment on aching joints.

September 16, 2006

Rain doesn't let up. When I finally put the rain cover over my backpack, within twenty minutes the rain stops.

Walked thirteen miles to the Devil's Racecourse Shelter. A hiker referred to the extremely rocky and rough terrain coming up here as the "High Rock Hellway." Someone wrote on the shelter's picnic table: "*Chicken Tits* was here" and a date in 2006. The three guys from Kansas are here.

We were surprised to find the shelter was only one-tenth of a mile away from a nearby road. We don't usually camp near a road. Occasionally, rowdy locals can reach your camp and possibly harass you. It had been a steep, rocky descent to the shelter and after an already long hike today we were not about to climb back up to the trail and endure a long hike to another shelter. Besides, with the three guys from Kansas, we knew we would be formidable opposition for anyone who might try to annoy us.

Like us, D. B., Boulders, and Road Runner are finishing their section hike tomorrow. They are cooking their last dinner consisting of everything they had left in their food bag: a Lipton's, a Ramen, tuna pack, dried beef, oatmeal, and anything else they could find. They asked me to join them for dinner. I tasted the concoction. It was good but too spicy for me because they put some rub powder in it.

Jim is tired and goes to sleep around seven o'clock. I talk with the three guys from Kansas for a while. Around midnight I am awakened by Jim shouting to some guys who are outside the shelter. "What are you doing here!"

Two youngsters outside said they came to the shelter for something to do, but they were walking around the area with a cigarette lighter and igniting pages of a magazine. Jim told them the shelter was filled. They stamped out the flaming paper and walked away. I watch the cigarette lighter flame disappearing in the direction of a road.

Just some kids looking for something to do on a Saturday night.

September 17, 2006

The fog is thick as chowder at Penmar Park where Maryland ends and, at last, Pennsylvania begins. We have a snack at a mist-covered picnic table.

As we approach the last few minutes of our hike, the sun comes out, humidity drops, and we get the kind of weather I had been hoping for throughout the last sixteen days. Unfortunately, it came at the very end of this section hike.

In bright sunlight we stand on Route 16, trying to hitch a ride to Waynesboro, Pennsylvania. Jim and I alternate holding up our thumbs, and eventually a pickup truck stops. Inside sits a smiling and bubbly young woman. She tells us, "My husband said it's all right to pick up hikers as long as they stayed in the back of the truck." We were destined to ride in the truck's bed anyway—two large dogs take up the truck's passenger seat. We throw our backpacks onto the back, climb in after them, and enjoy a zippy fifty-mile-an-hour trip up the highway to the Best Western motel in Waynesboro.

To me, this bouncy ride in the rear of a pickup truck, sun gleaming off the paint job, warm wind blowing over me, and rural American sliding by, is really living.

There's a sense of accomplishment in climbing. We hike because the scenery is so beautiful, the camaraderie is warm, and the excitement is exhilarating.

Rain and rocky terrain in places made it slow going this time. It's satisfying to reflect on the experience and know that I was able to endure the constant rain and muscle-burning climbs. I remember trekking 170 miles in this section—over a 1,000 miles altogether—going through a number of states.

Now it just feels good to get off burning feet and aching joints.

But, I need to finally prove something important to myself.

PART FIVE

Chapter Twenty-five

You may be disappointed if you fail,
but you are doomed if you don't try.
—Beverly Sills

Philadelphia has the nation's largest City Hall. It took thirty years to build in an ornate style known as French Second Empire. One feature of this design is a lofty rectangular tower with sculptured details; it makes the building grand and imposing.

Philadelphia's majestic tower rises 548 feet above the ground, topped by a gigantic statue of William Penn. When City Hall was completed in 1901 it was the tallest habitable building in the world and to this day is the world's tallest masonry building. For many years my office was on the eighteenth floor of the Widener building in center city Philadelphia, facing this magnificent municipal building's white marble and granite.

One spring day I looked out my office window at a wide ledge surrounding the City Hall tower where Peregrine Falcons had made a home. These formidable hunters hover high in the sky searching for prey, mainly pigeons. Diving in a spectacular swoop, falcon's strong talons grasp victims in midair and kill them. Center city passersby did not appreciate bombardments of sidewalks and themselves from pigeons that they called "flying rats." Some of us suspected Peregrines were brought in years before to alleviate the problem. The falcons succeeded. That day, perched on the ledge approximately eighteen floors above the sidewalk was a young falcon carefully looking out and down. Circling in the air in front of the young bird was the falcon's mother, trying to induce her inexperienced babe to leave the ledge and fly. The smaller bird craned its neck downward, gazed from its imposing height at the concrete far below, looked back up at its mother, flapped its wings, and screeched, seeming to say, "You want me to do what? Are you out of your mind?"

I could've spent all day watching nature take its course, but I had work to do. When I looked later in the day, the mother and child were gone. I assumed the young bird took a shot at it and jumped, or mom shoved it into its first great adventure.

Now it's my time to fly solo. Sure, people told me it's a bad idea to hike alone. The books on hiking advise: *never* hike by yourself. Even so, something inside demands that I hike Pennsylvania by myself, starting at the southern border and going diagonally across the state to where the A.T. leaves Pennsylvania. At this time of year, most thru- hikers are still hundreds of miles south—it is unlikely there will be people around, and I'll be alone for days at a time.

Many people said to me, "Al, are you afraid to be by yourself?" Some asked, "Are you taking a pistol?"

Dangers you need a pistol for are not the only perils. One slip on a glistening wet stone slab while descending a mountainside—rocks sliding beneath your feet—and you've got a broken leg with no doctor, no help from anyone. Several times before I'd slipped, fallen, and just missed hitting my head on granite. One unlucky day, I could take a bad spill and my head could have a contest with a boulder to find out which is harder. I'd lose—then what the hell would I do lying out in the hinterland with scrambled brains—without Jim!

According to U.S. Department of Justice statistics, in this country there are about six murder victims per one hundred thousand persons. "Considering 3 to 4 million people 'populate' the A.T. over the course of a year," says

Appalachian Trail Conservancy's Brian King, "people tend to put the odds of being a murder victim on it at 1 in 18 to 20 million."

The ATC has stated: "Don't let the potential dangers alarm you or discourage you from enjoying the Trail." Okay. Still, somewhere in the back of everyone's mind is the awareness that being by yourself in a vast uninhabited forest, you are vulnerable.

If I had an accident, injured myself, got lost—*or worse*—I'd be on my own. Still, it's something I have to do...without a wingman.

Are dangerous people out there?

How dangerous can it be?

CLAUDIA AND REBECCA

The Appalachian Trail runs through southern Pennsylvania, where I'll be hiking, along a mountain ridge in Adams County. In 1988, Claudia Brenner (thirty-one and petite with fine features) and Rebecca Wight (twenty-eight and athletically graceful) were out for a few days of hiking along this mountainous trail. When they reached the Rocky Knob Trail they turned off the A.T. to find a campsite. The two women stopped at an ideal place next to a small creek with brush and trees all around that gave them the feeling of solitude they sought on this sunny, pleasant mid-May afternoon. Claudia and Rebecca ate dinner, spread their tent fly out next to the slow-moving stream, and lounged in the late afternoon seclusion of greenery and peacefulness that is so often found along the Appalachian Trail in southern Pennsylvania. Other than birds singing in a nearby tree and easy flow of the small creek, it was quiet.

Gunfire!

Shots were being fired. Severe pain in Claudia's arm. Blood. Where in this tangle of mountain laurel and thick woods is the rifle fire coming from? Bullets tear into Claudia. She is hit in the arm and neck and screams at the impact. A third bullet hits the other side of her neck. The fourth and fifth shots strike Claudia's face and head.

Rebecca stood up to run toward the protection of a nearby tree. Rebecca took a fired metallic slug in the head and another in her back.

Their screams are unanswered. There is no one to help them in this secluded backwoods.

The green tarp they were on was splattered with blood.

The shooting stopped. Silence. The two women sought protection behind a tree. Afraid the gunman might return, Claudia urged Rebecca to walk with her to get help. Rebecca tried to get up—she couldn't, and fell. Rebecca was losing her vision, the world going dark, lips turning pale. Rebecca could no longer talk.

Claudia pressed a shirt to Rebecca's back wound and then Claudia wrapped a towel around her own bleeding neck. She spit blood and bits of bullet-shattered teeth.

With Amazon determination Claudia struggled almost four miles over rugged trail, the white cloth around her neck turning red. All the time afraid the sniper would reappear and sting her with a final fatal shot. At a road, Claudia stopped a car with two teenage boys in it. She wanted them to go back with her to help Rebecca. Instead, they took her to a police station.

Claudia was helicoptered to the Hershey Trauma Center, hospitalized, and—miraculously—she survived.

When the police found Rebecca, she was dead. The last shot had proved fatal to Rebecca Wight; it shattered her liver.

Stephen Roy Carr was twenty-one years old, tall, thin, sunken eyes, long jumbled reddish hair, wearing gray sweat pants. Carr drifted from place to place, managed to survive by fishing, trapping, and hunting in the woods—a fugitive from justice wanted by the state of Florida.

Carr had raised his .22 caliber rifle, lined up the sights on Claudia Brenner and fired. Each time re-chambering a shell in his bolt action rifle, sending speeding metal slugs into the body of Claudia—his first victim—then firing on Rebecca Wight.

The Pennsylvania State Police thoroughly searched the Appalachian Trail area and found a knife, twenty-six rounds of live .22 caliber ammunition and eight used .22 caliber shell casings. Those items were located behind a tree eighty-two feet from the spot where gunfire smacked into Rebecca and Claudia. The evidence pointed toward Carr as the shooter. A manhunt involving mounted police officers and dogs eventually led to Carr's arrest.

Why would Carr shoot two innocent people? Why shoot two strangers who had not harmed him—women who were not even aware he was nearby.

To reduce the crime from murder to manslaughter, Carr tried showing that at the time of the killing he was acting under sudden and intense passion resulting from provocation. The provocation? Let the proceedings of this case explain:

> Carr defended at trial on grounds, inter alia, that he had shot Brenner and Wight in the heat of passion caused by the serious provocation of their nude homosexual lovemaking [in backwoods near the Appalachian Trail]. In support of this defense and to show the existence of passion, Carr offered to show a history of constant rejection by women, including his mother who may have been involved in a lesbian relationship, sexual abuse while in prison in Florida, inability to hold a job, and retreat to the mountains to avoid further rejection. This was relevant, he contended, to show that he was impassioned when provoked by the "show" put on by the women, including their nakedness, they're hugging and kissing and their oral sex. The trial court refused to allow evidence of Carr's psychosexual history, finding it irrelevant.[21]

The problem with this argument, the prosecutor claimed, is that Rebecca and Claudia "changed campsites" and that Carr "followed and his act of voyeurism involved persons ignorant to his spying...They sought the solitudes of a location thought pristine. Many may frown upon what they did, but they broke no law and only pursued activities in which they have the right to engage."[22]

There was no evidence that Claudia and Rebecca knew that Carr was watching them. Therefore, it was up to the court to determine "whether two women engaging in intimate acts in the forest is a valid excuse for someone to kill them."[23]

It didn't think so, and judged that "The sight of naked women engaged in lesbian lovemaking is not adequate provocation to reduce an unlawful killing from murder to voluntary manslaughter."[24] Carr was found guilty of murder in the first degree and sentenced to life imprisonment without possibility of parole.

Neither Claudia nor Rebecca would ever return to the car they had parked before starting their idyllic Appalachian Trail hike. Ironically, they had parked it at a place called *Dead Woman's* Hollow Road.[31]

SCOTT AND SEAN

Wapiti Shelter is a log shelter surrounded by tall slender trees. Water is provided from the nearby Dismal Creek. Trekking the Appalachian Trail, before reaching the shelter is a pond some trekkers will swim in when the weather is warm. May 6, 2008, was a sunny, outstanding spring day—so glorious that two friends put out of their minds a horror that occurred here long ago.

Scott Johnston, thirty-nine years old, was an average-size man, a cook. He was going to meet his friend, Sean Farmer, at the Dismal Creek near the A.T.'s Wapiti Shelter for several days of camping and fishing in the backcountry. Scott arrived first and parked his truck. Fishing was fabulous. Scott caught six big trout.

Scrawny looking Randall Smith had been in the woods for weeks. Smith appeared underfed, facial skin slack, baggy under the eyes. He wore a camouflage jacket. His dog's ribs showed through its spotted fur. Smith walked up out of the creek bank and said to Scott, "Oh, you know, there's no fish in this creek."

Scott fixed his eyes on the hungry-looking stranger, opened his cooler and, handing a bag of fish to Smith, said, "Here, you can have these." Scott went on to say he was setting up a camp nearby and was waiting for a friend to arrive. Randall Smith left.

The campsite was a level green area with woods to the rear that curved to the right where it met a dirt road. In the afternoon Scott's buddy Sean drove up this road in his Jeep, and pitched a tent. Sean, thirty-three years old, was a truck driver, a tall man, big in every dimension.

The gaunt Randall Smith returned to the campsite and talked to Scott and Sean. They invited Smith to stay for dinner and cooked up trout and beans, and grilled an extra trout for Smith's emaciated dog. Scott, Sean, and Smith sat around the campfire, occasionally adding wood from a pile next to it, and chatted.

It was getting dark. The stranger, Smith, walked toward his dog and patted his leg to attract the pooch, "Come on, boy. We need to get back to the camp." Calmly, the withered Smith sauntered behind Sean. Smith put a hand in his jacket pocket, took out a .22 caliber gun, pointed it toward Sean, and *bam!* Smith shot him in the right temple.

Sean saw fire coming from the stranger's hand, heard the boom, and felt a huge ringing in his head. His mouth swelled; Sean couldn't speak. Sean stood, and his massive body staggered back. In the dark he could see the firing of bullets toward his friend Scott.

Scott was hit in the neck. He got up and started to scurry away, ducking down. Scott was shot again, this time in the back. To shield himself, he got behind a clump of trees. With every heartbeat blood squirted from his neck. He felt the bullet hole, stuck his finger in the small opening in his neck to stop the flow.

The shooter turned back toward Sean who was bleeding from the right temple. There was a blank look on the gunman's face when he fired a shot into Sean's chest. Over six feet four and upwards of 325 pounds, Sean was a bull of a man. He staggered but didn't collapse. There was blood in his eye. Sean stumbled to his Jeep and got in. Surrounded by darkness he wondered *Where is Scott? Where is the shooter?* In campfire light, Sean saw the gunman approach the driver's side, a firearm aimed directly at him. The stranger squeezed the trigger. The gun did not fire. Out of ammunition! Sean started the car, ducked down toward the passenger seat, and sped away.

Scott had moved toward the woods for protection. When he heard Sean's Jeep he stepped into the road. Sean stopped and Scott stumbled in. They were both heavily bleeding, critically wounded, trying to stay conscious. The vehicle accelerated down a dirt road with sharp turns. There were drop offs at the edges of the road. Wildly, they skidded sideways around a curve.

A bullet in his head, Sean was losing sight, blacking out. Scott said, "You just listen to me, and I'll tell you when to work the pedals." As they went down the mountain, Scott directed what pedals to use—"…gas…brake…" They took S curves, Scott steered from the passenger side, holding a finger in his spewing neck wound to keep from bleeding to death. They had to stay ahead of the gunman who would soon chase after them in Scott's truck— Scott had left the keys in the ignition.

At the bottom of the mountain the two wounded men found a house where the people helped stanch the bleeding and called 911. Sean could not talk. Scott gave a description of the assailant. He was well known to the police.

Who was Randall Smith? For that, we go back to the same Wapiti Shelter on the Appalachian Trail, years earlier, 1981.

Robert Mountford, Jr. and Susan Ramsay, both twenty-seven years of age, were from Maine where they were social workers at a residential center for troubled teens. Robert, sincere eyes and a flourishing mustache, and Susan, her long hair parted in the middle with two pigtails, were hiking the Appalachian Trail together. When they didn't show up in Pearisburg, Virginia, law officers went to the A.T. to check out the Wapiti Shelter because it is the shelter on the Appalachian Trail closest to Pearisburg. One of the investigators, Tom Lawson, said that the flooring of the shelter "was very black, like someone had rubbed a substance on the floor. I kind of bent over to kind of look down between the boards and I could see a red substance through the cracks. And once the boards came up—we saw that there was a large puddle of blood."

They searched the neighboring woods. Poking up from beneath leaves was a sleeping bag and the body of Susan Ramsay. A blunt instrument had struck her in the back of the head. Susan was stabbed repeatedly in the chest. The next day they found the body of Robert Mountford, shot in the head.

A paperback book that belonged to Susan Ramsey was found with a bloody fingerprint on one of the pages. It was the fingerprint of *Randall Smith*. Eventually, Smith made a deal with law enforcement, pleaded guilty to the two killings and received fifteen years imprisonment, seven and a half years for each of the murders.

In 1996 Smith was released from prison. Despite previously murdering two innocent hikers on the Appalachian Trail, Smith could not be prevented from lurking the A.T. And now, in 2008, he had struck again, and the police knew him all too well. Shortly after Scott and Sean were shot, the police began to hunt down Randall Smith. That evening, a state trooper spotted Smith driving Scott's gray pickup truck. Smith tried to speed away along Sugar Run Road but lost control and ran up an embankment, flipping the Ford Ranger on its roof. So severe was the crash that Scott's fly fishing rod in the truck broke in two. The authorities had never before found the gun used in the 1981 killings of the two hikers in the Wapiti Shelter. When the police pulled Smith from the truck wreckage, a .22 caliber revolver was within his reach—the same type of handgun Smith used in 1981 to kill the two hikers, Mountford and Ramsay!

Smith was taken to Carilion Roanoke Memorial Hospital. Several days after his latest attempted murders Randall Smith died.

Sean and Scott survived. Scott was told by his physician that the shot into his neck came within one millimeter of Scott's carotid artery. Had the bullet cut this major blood vessel, he would have bled to death. Sean still has bullet shrapnel in his rib area and a bullet in his sinus.

The miraculous teamwork of two critically wounded men struggling to drive a vehicle down a winding mountain road at night, one steering and the other using the accelerator and brakes, produced inspiring outlooks on life. In a 2009 *Dateline NBC* interview, Sean said, "Well, I'd say the most important part is, you know, just don't give up. Ever. No matter what." Scott added, "And live life to the fullest. And be thankful for all the things you have, because it could be taken from you in a split-second."[25]

MOLLY AND GEOFF

Through a Pennsylvania pine and oak forest, the A.T. comes to a blue blazed trail leading to an older log shelter with a spring behind it. Few hikers stop at the Thelma Marks Shelter because of a disaster that happened on September 13, 1990.

Molly LaRue, twenty-five years old, was outgoing, an artist. For three months she had been hiking the Appalachian Trail with her boyfriend, Geoff Hood. He was twenty-six years old, quiet, an admirer of Gandhi. They didn't know they were spending the last hours of their lives in this shelter.

As a husband and wife hiked up to the Thelma Marks Shelter, they knew something was wrong. Food and equipment were thrown around...In the shelter were two dead hikers.

Molly was bound, raped, and repeatedly stabbed in the neck and upper back. A boot mark on her left elbow and a rope around her neck are evidence she had been tortured. Molly died approximately fifteen minutes after the knife went into her neck.

Geoff had suffered multiple .22 caliber gunshots in the head, back, and side. Geoff died five to eight minutes after being shot.

The killer covered their bodies with their sleeping bags and left them in that Appalachian Trail shelter. The search was on for the killer.

Hikers didn't know they shared the Appalachian Trail with a man under extreme mental or emotional disturbance—a murderer who was also sought by the F.B.I. in connection with slashing a woman's throat in Florida. F.B.I. records revealed that the Florida woman's naked body was found next to an alligator infested swamp near Paul Crews' makeshift home. In the dead woman's car trunk were Crews' bloody clothes and knife.[26]

Hikers on the trail had noticed Paul Crews carrying Molly and Geoff's belongings. This transient had Geoff's unusual green and purple backpack and wore Geoff's hiking boots. Eight days after their murders, the police found and arrested Paul Crews. He had the dead hikers' gear and a .22 caliber revolver and a long knife. This drifter fit the description of a man seen by witnesses near the Appalachian Trail murder scene. Crews' gun had been used to kill Geoff; traces of blood on the knife matched Molly's blood type.

Crews was tried and convicted of murdering Molly and Geoff, and he received two consecutive death sentences."[27]

According to the Keystone Trail Association, "This rape and double murder was the worst crime ever recorded on the AT in Pennsylvania."[28]

Hikers avoided the Thelma Marks log lean-to, a reminder of gruesome crimes committed on the same floor where hikers were expected to sleep. So it was, in September 2000, men bearing axes dismantled the old fated refuge and replaced it with a new Cove Mountain Shelter.

These were not the first grisly homicides on the A.T., and would not be the last. Since 1974, about ten murders took place on or near the Appalachian Trail. The Appalachian Trail Conservancy website provides Personal Safety & Awareness Tips for A.T. Hikers. Among the info is this:

> **Use extra caution if hiking alone.** When you hike alone, you are more vulnerable…If you encounter someone who makes you feel uneasy, avoid engaging them and put distance between you…

A cell phone may help in an emergency, but is useless if there is no reception. It's possible to go for days without a signal on the Trail.

Be wary of people who make you uneasy. Avoid or get away quickly from people who act suspicious, hostile, or intoxicated or exhibit aggressive curiosity or any other behaviors that just don't feel right, even if you can't explain why. Trust your instincts, even when someone claims to be an authority figure or "trail angel." Don't worry about being judgmental or hurting someone's feelings—your safety may depend on it. Don't stay in a shelter or engage in conversation with anyone who makes you feel uncomfortable. Criminals are often opportunistic—even engaging in polite conversation with someone who is overly aggressive may signal to them you are an easy target. Don't reveal your itinerary. Make note of as many details about the person as you can, and report them to law enforcement or ATC.

The ATC leaves us with this final caution: *"remember you are responsible for your own safety."*[29]

We size people up in the first seconds we meet them. When a stranger approaches me on the trail, I'm reasonably cautious until I give them a quick once-over. So far, no one failed my evaluation. Gorilla Jim was different— Jim was wary of many people.

Everyone has to decide for themselves what risks they will or will not take.

Are you 100 percent safe anywhere?

Pennsylvania's Michaux State Forest—where Rebecca Wight was cruelly killed and Claudia Brenner was viciously shot five times—*is exactly where I'm headed.* Alone.

This doesn't prevent me from hiking by myself and enjoying the backwoods. On the other hand—since Molly LaRue and Geoff Hood were killed as they slept in a Pennsylvania shelter—much as I hate the sounds of mice scurrying, I may never again use my sound-deadening ear plugs when alone in a shelter.

It's time for me to fly into enemy territory…without a wingman. Alone.

Chapter Twenty-six

Pennsylvania– The Ankle Buster State!
Pennsylvania…Where boots go to die.

April 20, 2007

Early this morning I meet Lou near the Pennsylvania Turnpike. We drive three hours to Waynesboro, Pennsylvania.

In warm weather, I hike six miles to Tumbling Run Shelters, which consist of two log shelters. Comically, one shelter has a sign on it: "Snoring." The other shelter has a sign: "Non-snoring." There is a fresh spring coming down the mountain on the other side of a fast-moving stream. Large stepping stones with water tumbling over them are slippery and out of the question. I walk downstream and go over on a log that had fallen across the rushing water.

Dave, a man who is here at the shelter overnight, talks about packaged meals used by the military known as MREs [Meals Ready To Eat]. Because these rations are not favorite food on the trail, MREs are also known as *Meals Refused by Ethiopia.*

In late afternoon, local residents Dick and Cheryl come by the shelter. Dick is a wiry man in his forties, steel-gray bushy beard and a daypack. Cheryl has a smiling, goodhearted appearance. They ask if we need anything; Dave and I say we don't. They are quite insistent that if we need anything from food, a drive, shower, place to stay for the night, or if we have any problems, to let them know. Dick writes his telephone number on a card. "If you run into any problem in the next hundred miles, call me." As Cheryl gets ready to leave she asks, "Is there anything at all that I can get you?"

"Yeah..." I couldn't resist and slowly start to say, "Twenty-one year old—"

She interrupts with a broad smile. "I can't get you any twenty-one-year-old *girls*."

"No, no," I say red-faced and flustered. "What I need are twenty-one year old *legs and lungs*."

Her merry face explodes into laughter. She holds one hand up to her mouth to help compose herself and giggles. "I can't get you that either." Then pleasantly and genuinely, "But, if there is anything else you need, call us."

They put Oreo cookies and pieces of wrapped chocolate on the table, and went on their way.

While Dave and I continue talking, four Penn State students show up.

Dave says, "Here come the twenty-one-year-old girls."

April 21, 2007

In the morning, hiking out of the bowl in which the shelter is located, the temperature rises and becomes warm. Yesterday's terrain was rather easy. Hiking by myself is fun. I stop when I want to, hike as fast as I like, and enjoy the scenery and solitude.

At midday I stop high atop a mountain, and sit behind boulders to shield myself from the sun. Buzzards are nature's undertakers, disposing of the animal kingdom's dead carcasses. Three famished turkey buzzards—dark wingspans as wide as my arms span—glide above, slowly circle, and look me over. They crane their necks, eyeballing me like a funeral director looking for business. I yell up to them, "I'm not your next meal."

Today finds me treading over large rock after large rock, stepping up onto stone masses and down into gullies between them. There is a rugged beauty to the jutting landscape; still, it slows my pace and twists my ankles.

At night, Quarry Gap Shelters is shared with various hikers, including a woman who is solo backpacking for the first time. At times she seems worried about hiking by herself, but looks as if she enjoys the camaraderie of everyone at the shelter.

April 22, 2007

Before 11:00 a.m. I reach the Birch Run Shelter, a fine place with bunks in it. Lots of time to do things such as wash underwear and socks and hang them on a line, fix my camera case which is sliding down on the backpack's shoulder harness. I wash up at a stream nearby. Weather is gorgeous, high of seventy-four degrees.

Being Sunday, a number of day-hiking families come by. Scout leaders stop to eat lunch and look over the Birch Run Shelter area for a campout and hike they're having here next weekend.

Everyone has left. It is now tranquil, quiet, except for the sound of a lightly babbling stream about two hundred feet away. A happy chipmunk goes in and out of ground cover, pauses, then moves on. The bottoms of my feet burn from the long trek yesterday. I soaked them in the cold stream and then put tape across the balls of each foot and on other areas that look rubbed and could form blisters. It doesn't seem like anyone else will be here tonight so I gather wood for a fire. Scouts must have been at the shelter recently—it is picked almost clean of fire wood.

With nothing else to do, I read entries in the Birch Run Shelter Register:

7/24/06

"Pro is the opposite of con, right?

So what is the opposite of progress? Congress."

9/20

"In for shelter check. Swept out bunks and shelter. Swept out a mad amount of bat guano [bat poop] off of the top right single bunk. Beware, little guy living in the rafters above. Sorry, too terrified of them to chase him out! * * * *"

— Overseer K. T. and Sally (the dog)

9/29

"Third grade from G B Lahrs had fun. We saw a caterpillar, a spider, a centipede, egg sacs, water bugs. We learned lots.

— Mrs. Cook (aka The Turtle) and her gang"

9/30

"So a bear and a rabbit are out in the woods answering nature's
call. The bear says, 'Hey rabbit? '

'Yeah? '

'You ever have trouble with shit sticking to your fur?'

'No, not me.'

'Oh.'

...so the bear wipes his ass with the rabbit."

Although Birch Run is a big shelter, no one shows up. Slept here by
myself. Had a great night's sleep.

April 23, 2007

It takes only three hours to go six miles to the Toms Run Shelters. It's
seventy-five degrees outside. I go into the shelter's shade, take off my boots,
lay down on my sleeping pad, and, using my backpack for a pillow, take a
nap while listening to a song bird and meandering brook close by. Mild air.
No one around. Peaceful. This is heaven. Awoke, ate an early lunch. Lay
down to take another nap.

A woodpecker rapidly pecking on a tree wakes me with a reminder it is
time to move on—even though it's only 10:45 a.m.

I had hoped to stay at Ironmaster's Mansion Hostel, a brick building
dating back to colonial times, but there was no room for me because a high
school class would be occupying the entire premises. I stop to pick up a mail
drop box I had sent there, go through my package of goodies while sitting at
a table on their covered porch.

Instead of people to talk to and a real bed tonight, I stay alone in my tent
at the state park, which is down the road from the hostel. At this campground
there are no other hikers except me. Instead, people are holed up in their air-
conditioned RVs. I have the whole afternoon to take care of things. I take a
shower, my first one in five days. And I take care of my feet. My little toes
have been bothering me and the side of the left ankle is painful. I tape the
toes and put moleskin on the ankle.

April 24, 2007

Last night I slept in my new lighter tent for the first time. Very comfortable. During the night it drizzled—the tent stayed dry.

This morning on the trail I met a young man bounding over rocks, heading south. He said he started at Bear Mountain, New York, on April 1. I asked what kind of mileage he was averaging. He said, "In the low twenties." I thought, *How great it would be to average miles in the low twenties and have a similar age.* When I last saw him, he was skipping over this stone mason's playground going south.

April 25, 2007

I wake up this morning and go outside—it's chilly, hospitably damp as though the dew came to greet me. I stretch and shiver the good shiver of feeling alive—all my senses taking in and enjoying the morning.

The terrain has been good—relatively easy compared to what I've heard about the steep and rocky areas farther north. It was forty-six degrees when I left at 6:20 this morning. Two hours later, it is fifty-one degrees, cool, invigorating. I hike in shorts and T-shirt, moving at a good speed.

I feel wonderful. All around me it is calm and silent. A certain tranquility here in the woods. Today is Wednesday, unlikely anyone will be out.

Hiked across many broad farms and finally reach Boiling Springs, Pennsylvania. Spent the evening at Galinas Manor, an immaculate 1800s Victorian B&B loaded with chotchkas (dolls, knickknacks, toys, pictures and furniture of every kind). My bedroom has a doily covering on top of the dresser. There's a wash basin and pitcher, canopied bed and a chamber pot. Everywhere you look are things to occupy space. Kitty Galinas washes my clothes. It had started raining when I was a mile or so from Boiling Springs. The rain has picked up. Lee Galinas lends me an umbrella and directs me up the street to a great dinner at the Boiling Springs Tavern.

April 26, 2007

The first part of today's hike is easy; the ground is muddy. It's cold, damp, and breezy. No place to stop because everything is wet from last night's downpour. My boots are not waterproof and my socks are soaked.

It's fourteen miles to the Darlington Shelter. This shelter sits in the woods off the A.T. amid tall trees with a stream a quarter mile away. No one else shows up; I have the shelter all to myself.

April 27, 2007

I awaken at 3:00 a.m. Where did all this fog come from? Looks heavy and it's rolling in fast. I'll sleep a few more hours, then get an early start at five o'clock.

When I next pull my hand out of the sleeping bag, I press the button that lights my watch. It is after five, very foggy—*a* murky darkness. It's bone-chilling damp. Stiffly I get up, put on a warm layer, and eat breakfast with my gloves on. Grudgingly, I pack up.

At this time of year, way after 5:00 a.m., the sky should be getting brighter—but it's still dark. Waiting. At this time of morning daylight should show through the fog!

But everything around me remains encased in murk the dirty gray color of rats. Eerie! It's like time is standing still. Is this a permanent eclipse? Is an astronomical phenomenon blocking out the sun? Am I in a black hole? Am I going nuts out here by myself in the woods?

It is cemetery quiet. Shivering.

The cracking of a twig breaking underfoot. I stare into deep opaqueness that can't be slashed through with a machete. I'm straining to detect what is moving across the forest floor. Dead silence. My little flashlight aims out at what should be tree trunks and undergrowth, but they are darkly tangled and enshrouded in the fog.

If it doesn't get light, I'll have to stay in this small wooden lean-to all day. I don't have enough water. I couldn't go down to the spring because it would be like walking into a world of fiberglass insulation—I'd never find my way back. Inside, I'm trying to ignore a gnawing feeling of anxiety.

Nature has run it's course and I have to take a trip to the privy. Fifteen steps away I lose sight of the shelter in the engulfing murkiness. I shine my small light toward the privy. I can't even tell how far away it is. It is as though I'm looking through a steamed up window or two or three. I return to the shelter, take a second little flashlight and rig it to shine out of the shelter.

This will be a beacon to find my way back from the privy. With every step I turn around to see if the beacon is still visible—it has turned into a blur. That fuzzy glow floating in the woods is all I have to aim for on my return trip to the shelter.

Back into my sleeping bag to keep out the damp and cold. Still very dark for this time of the morning. I'm in a time warp of bleary never-ending night. When I look at my watch again, something is strange. I press the watch's Mode button several times and finally get to the *date-time* mode. The mystery is solved—I had been looking at the *wrong mode*! It is only *4:30 a.m.*!

Gradually ebony inkiness dissolves. I pack my sleeping bag and get ready to hike. It's now lighter, and, although somewhat foggy, I'll be able to make my way out of here.

This morning I come to a small creek. A split log bridge crosses the stream. The bridge is shaky, tilts downward to the left. Its log planks are slippery from last night's rain and mist—coated with a thin, damp slime. My feet start slipping sideways. No guardrail! I'm sliding left off the edge of the bridge and drop over five feet. My boots plunge into cold water, soaking my pants up to the knees. The water is not deep; I laugh to myself, thinking: *This must have looked like a children's cartoon.*

Feeling strong, independent, and self reliant I spend the day hiking in cool drizzle. It's peaceful—no usual problems of business and social life. I walk through extensive farmlands and empty woods. I amuse myself by pretending to be an Indian sneaking up on wild game, my footsteps soft and quiet. Finally, I arrive at the town of Duncannon and go to the Doyle, as it is known to hikers. This hotel was erected a hundred years ago. It is a grand old structure built by Anheuser-Busch near the Susquehanna River for the enjoyment of folks of a prior century. The Doyle's glory days have long since gone. Today, it is a weary hotel run by Vicky and Pat, two friendly people who welcome backpackers. It is a thru-hiking tradition to stay at The Doyle. I feel the spirit that a century of hikers before me brought to this place.

Vicky greets me in the bar, which serves as the main point of entry to the Doyle and is the only place downstairs where people congregate to drink, eat, and shoot pool. I ask for a room with its own bath, but Vicky tells me the Doyle wasn't built that way and there are two bathrooms in the hallway (for the approximately dozen rooms on the third floor). Vicky says there are two boxes waiting for me. I schlep my backpack and boxes up creaky dark wood stairs three floors to a long dim, musty corridor. The key turns and unlocks the door to a monastery-cell-sized room. It's tiny and old but neat.

There is a coin-operated washing machine and drier located in the bathroom on the fourth floor where I wash my clothes. A shower is next to the washer so I decide to wash up as my clothes get washed. Vicky had warned me that the water at the Doyle is very hot, and it is. The problem is that when the hot water goes into the washing machine it suddenly turns the water in the shower cold.

Around seven o'clock I go downstairs to the small dimly lit bar and restaurant on the ground floor. In come two thru-hikers: Woodstock and Osprey. They get lodging, shower and come back down. Osprey is eighteen years old and is doing the Appalachian Trail before starting college. He hiked parts of the Pacific Crest Trail and the Continental Divide Trail by himself. He is an incredible young man, friendly and well spoken. Osprey and Woodstock hiked thirty miles today.

April 28, 2007

This day is Pennsylvania on the rocks. I trek eleven miles over ankle-twisting, rocky terrain to Peters Mountain Shelter.

Woodstock and Osprey show up. We talk and have dinner. Two fathers arrive with their sons. Peters Mountain is a large, contemporary, two-story shelter. I was going to stay up top by myself so it would be quiet, and I'd be able to get up early for the more than seventeen-mile trek to the Rausch Gap Shelter. Instead, I let the fathers and sons have the top level, making it easier for me to get out in the morning.

A fire blazes in the fire pit. Osprey tells us about the time a grizzly bear "bluff charged" him. When I asked how he knew the grizzly was bluff charging, he said he didn't know for certain. He had to empty a canister of pepper spray in the bear's face. The pepper spray—made of cayenne pepper—causes pain. It doesn't cause any permanent damage, just gives you enough time to get away from the distracted bear. Another time, Osprey had gotten between a black bear sow and her cubs. He knew he was in trouble when he heard the cubs making a "Ma…Ma" sound. That's when the mama bear charged towards him. He unloaded a canister of pepper spray at her and was able to escape.

Ah, this is what life is about—swapping chilling adventures and funny stories, the camaraderie of kindred souls bound together in a common venture of hiking the A.T.

April 29, 2007

At 4:45 a.m. I'm up and ready to get on the trail for a long day. The sheer hike down and then steep rise up from the Clarks Creek area are difficult but not as bad as I expected.

Later on the A.T., I hear a rough hissing sound next to the trail; then a rattling sound coming from…a rattlesnake! A large long rattlesnake! Maybe I'm nuts, but I'm not seized with fear. Rather, I'm elated to finally meet an interesting wild animal. This may seem even goofier: I said, "Stay where you are, I'm going to take your picture!" I get out my camera and stupidly move in closer to take photos. Within how many feet can I get before this venomous snake lunges and sinks its fangs deep into my bare legs? It let me take photos but continues to rattle and stay in a coiled strike position. I'm fascinated by the shaking tan tail and ice cold dark eyes in its wide head, which is weaving from side to side, waiting to spring.

They say a snake can strike two-thirds of its total length, but I don't want to find out. My attention remains riveted to that head until I slowly back away to a bend in the trail and out of sight. Then I make a crazy laugh and my heart thumps wildly.

Magnificent weather! Sunny, dry, and by one o'clock it is seventy degrees, temperature rising. Woodstock and Osprey passed me about an hour and a half ago. It doesn't matter, I'll be able to make it to Rausch Gap, and

I'm loving this day. Except for Osprey and Woodstock, I do not see any thru-hikers, just people out for a Sunday hike. The almost eighteen miles to the Rausch Gap Shelter are long, somewhat difficult, and hot. I had doubts I could do such a distance, having been out only ten days. But I make it. It's 8:00 p.m. and no one else has shown up. Spend another night by myself.

Chapter Twenty-seven

April 30, 2007

Rausch Gap Village was a coal mining town at one time. When I came into the Rausch Gap Shelter yesterday I saw coal on the trail and smelled the black rock's musky, oily odor.

Pennsylvania rocks are similar to those in Virginia and North Carolina except here they are endless. It slows down hikers, causing you to slide around, ankles turning from side to side, catching yourself with hiking poles. On the side of a round rock, my foot skids enough to turn it crooked, just short of twisting the ankle into a sprain.

An Indiana backpacker who had hiked Pennsylvania once told me, "Pennsylvania may be a beautiful state. I wouldn't know. I never looked up." Some trekkers say they "only saw Pennsylvania three feet at a time."

Today the weather is glorious, sunny. It's unusually hot for April. I find some relief in a tunnel of Rhododendron. Unfortunately, it doesn't last very long.

The trail comes to a wide rushing creek. I cross by stepping down into surging water and onto slippery rocks. Each foot is carefully placed so not to slip into the creek's racing deluge. The water looks dirty; maybe it comes from a coal area and has a deleterious chemical in it—so I only filter one liter.

That was a horrible mistake—one of the worst mistakes I ever made!

The day gets hotter. This early in the year trees here have no leaves to provide shade. The trail is out in the open. Up on exposed ridges the sun gets hotter. It is unseasonably sweltering. There is no escaping the heat. Off comes my shirt and pant legs. Like a vampire, the heat sucks away strength.

With sweat soaked miles water goes fast. I drink all the water I have—on a cool day it would have lasted. There's no place to get out of the glaring sun.

Perspiration drips salt into my eyes. I take off my hat and run a finger around inside its band, sweat trickles down my hand. The day wears on, I'm parched... throat and mouth scratchy dry...thinking of the time Jim got dehydrated. I'm uneasy...head hot, slightly dizzy. Being by myself and getting dehydrated, maybe heat crazed—weak, stumbling around in a stupor, confused—I might make some dumb judgments. Stray off the trail. Fall off a mountain.

Hours in scorching heat...woozy. There's a slender tree, providing some shade. I ease off the pack and let it fall against the tree. The air is almost too hot to breath, too thick with humidity to draw into my nose. I am sun-beaten. Wearily, I flop into the shadow of the narrow trunk. Tired...head swims in a dizzy sea of confusion...Have to rest awhile...My eyes close. Barely this side of consciousness, being pulled down into a torrid box. My head falls to my chest.

In my daze I hear music in my head—sultry women singing a ballad. *Have I heard this song before?* I don't know where I heard it...or when. A dense world of heat and muddle of thoughts. Am I starting to go mad? Who the hell cares about this damned song! I'm out of water, heat choked...can't focus on what to do...and I'm concerned about a song! I do hear...a duet.

Two women look down at me and talk, their rumpled shirts are sweat soaked, hiking shorts wrinkled, heat beat, limp. In a faraway echo they are saying something about "...day hiking...coming up a side road..." but it did not register. "Are you okay?" they ask, with voices distant and faint.

Is this a dream?

I cannot see their faces, only shadowy silhouettes against intense sun-stained sky. I want to ask for help, can't find the words. My dry mouth opens, and a voice comes out weakly, "I'm out of water."

They say something...also being low on water...the words glide through my head. The sun-haloed women both lean down, look into my face for a moment, reach into their daypacks, and each gives me a little water from their own water bottles. I drink eagerly...say a feeble thanks as they depart.

This was my last chance. I know I have to get moving. Gradually I begin trudging again. I don't think I can make it to the William Penn shelter. There are no streams, springs, or creeks ahead of me. Looking skyward, I mumble, "Please send me more water." I eke out what seems to be miles...getting drier, my tongue sticks to the roof of my mouth.

I'm not one to believe in miracles. My lawyer's mind doesn't allow me to believe in water miraculously appearing out of arid ground. Yet, seeping from beneath leaves and twigs, trickling across the A.T., is water forming a puddle in an indentation in the ground. While I ordinarily avoid taking such questionable water, it is better than passing out from thirst. I fumble with my water filter, and pump it like an amateur. I gulp over a liter and a half, wait for the puddle to refill, and pump another liter to take with me. I know I'll make it all the way.

Eventually, I reach William Penn Shelter, throw down my sleeping pad, lie down, and give way to the sleep of exhaustion. When I get up I go to the spring and drink another liter and a half. I have avoided a total disaster.

May 1, 2007

Two previous grueling days took their toll. Today I will not hike the planned nineteen miles to Eagle's Nest Shelter. Instead, I'll stop at the Hertlein Campsite, ten miles from here, and the next day do another nine miles to Eagles Nest.

On the way to the Hertlein Campsite a man approaches me, a shotgun cradled in his arms. His face is covered by camouflage netting. I ask, "What hunting season is this?"

"Turkey."

He tells me, "Be careful, there are hunters in this area. Wear an orange hat like the other hunters are wearing."

I wonder two things: 1) Where am I going to find an orange hat in the midst of deep Pennsylvania woods? and 2) Haven't the turkeys figured out that people wearing orange hats are out to shoot them?

Much later I see a goofy looking large gray-brown game bird, swan length neck, small brain-box head, and warn it, "Watch out for the guys in the orange hats!" It stupidly looks at me and ambles into the brush.

Hertlein Campsite is in a valley, mountain ridges all around, a gurgling brook and waterfall close by. There is no one here just as there was no one at the shelter last night. I didn't see any hikers today and I haven't seen thru-hikers since Woodstock and Osprey. If you like solitude, this is the place to be.

After lunch I lie down on the bench of a nearby picnic table, enjoy the sun on my face and listen to a waterfall. Two white butterflies slowly follow each other in casual play. This is heaven without a bunch of jabbering angels. My tummy is full, it's a sunny, dry, lazy spring day where you lay around contemplating your navel. I'm halfway between awake and snoozing, dreamingly looking up through leaves. Everything eases into comfy, pleasant relaxation, blurs, fades and I slip into nap-sleep

Little things break every day. A piece broke off my headlamp; I use duct tape to put it back together. My metal cooking pot support disintegrated and I now use stones to hold up the pot while I'm cooking. My leg got scratched and I went to the brook to clean it up. My camera fell into the water. I grabbed it just in time and quickly wiped it off to keep water from getting inside.

I had not heard about bears being here in the Hertlein area, but I hang a bear line anyway. I wrap my food bag and cook pot in a plastic bag, tie it securely to make sure it is watertight, and hang them up in a tree. By the time I finish and settle back in the sleeping bag, it starts drizzling. There is lightning and thunder off in the distance. The rain increases, light flashes brighten, and thunder claps get louder. I count the seconds between flash and thunder. A close lightning strike is less than two city blocks away. Only thin silnylon fabric protects me from over 100 million volts of electricity or a 300 pound oak limb smashing through my tent. (Pennsylvania is among the three states with most deaths and injuries due to lightning.)

Blasting wind roars, the tent shivers. Strangely, it feels okay, happily at peace with myself. It's comforting that I'm making it alone. I feel I should be more concerned—I'm not. I'm looking forward to seeing Barbara at the Delaware Water Gap and some time off from the trail. It's warm and cozy in the sleeping bag. Sleep overtakes me and carries me off, far from this place.

May 2, 2007

With last night's rain there would be no problem getting water. Rain had seeped onto the boot-rutted trail, formed a stream, burgeoned to a brook and then—river-like—burst across the adjoining sides of forest plants. To keep from stomping through the mud, mess and slippery rocks, I hike in the woods alongside the trail.

Leaning against an inside wall of each shelter is a broom. At the Eagles Nest Shelter I follow my usual routine of sweeping the place of dirt, possible mouse droppings, and blown in leaves. I can't lay my ground cloth in this earthy grunge and sleep with my nose inches away from the dust.

I start sweeping at the rear and sweep forward…last broom strokes sending dirt flying off the open front. Then it feels like home.

A deliriously happy bird is tweeting away in a low tree. It has turned into a kiss on the cheek perfect day, temperature in the sixties and an arid breeze. I expect to be at a motel tomorrow, so I'll get my wash done then. Haven't seen anyone all day, and there is no one else at this shelter. I haven't spoken to another hiker in days. I call Barbara for a little human contact. I tell her I'd be at the Microtel in Hamburg tomorrow if she is able to come out. If not, I would see her at the Delaware Water Gap.

Have a good night's sleep alone at the shelter.

May 3, 2007

I see a distant hunter. Closer, I say to him, "I'm not a turkey."

"I saw this large gobbler…trying to find it in the woods. What's your trail name?"

"Avalanche."

"Where you from?"

When I tell him I started in Georgia, he's surprised. This hunter is not wearing an orange hat. He knows the turkeys figured out that the guys with the orange hats are trying to shoot them.

It's a bone-jarring steep drop from the adjacent mountain down to the Schuylkill River. Port Clinton is an old river town. At the outskirts of Port

Clinton I hobble over sets of railroad tracks. The immovable, level wood railroad ties beneath my feet is a welcome change from the loose rocks, but the little toe on my left foot is killing me. I stop at a shaded picnic table next to the river and put tape on my ailing toe. Listening to the river flowing by, sitting in the balmy spring air, I get drowsy but decide I should get going.

Standing at a Port Clinton intersection looking at my map, a woman in a compact car stops, pokes her head out the window and asks, "Do you need help?"

"Where's a restaurant?"

She looks around as if she's looking for a place to recommend. "The only restaurant that's open is blocks away."

"How far is that if you have to walk carrying a backpack?"

"Oh, it's a good walk."

I decide to continue trekking to Hamburg. It's hot out. At Route 16 near Pa 61, off comes my backpack—my back is soaked in sweat—on goes my most pleasant smile, up goes my hitchhiking thumb. A few cars pass by, mostly occupied by older couples. No one stops. One man coming from the opposite direction slows, makes a U turn, looks at me, and continues in the direction I want to go, but without me. No one gives me a ride.

After a hot boot-slogging *mile and a half*, I reach a Burger King. In I go, have a sandwich, call the Microtel, and talk to the desk clerk. He says, "You're not too far away." Through the Burger King window the Microtel appears about a quarter of a mile away. Fortunately, it's a pleasant day; anyway, that's what I told my burning feet.

May 4, 2007

Barbara comes to visit, drives me to an outfitter near Pottsville, to a supermarket, and a convenience store where I resupply. Just having her here gives me a needed boost.

May 5, 2007

On the way to the Windsor Furnace Shelter I stop to talk to a couple and their teenage son. They are out hiking for the day. I tell them I started in Georgia and the wife says, "You're my hero! This is something I'd like to do."

The husband looks up into the trees. "Retirement is not too far off."

"Better do it while you're young enough. It's rougher when you get older."

The view from Pulpit Rock is magnificent. Maybe more beautiful than the view from Macafee's Knob and from Max Patch. A day hiker at the Pulpit takes my photograph, and I take a picture of a couple sitting on an interesting rock formation jutting up from a great depth.

After Pulpit Rock it's extremely rocky and poorly blazed. This area looks like nobody has been up here with a paint brush in years. Two men out for a weekend hike talk about how this vicious terrain tears up everyone's boots. "The day after tomorrow you're going to hit real Rocksylvania!" one of them tells me. "Two days of rocks. The going will be terribly slow." He wipes his hand across his brow as an expression of how exhausting it will be.

There's a shady spot next to a big tree composed of several different trunks coming up out of the ground. It doesn't matter that there are ants and bugs flying around—I just want to get out of the roasting sun. While eating, a guy climbs up the ridge, out of the woods, and approaches me. Between swallows I say to him, "You must be bushwhacking." Bushwhacking is hiking where there is no trail.

He wears long tan pants, a green T-shirt, and has an untrimmed mustache and tousled hair. His voice is strong but slightly out of breath. "Bushwhacked from that ridge—" points with his arm "—and do it often." He tells about off-trail hiking he's done in the Catskill and Adirondack Mountains.

"Ever get lost?"

"Never! Use a compass and maps."

As I sit eating lunch, many day hikers pass by. This must be one of the most popular parts of the trail in the state of Pennsylvania.

The view from the Pinnacle is dramatically beautiful. We are over sixteen hundred feet above sea level, looking over a valley below. Hikers standing on extensive rock outcroppings say this is the best view on the A.T. in Pennsylvania.

A day hiker walks with me along a mountain road. He is looking for a blue blazed trail that goes off the side of the Appalachian Trail, but he can't find it. I bring out my map. The man checks it carefully. "Has to be around here," and as he looks up from the map, immediately to his left is a trail with a blue blaze. It's difficult to see because a tree had fallen diagonally across it, blocking the trail and the blue blaze. He goes around the downed tree, waving goodbye.

I cross Hawk Mountain Road, continue into woodlands and look for the Eckville Shelter. After walking an additional twenty minutes I reread the directions. Unfortunately, I had not originally read the directions correctly because the shelter was on Hawk Mountain Road—not on the A.T. Although worn out from today's trudging, it's necessary to backtrack through the woods, and go up Hawk Mountain Road. There's the shelter—a good bunkhouse with a caretaker who lives next door.

It's been a strenuous fifteen-mile hike. Rocksylvania has taken a lot out of me. Time to consider the situation: My arms are blistered from sun and poison ivy, and I must wear long sleeves all day to protect them; I'm strained from several weeks of long, hard trudging; they tell me the hardest part is still to come. That's it! Time to call it quits for a while, maybe forever. I call Barbara and arrange for her too pick me up the following morning and end my Appalachian Trail excursion.

It has been a most wonderful experience, particularly this last two weeks when I hiked by myself. I wonder if I'm getting too old for this type of grind.

At home resting from trail-hiking rigors. Barbara has a suggestion. "Break the remaining part of Pennsylvania into shorter hikes. I'll resupply you often, so you can carry less. If you want to do that, I'll help you finish the strenuous remainder of the Appalachian Trail in Pennsylvania."

It appealed to me. I could carry much less and get some use out of the lighter, smaller backpack I previously bought.

Chapter Twenty-eight

Where you end up isn't the most important thing.
It's the road you take to get you there.
The road you take is what you'll look back on and call your life.
—Tim Wiley

May 20, 2007

After two weeks I'm back and start hiking from Hawk Mountain Road. It feels better carrying a lighter backpack. The pack is loaded with everything needed to stay out overnight. I leave my inflatable sleeping pad, extra pants, and shirt at home. I carry minimal food plus emergency food and snacks—the load weighs about twenty pounds. It's clear why guys who carry much lighter packs easily do so many more miles. Decreased weight makes trekking a pleasure.

Dan's Pulpit has excellent views. On the way up I meet teenaged Boy Scouts hiking down with their dads. The fathers, as usual, are at the rear lugging enormous backpacks. I say to one dad, "Why do fathers always carry the large backpacks?" He laughs. Yet, walking away, he seems to be asking himself the same question. Maybe he just realized that formerly younger and smaller scouts are now young men capable of handling heavy loads.

The rest of today is spent walking on rocks. Stretching to climb big blocks of stone slows you down. You look out at a rock wilderness, try to figure out which way the trail is going and how to go from massive rock to

279

sloping rock, sometimes hopping, sometimes stepping between them, going up and down endless stacks of broken stone. Sometimes I feel hidden amid car-sized shapes.

I sit at Balance Rocks, pulling up socks that started to creep down into my boots. A guy comes by looking like an old-time peddler with his cup and pans tied to the rear of his backpack, rattling with each step. The thru-hiker says he feels a little tired—in the last three days he'd gone eight-five miles. The man has a Gu pack in one hand and ambles over rocks while sucking on the energy gel pack.

I reach the Allentown Hiking Club Shelter. The peddler-appearing hiker sits on the edge of the shelter's floor drinking a Budweiser, a leg stretched out lazily onto the front step and the other dangling next to it. "Somebody left a six pack here," he says.

"Is it cold?"

He laughs. "It's cold enough!" and goes on, "I'm finishing my second," places the now empty can on the step and crushes it flat with the heel of his boot. "Want a brew?" He motions my attention to the floor inside the shelter where four cans cool in the shade.

I think of the miles ahead and decline. His trail name is No Joke. He hiked from Springer Mountain. He saw a puma (mountain lion) in Tennessee, but he really wants to see a bear.

No Joke drinks a third beer, crushes the can with his boot, and by the time we finish our conversation he crushes the fourth beer can. No Joke says he gets lost every day. I think to myself, *After four beers he just improved his chances of getting lost today.* He says he's going to the Blue Mountain B&B for lunch.

"You know what. My wife is waiting for me there. She's short with blond hair. Surprise her by telling her Avalanche is eating lunch at the Allentown Shelter and will be along soon."

He stands with a slight sway, gathers up his stuff, shakes my hand, and says goodbye. Later, I'm getting out my lunch when I notice a small pair of eyeglasses on the shelter floor. No Joke had long since gone. I'll take the spectacles with me after eating and hopefully catch up with him at the Blue Mountain B&B. When I start on my way it's not yet noon, sun filters through the trees, and the air is dry.

An elderly man with a backpack and a dog are hiking toward me. I ask if he's seen a hiker ahead of me. He says he saw someone by the name of "Mo Jo," mispronouncing No Joke's name.

"I'm trying to catch him because I have his glasses."

"Okay, I won't hold you up. He's about fifteen minutes in front of you and he's probably going to be slowed by some rocks ahead."

I think to myself, If No Joke is going to be slowed down by the rocks, imagine what they'll do to me.

I make good time and in early afternoon reach the bed-and-breakfast, which is also a restaurant and bar. Barbara is on a deck behind the restaurant reading at a table with a large umbrella. No Joke is at the restaurant's bar eating a sandwich and drinking a beer. He's delighted to get his glasses and offers me a beer. I have a sandwich and the three of us talk. No joke has another brew, and with six beers under his belt he wends his way to do eleven more miles.

After drinking six beers I couldn't even find the Appalachian Trail.

May 21, 2007

I hate the Pennsylvania rocks....
I hate the reek of third day socks.
From a poem, "Why I Hate the Appalachian Trail," by Robert Rubin
Appalachian Trailway News, Nov-Dec 2003

Into an hour and a half of hiking I come to the Knife's Edge, a mountain ridge rising so sharply on both sides it looks like a dagger's edge. Instead of one smooth long line, it is a serrated blade of sharp jagged blocks with spaces between to jump over. Straddling this long thin mountaintop, looking down into bottomless space, is not for the faint hearted. A boot steps on one side of the narrow ridge and the other boot lands on the ridge's opposite side, constantly shifting weight from side to side, jumping over breaks between the rocks. I've been up in tall buildings such as the Sears Tower, but falling from here would be greater than plummeting from the top of even that lofty building. It's exhilarating standing on the Knife's Edge looking out and down—and for the next place to put a foot and hand. Strong wind tries to blow my hat away, but hat strings are tied tight under my chin. It's sunny and a crisp forty-eight degrees. It's perfect other than the high wind trying to shove my hat, and me, off the sharp ridge.

There's a hell of a lot of big rocks both south and north of the Knife's Edge, making it slow going. At times I have to pull myself up over stones the size of several stacked up refrigerators or lower myself from boulder-sized stones. Sporadically, it's necessary to sit and slide. I ask myself, *Where do I go next?* You don't know where to place your next footfall—or hand grab—or where to leap. Hiking poles are useless. One hand holds them while I grab rock with the other.

The trail down from Bake Oven Knob is hard to follow—twists and turns that are not obvious—all you see are huge slabs. You constantly need to use hands to lower yourself from one ledge to another or from a block of stone to another.

Coming out of the worst rocks, I meet a man and woman heading up to the Knife's Edge. They mention having hiked much of the A.T. in New England and south of Pennsylvania. She looks nervous, her eyes go up to the crest I had just done. "I dread going up there because I read in a book about jumping from rock to rock." She clings to her husband's arm. "And it's going to be real scary."

A reassuring smile comes to my face. "Take your time, think about where you're putting your feet and hands; you'll love the views up ahead and really enjoy it when it's all over."

The Bake Oven Knob Shelter was built in 1937, the smallest shelter I've ever been in. I eat lunch, rest, and then look for water. Almost always, it's a steep climb down to find water. Descending sharply from the Bake Oven Knob Shelter, the first spring I come to is dry. The blue blazed trail continues steeply down to a second spring, and I hope there's water here because it is an almost vertical climb down and a sign indicates a third spring far below this one. The second spring is flowing. I filter the elixir of life, drink, and sit in crystal clear air listening to birds and water bubbling out of the piped spring.

Back up at the shelter, two guys in their early twenties stop for a break. They say they impulsively decided to take a hike. They don't have a filter and are carrying *three gallons of water*. "That's a lot of weight!" I say. One guy shrugs his shoulders. They move on.

A hiker, trail name of Traveler, stops at Bake Oven Knob Shelter for a break. Traveler goes down to the spring to get water. He comes back somewhat depleted. "It's so steep that by the time you come back up you need to go back down for some more water!" Before he leaves, Traveler says there will be thru-hikers showing up here tonight.

No one else showed up, so I had the shelter to myself.

Here are some entries from the Bake Oven Knob Shelter register:

5/8/07

"Rocks all morning from [route] 309. Only 40 or 50 miles of Pennsylvania left.

The rocks do know to stop at the border, right?"

— Medicine Man/07

5/15/07

"My, oh my!…those rocks sure made me blue. First time the AT made me frightened (Knife Edge). Am anxious about doing this solo stuff. Sleeping tight tonight. (But ain't it great to be high in the sky!)"

—Blue Skies

5/20

"Staying here to miss a little rain. That and I think I drank too many Budweisers today…[something illegible]"

— No Joke

May 22, 2007

The trail leading off the [Bake Oven] knob and through a rock slide on the north side of the mountain presents some of the most challenging hiking on the AT in Pennsylvania. Hikers must traverse large boulders and slabs canted at odd angles. Some require daring, broad leaps— especially daring with anything more than a day pack on one's back.

Trail markings can also be hard to follow on the light-colored quartzite
and sandstone. *Take care here. This is a test.* [30]

Awake by 4:45 a.m., eager to get started. After hiking the heavily rock-
strewn regions of Pennsylvania, you can go back south and dance through
North Carolina and Virginia's tiny stony sections.

The rocks here are often poorly blazed. There's no trail. Only expansive
fields of stone with far distant paint marks on them. Don't see the white
inscriptions? You'll be lost in an endless mass of huge broken slabs.
Yesterday, Traveler said how irritating it was not being able to find his way,
squandering time searching for blazes. Another irritating thing is that the
Pennsylvania Game Commission uses white blotches of paint on trees to
mark the boundaries of state game lands. From a distance the marks look like
white blazes, and it's easy to get off the trail and head for hunting lands. Why
the Game Commission can't use another color like yellow or safety orange
(which makes more sense) is beyond me!

The first time Gorilla Jim and I got lost—the trail abruptly ended—I was
alarmed. If I had been alone then, it would have been traumatic. Jim was with
me, and he was not bothered by it. He did what the experts say to do: calmly
assess the situation, backtrack until you find where you got off the Trail, then
continue again on the A.T.

Despite his cool demeanor, Jim once said, "When I went through the
Pennsylvania rocks, there were times I felt like crying."

During the day I'm lost in a wilderness of rock...can't find a blaze.
Where am I? No one else is up here, and I don't know where the hell I
am! Disoriented—on my own. A scare washes through me like a long time
misplaced sensation.

I reach up to the loftiest edge of a slab, pull myself to a higher vantage
point. From this perch each direction appears the same: Boulder world
everywhere.

Where the fuck am I!

There is no where to go.

Jim, where are you when I need you?

Jim is not here. I backtrack, look around; everything looks the same—
endless huge rocks everywhere. No trail on the ground to trace back.

I'm lost and confused—feeling disoriented and panicky as I had long ago in the Pennsylvania snow.

Time lapses in measures of anguish. I talk to myself: *This is bullshit! There has to be a way out.* I climb down from high rocks, sometimes having to sit on my rear end, sliding to the next level below, searching. I shade my eyes with my hands, searching each rock for any signs of a white blaze.

Far above me and to the right is something—there it is! A pale smudge.

I'm back on track and glad to be trekking up through a mountain of tilting oversized gravestones.

I have apprehensions about climbing the rocks out of the Lehigh Gap alone tomorrow. Since I got lost today, I'm deeply concerned about what would happen if I get disoriented in the sinister rock world climbing high out of that notorious, forbidding gap.

May 23, 2007

I'll try it. If the trail isn't well blazed, I'll come back down, call Barbara who's at a Palmerton hotel, and bag it. It's 6:20 in the morning, temperature in the low fifties. Another beautiful day.

You look up from the Lehigh Gap at near vertical slopes, there is no trail. The sheer rise ahead can only be described as a massive, over one-thousand-foot-high pile of jagged rocks and boulders thrown together by a pissed-off giant. It's all barren, a steep, angry mountain.

Why does this place have no trees and plants?

At the base of Blue Mountain, in Palmerton, a flourishing zinc smelting industry began in 1898 and continued for ninety years. Zinc smelting emits large quantities of toxic metals carried by wind and dropped onto surrounding areas. Metal particles settled into the soil. The greatest contaminants were arsenic, cadmium, copper, lead, and zinc. Heavy metals such as these cause severe contamination and kill plants. Blue Mountain plant life was slaughtered by air and soil toxic waste. Defoliation was so complete that rocks were torn clean of vegetation. Not even weeds could grow here. Runoff and erosion followed, leaving a barren mountainside, a biological wasteland.

The Palmerton zinc pile is a federal government Superfund site which has been subject to a hazardous waste clean up. Yet, even now, winds here blow through barren rocks.

Climbing out of the Lehigh Gap, rocks become boulder high. Picture a junk yard of crushed and wrecked cars heaped higher than the world's tallest buildings side–by-side. It's going to take work climbing, which I don't mind. It will be treacherous because of the crags. I just didn't want to get lost in a rock jungle.

I tilt my head back as far as it will go to look straight up. In many places the blazes are high above and I wonder how I'll reach them. Often say aloud to myself, "They want me to go where?" And, "How the hell am I going to get up there!" This is not backpacking. This is hands and knees mountain climbing. Just take one step at a time, one handhold. Again, my poles are of little use and sometimes they just get in the way. I reach up, put the poles on a ledge above and pull myself up using my hands and legs. There are moments when I'm not sure there is a place to put my feet, and some places hold only my toes or support only one part of a boot's sole. If anyone had been below, the only part of me they would have seen is the soles of my boots. This is not for people who fear heights.

At the highest point I stop...filled with emotion. I'm doing it...alone.

An expanse of stone surrounds me. Spectacular world high views. Way below, the bridge I crossed this morning is a thin pencil line across a royal blue Lehigh River. Adjacent towns are green areas with houses the size of dots. A passing fluffy cloud casts a huge moving shadow that temporarily darkens the river to battleship gray.

Crossing saw-toothed rocks, a trickle of blood seeps down my left knee. Without feeling it, a razor-like spike of stone pierced my skin. At the time, I'm on a precarious perch. In a few minutes the footing is better. I loop both poles around one wrist to prevent losing them down the mountainside. I press a wad of clean tissues against my cut.

I'm grateful for the abundance of today's blazes, which now are turning down the mountain. Facing a wall of stone, one hand clings to a rock formation. Looking down, between myself and the stone wall, I see an outcropping of rocks below that I have to drop to. Firmly grasping a crag with my hands, I let my feet slowly slip down the rock face, hoping the small ledge will stop me. I watch the rock face glide by me as my body slides downward. My foot scrapes along the stone face.

There is the uneasiness of jumping out of an airplane and the parachute has not yet opened. I expect the outcropping of rocks to stop my right foot. It doesn't. Instead, the quartzite gives way—clunking stones dropping and bouncing into the valley below. My right hand is yanked loose and slips from the top of the rock I was clinging to, stone particles imbedding themselves into my palm. Hiking poles in my left hand jam into the first thing they contact, my right foot slips into a small crevice and stops—there is no place to put my other foot. One foot is supported in a shallow cleft in the rocks, the other foot hangs out over air. I peek over my shoulder. It looks like a thousand foot drop into the Lehigh Valley below. I ask myself out loud, "What the hell are you doing here?"

No answer. There is no one up here but me.

With the weight of my pack pulling me backward, I waver toward the rear, try to balance on one foot, steady myself, shift my body weight first to the right and with a lurch to the left, I free my foot and jump to a rock that firmly holds both boots.

Crossing this part of the mountain's face is exhilarating—scary at times. I talk to myself, "Everything is coming along okay. Just keep taking one step and then another, and eventually I'll finish crossing this dicey part of today's trek." Sometimes I have to slide on my butt. A momentary stop to take photos, but I doubt they will show the height and difficulty of this climb. Eventually I start coming out of rock world. There's a little bit more of going up and onto a bald. Then, I'm on an old gravel road, a blessed reward to make the journey easier going down to Little Gap.

It has been written many times before, but I finally realize the truth: It's not the *destination* that counts—it's the *journey* that's so precious.

What a journey I had!

I would go on to complete Pennsylvania, New Jersey, New York, Connecticut, Massachusetts, and end at Vermont. From Georgia, altogether, trekking 1,590 miles over mountains, through forests and fields, crossing streams and railroad tracks, under high-tension power lines, through rain, sleet, snow, and brilliant sunshine, enjoying the most beautiful mountain high views of sleepy villages and farmland, meeting the greatest people, and having the adventures of a lifetime.

But, when I came to the top of those rocks, standing alone in the wind, high up on that rugged mountain, looking down into the Lehigh Gap, I knew I finished what I came here to achieve.

Epilogue

"I have always depended on the kindness of strangers"
—Blanche DuBois in Tennessee Williams',
A Streetcar Named Desire.

He that gives should never remember,
he that receives should never forget.
—The Talmud

Unlike Blanche DuBois, I never before depended on the kindness of strangers. I wasn't aware you could depend on strangers for anything. Or that strangers—people you never knew before—would come to your rescue or help you at all. So I learned there are decent people in the world who offer help even though they don't know you. They want nothing in return, except—if the opportunity ever comes to help someone else—we should do the same for others. "Pay it forward" is one way of expressing this wonderful bit of philosophy. I did that with a little trail magic the day I waited to pick up Jim on the A.T. the summer of 2002, and whenever else I could do something for others—particularly hikers. Quite frankly, I don't think I'll ever be able to do enough to return all the kindnesses strangers sprinkled on me during my hikes on the Appalachian Trail.

Gorilla Jim would have put his life on the line for me. Yeah, Jim—you taught me one other lesson: In the great poker game called life, sometimes you have to ante up your own security to help a true friend.

The Appalachian Trail changed my life for the better. I had more adventures trekking those woods and mountains than I had enjoyed in the rest of my life.

Perhaps my account of these adventures seems as though it was overwhelming at times. It was. It would have been less difficult if I had done this in my early twenties, the age of the vast majority of hikers on the A.T.

I was born the year the Appalachian Trail was completed, 1937. I can never get twenty-one-year-old legs and lungs. I'm over fifty years too late.

—**Avalanche**
(Al Dragon)

Acknowledgements

I f you have good friends for a lifetime, you are many times blessed. Lou Shane and Bob Freedman have been my friends since teenage years. They shared my adventures on the A.T. by driving Jim and me to and from Virginia and other trail sites, in lousy weather and sunny days, so we could have the experiences written about in this book. For all of this I am truly grateful.

It takes 5,000,000 steps to hike the entire Appalachian Trail. I hiked about 3,655,000 steps. My abundant thanks to everyone I met during my years hiking the Appalachian Trail. Each person added something to this journey. Maybe some people stand out more in my memory, but each acquaintance put his or her seal on the journal of this voyage—and you have my profuse thanks and hope that I added a gram of pleasure to your journey. No matter how far you get along the trail, may your experience be as fulfilling as mine.

To my niece Laura, thanks for being the sparkle in my hike through New Jersey and for being like a daughter for those precious days.

Cindy McMahon, my former secretary, patiently listened to tapes dictated on the trail and deciphered my voice through a background of high wind, pounding rain, garbled tape and produced a transcript of most of my hiking notes. While I'm at it, thanks for twenty-three years of being my right arm, friend, and person whose suggestions were always appreciated.

I'm grateful to these folks who read my manuscript and offered suggestions or support: Barbara Dragon, Deborah Dragon, Aileen Freedman, Bob Freedman, Sheldon Levy, Cindy McMahon, Hon. Sandra Mazer Moss, Jim Saxton, Lou Shane, and Helen Wilson.

Geoffrey Stone edited this book, was very helpful cutting it down in size, and kept in check the more ribald parts of my sense of humor.

Two people stand out for particular mention:

First, my wife, Barbara, who got me started on this adventure, supported me in every way, and was understanding of my need to go back to the trail time and time again. And for many years of marriage filled with interesting and loving times.

Second, Jim, for the reasons you've seen when you read this book.

To all of you, thanks for the memories.

—Al

Bibliography

See endnotes.

Information about Claudia Brenner and Rebecca Wight was obtained from various sources. Among them was Brenner's emotionally moving account, *Eight Bullets*, by Claudia Brenner with Hannah Ashley (New York: Firebrand Books, 1995).

Endnotes

1. "Rudolph Pleads Guilty to Bombings in Atlanta and Birmingham," U.S. Department of Justice press release, April 13, 2005.

2. Patrick Rogers et al, "Manhunt," *People*, 00937673, (November 16, 1998), Vol. 50, Issue 18, reported in Ebsco Host Research Databases, http://web. ebscohost.com/ehost/detail?vid=13&hid=108&sid=1f61dac-d488-4eaf-8a00-d.

3. Patrik Jonsson, "How Did Eric Rudolph Survive?" *The Christian Science Monitor*, June 4, 2003, http://www.csmonitor.com/2003/0604/p01s02-usju. htm.

4. Henry Schuster with Charles Stone, *Hunting Eric Rudolph* (New York: Berkley Books, 2005), 272.

5. "Where's Eric Rudolph?" CNN, March 5, 2001, http://archives.cnn. com/2001/US/03/05/wheres.eric.

6. *Hunting Eric Rudolph*, 148.

7. "Out of the woods," *Economist*, Vol. 367 Issue 8327, reported in *Ebsco Host Research Databases*, http://web.ebscohost.com/ehost/detail?vid=13&hid−1 08&sid=1f616dac-d488-4eaf-8a00-d.

8. "Trail Hikers Told of Bombing Suspect," *The New York Times*, May 17, 1998, Section 1, Page 16, Column 2.

9. "FBI Puts Rudolph on Most Wanted List," CNN, May 5, 1998.

10. Maryanne Vollers, *Lone Wolf: Eric Rudolph: Murder, Myth, and the Pursuit of an American Oultaw* (New York: HarperCollins Publishers, 2006), 152.

11. Becky Johnson, "Rudolph's capture ends WNC saga," *Smoky Mountain News*, June 5, 2003, http://www.smokymountainnews.com/issues/06_03/06_04_03/fr_rudolphs_saga.html.

12. "Two Jailed For Lewd Conduct On Top Of Chunky Gal," *Clay County Progress*, vol.16, no. 50, reported in the Best of Randy and Spiff, http://www.youtube.com/watch?v=gxroHUbc2jo.

13. *Heartbeat AT,* "For the Love of Ox," in *Heartbeat AT,* a blog by Bill Newman, aka Circuit Rider, http://www.heartbeatat.com/2008atblog.htm.

14. National Park Service, "Great Smoky Mountains National Park Air Quality," http://www.nps.gov/grsm/naturescience/air-quality.htm.

15. *Backpacker*, April 2007, 13.

16. *Heartbeat AT,* "2009 Daily Schedule for Circuit Rider and Sherlock," in *Heartbeat AT,* a blog by Bill Newman, aka Circuit Rider, [emphasis added], http://www.heartbeatat.com/2009schedule.htm.

17. Appalachian Trail Conservancy, "Health & Safety," http://www.appalachiantrail.org/hiking/hiking-basics/health-safety.

18. The Atlantic Coast Observer Network, "Summary of Climatological Data, May 2004," http://members.cox.net/pwrs/acon/may04.htm.

19. National Weather Service Baltimore/Washington, D.C., "Flash Flood Watch, Shenandoah (Virginia)," 341 PM EDT THU AUG 31 2006.

20. Appalachian Trail Conservancy, "Safety Tips for A.T. Hikers," http://www. appalachiantrail.org/hiking/thru-section-hiking/safety-tips.

21. Commonwealth v. Carr, 398 Pa. Super. 306, 308–309 (1990).

22. Commonwealth v. Carr, Opinion On Post-Verdict Motions, pages 12–13 (Court of Common Pleas, Adams County, Pennsylvania, Criminal, No. CC-385–88).

23. Commonwealth v. Carr, Brief for Appellee [prosecution] pages 5-6 (Superior Court of Pennsylvania).

24. Commonwealth v. Carr, 398 Pa. Super. 306, 310 (1990).

25. Chris Hansen, "Escape From Brushy Mountain," *Dateline NBC*, February 15, 2009, http://www.msnbc.msn.com/id/29187510/ns/dateline_nbc-crime_ reports.

26. Terry Mutchler, "Troubled Loner Faces 3 Charges of Murder," *Los Angeles Times*, April 28, 1991, http://articles.latimes.com/1991-04-28/news/mn-1470_1_appalachian-trail; *People* Vol. 35 No. 21, June 3, 1991; and Crews v. Horn, Commissioner, et al, 360 F.3d 146, #7 – 8 (U.S. Court of Appeals, 3rd Cir., 2004).

27. Crews v. Horn, Commissioner, et al, 360 F.3d 146, #7 – 8 (U.S. Court of Appeals, 3rd Cir., 2004).

28. Maurice J. Forrester, Jr., "1986-1995: KTA Hosts AT Biennial Conference," Keystone Trails Association, http://www.kta-hike.org/index. php?option=com_content&task=view&id=17&Itemid=33

29.   Appalachian trail Conservancy, "Safety Tips for A.T. Hikers," http://www. appalachiantrail.org/hiking/thru-section-hiking/safety-tips.

30.   Scherer and Hopey, *Exploring the Appalachian Trail, Hikes in the Mid-Atlantic States* (Stackpole Books, 1998), 175–176 [emphasis added].

31. Information about Claudia Brenner and Rebecca Wight was obtained from various sources. Among them was Brenner's emotionally moving account, *Eight Bullets*, by Claudia Brenner with Hannah Ashley (New York: Firebrand Books, 1995).

BUY A SHARE OF THE FUTURE IN YOUR COMMUNITY

These certificates make great holiday, graduation and birthday gifts that can be personalized with the recipient's name. The cost of one S.H.A.R.E. or one square foot is $54.17. The personalized certificate is suitable for framing and will state the number of shares purchased and the amount of each share, as well as the recipient's name. The home that you participate in "building" will last for many years and will continue to grow in value.

Here is a sample SHARE certificate:

YES, I WOULD LIKE TO HELP!

I support the work that Habitat for Humanity does and I want to be part of the excitement! As a donor, I will receive periodic updates on your construction activities but, more importantly, I know my gift will help a family in our community realize the dream of homeownership. **I would like to SHARE in your efforts against substandard housing in my community!** *(Please print below)*

PLEASE SEND ME _____ SHARES at $54.17 EACH = $ $_____

In Honor Of: _____

Occasion: (Circle One)   HOLIDAY   BIRTHDAY   ANNIVERSARY

       OTHER: _____

Address of Recipient: _____

Gift From: _____   *Donor Address:* _____

Donor Email: _____

I AM ENCLOSING A CHECK FOR $ $_____ PAYABLE TO HABITAT FOR HUMANITY <u>OR</u> PLEASE CHARGE MY VISA OR MASTERCARD *(CIRCLE ONE)*

Card Number _____   Expiration Date: _____

Name as it appears on Credit Card _____   Charge Amount $ _____

Signature _____

Billing Address _____

Telephone # Day _____   Eve _____

PLEASE NOTE: Your contribution is tax-deductible to the fullest extent allowed by law.
Habitat for Humanity • P.O. Box 1443 • Newport News, VA 23601 • 757-596-5553
www.HelpHabitatforHumanity.org

CPSIA information can be obtained at www.ICGtesting.com
Printed in the USA
BVOW02s1442160915

418276BV00006B/167/P